A MATTER OF LIFE AND DEATH

A History of Football in 100 Quotations

Jim White has written for the *Independent*, *The Guardian* and *The Telegraph*. He is the author of *Premier League*, *Manchester United the Biography* and *You'll Win Nothing with Kids*.

A MATTER OF
LIFE AND DEATH

A History of Football
in 100 Quotations

JIM WHITE

HEAD
ZEUS

First published in 2014 by Head of Zeus Ltd

1 3 5 7 9 10 8 6 4 2

A CIP catalogue record for this book is available from the British Library.

ISBN (HB) 9781781859278
      (E) 9781781859261

Printed and bound in Germany by GGP Media GmbH, Pössneck

Designed by Austin Taylor

Head of Zeus Ltd
Clerkenwell House
45–47 Clerkenwell Green
London EC1R 0HT

www.headofzeus.com

For my mum

CONTENTS

INTRODUCTION

Alan Hansen was lost for words. It was the evening
of 8 July 2014 and the whistle for half-time had just
sounded in the World Cup semi-final between Brazil and
Germany when a BBC camera panned onto the face of
the corporation's leading football pundit. It revealed a
brow creased in perplexity. What he had just seen had
rendered Hansen flummoxed, flabbergasted, floundering.
A man who had developed a sizeable reputation for
the rigour of his analysis and the speed of his verbal
dissection of football's defensive arts was temporarily
rendered mute by the shambles he had just witnessed.

What made his reaction all the more astonishing was that this was
the Brazilian football team he was reporting on. Custodians of the
most vaunted international tradition in sporting history, these were
the representatives of a nation which had won the World Cup on
no fewer than five previous occasions, the five stars atop the crest
on their chest testament to the glories achieved by former national
sides. And here they were, in the space of just ten first-half minutes,
conceding four goals to a rampant Germany. By half-time they were
trailing 5–0 in the semi-final of their own World Cup in front of their
own supporters. A competition many thought they were predestined
to win was rapidly turning to dust.

But it wasn't the manner of German superiority that momentarily
muted Hansen. Joachim Low's team was good – very good – and would
rightly ultimately triumph in the competition, the first European side
to lift the World Cup in the Americas. But they were not sufficiently
stellar to stop the eloquent Scotsman in his chat-tracks. Besides,

excellence generally encourages words, rather than preventing them from emerging. It was the Brazilian haplessness that he found so hard to explain. How had a side that had been ruthless in its demolition of Chile and Colombia in the earlier knock-out rounds apparently transformed into jelly at the point where it really mattered? How had players at the very pinnacle of their profession, who had sung the national anthem before kick-off with a passion rarely before demonstrated on a football pitch, played with such a spineless lack of resolve, resembling in their organisation a particularly shambolic Sunday morning gathering of under-nines? This was embarrassing. This was enough to tie even the most eloquent tongue.

When Hansen finally composed himself – and in truth his silence was but a fleeting thing – he did not hold back. His assessment was as withering as it was heartfelt. 'In forty years in the game I have never seen anything like it,' he announced.

Looking back on that excruciating 7–1 defeat in Belo Horizonte, a night on which – as the German goals flew in – the mood among the watching Brazilians switched from open-mouthed astonishment through anger and humiliation to a kind of self-mocking laughter, it is hard to better Hansen's response. The team's capitulation really was extraordinary, a landmark moment in the game's history, a unique instance of incompetence. His words succinctly encapsulated its significance.

Not that he was alone in voicing his opinion. Across the globe, as fans put their jaws back into place after they had collectively hit the floor, we couldn't stop talking about it. The match was the most tweeted-about event in Twitter's existence, as millions sought to emulate Hansen and put their own assessment down in 140 characters. The tears, the astonishment and the jokes – lots of jokes – kept on bouncing across the ether. Twitter simply couldn't shut up about the game: 36.5 million tweets on the subject were sent during its ninety-minute course. What a useful resource the site was that night, a sort of universally available watercooler across which to express our feelings.

But then Twitter is just the modern vehicle for communicating our thoughts on the game. Because this is what we have long done when we watch football: we talk about it, we write about it, we laugh about it. Non-stop. 'The beautiful game' was the phrase Pelé borrowed from his colleague Didi to characterise the sport that made him. But the reality is that the adjective that best describes football is not 'beautiful', it is 'noisy'. For a game that can be the ultimate expression of physical agility, of balletic grace, of muscular power and technical skill, football is unyielding in the din it generates. The brouhaha that surrounds it is incessant, a broiling torrent of words.

It is pretty obvious why. Few of us can kick like Steven Gerrard, not many of us can express ourselves with a ball like Cristiano Ronaldo, perhaps only a couple of others in human history have been as eloquent with their feet as Lionel Messi. So how else are we going to articulate our passion for the game except through what we say about it? And we can all talk about it. Everyone, as the talk radio shows endlessly insist, can have an opinion. So much so, this is a game that can be best addressed not through its movement, its structures, its procedures, but by what we say about it. Football is a game defined by words.

Given that football is so surrounded by verbals, the odd thing is that so many have traditionally dismissed it as the least articulate of sports. Football and its practitioners have long been snobbishly characterised as collectively tongue-tied. Its players – young men almost entirely lacking in extensive education – are mocked for their adherence to cliché. They are invariably 'over the moon' with victory, 'sick as a parrot' at defeat. If they say anything interesting they find themselves and their words picked at like a ball of lard hanging from a washing line. Managers are satirised as mumbly, grumbly sheepskin-coated Rons invariably spouting self-defence while moaning about the referee.

Those who talk about the game professionally are equally lambasted. *Private Eye*'s long-running 'Colemanballs' column sniggers fortnightly at the nonsense that spews from the mouths of those who are paid handsomely to deliver what passes for communication on the game. Like the pinpoint accuracy of Murdo MacLeod's assessment of a passage of play: 'that was only a yard away from being an inch-perfect pass.' Or Ian Wright's confused geography when talking about the future employment possibilities for Wayne Rooney: 'I don't want him to leave these shores but if he does, I think he'll go abroad.' Or this, one of the thousands of similar offerings – enough to fill a sizeable library of collected volumes – from David Coleman, the doyen of football commentators who died in the winter of 2013, having bequeathed his name to posterity in the title of the column: 'Don't tell those coming in the final result of that fantastic match,' he once instructed viewers of the BBC's *Sportsnight*. 'But let's just have another look at Italy's winning goal.'

And why is it that football has so rarely been comfortably addressed in literary fiction? How come, while many an ambitious American state-of-the-nation novel is replete with references to baseball, the game that best associates itself with dissection of the American psyche, our favourite sport has barely ever featured in Booker Prize nominations? Aside from Nick Hornby's beautifully observed memoir *Fever Pitch*, the canon of English literature has not been added to by tomes addressing the country's principal cultural obsession. It can't simply be that the natural drama of the game is not comfortably replicated in fiction, can it?

More likely it is something the great Martin Amis, in his younger days an obsessive fan of the game, once observed. He revealed in an essay that the game is widely dismissed as a little too vulgar for legitimate inspection in the more elevated art of novel-writing.

Football-lovers like him, he wrote, were 'a beleaguered crew, despised by intellectuals and football-lovers alike, who regard our addiction as affected, pseudo-proletarian, even faintly homosexual'.

The paucity of literary reference to football is all the more odd, given that writing about the game of the highest order can be found in every newspaper in the land. On the sports pages there is little evidence of Amis-like shrinking from words describing our national addiction. From the match reports of Henry Winter and the cunning, punning wordplay headlines in the tabloids, through the tactical analysis of Jonathan Wilson and acute observation of Paul Hayward, to the arch reflections of Barney Ronay and chortling sarcasm of Matthew Norman, here are original, elegant and pertinent words being delivered on a daily basis. Funny words, too. Sometimes emotional, sometimes unhappy, sometimes thrilled, always engaged, they neatly sum up our own sense of what we have seen. Even if we vehemently disagree with every single one of them.

According to Winter, what those involved in writing about football crave is not just words, but memorable ones. What they seek is the epithet, the citation, the pithy distillation which perfectly sums up what they have seen. Whether it comes from the manager, a player, a commentator or their own keyboard, that is the holy grail of their calling: the quote. 'All we need to sustain us in our job', Winter once told me as we trawled the buffet at Stamford Bridge, 'are quotes and sandwiches.' Well, that and functioning wi-fi.

And when the quotes come, how the game relishes them. Every summer newspapers mark the close of the season by publishing a list of the most memorable utterances of the footballing year. Compiled by such diligent archivists as the redoubtable Phil Shaw, these have been collected in volumes, packed with the funny, the silly, the obtuse and the eloquent and occasionally the grammatically challenged: verbal flourishes which immediately remind us of time, place and character. Quotes that mark the history of the game.

Which is where this book comes in. Its purpose is to track the story of football through just a short selection of the many thousands of quotes that Shaw and others have noted through the years. Plus a few they might have missed. By analysing the verbal pearlers of managers, players, fans and administrators, seasoned with a selection of headlines, rulings and literary observations, its aspiration is to tell the story of the pastime that consumes so much of modern life. From football's early days of medieval rough-and-tumble to the modern, sophisticated, civilised sport it has latterly become, as characterised by Luis Suárez biting an opponent in front of a television audience of some half a billion people, the game's rich heritage and variety is explored in the pages that follow.

Unavoidably it is a partial history, selective and subjective. It is impossible to cover every by-way in the space allowed. There will, inevitably, be some telling omissions. Some avenues were further restricted by legal considerations. My first instinct was to include some reflections on the first line of Lord Justice Taylor's report on the Hillsborough disaster.

'On 15 April 1989 Liverpool and Nottingham Forest were scheduled to play in the semi-final of the world's oldest and most celebrated soccer competition – the Football Association Cup (FA Cup).'

In many ways, these cold, unemotional, deliberately legally neutral opening remarks of his report form the most important football quote of the past thirty years. They were the words that changed so much in the way that the game was watched and administered. This is a quote that matters.

But given that the inquest into the ninety-six who died on that cruellest of April days will still be ongoing when this book is published, the last thing anyone would wish to do is to prejudice the legal process. Those who lost loved ones in the disaster deserve finally, after more than a quarter of a century, to have answers delivered without any obstacle. Analysis of Taylor's meaning will thus have to wait.

But there is still plenty to detain and entertain – from the chirrupings of Gazza and the musings of Jürgen Klopp, through the thoughts of Bill Shankly and the defenestration of David Moyes, to *The Sun*'s cruel reduction of Graham Taylor and Roy Keane's withering dismissal of his international manager. Not to mention Ryan Giggs on sex, Brian Clough on bribery and Jermaine Jenas's fiancée on the romantic beauty of her other half's body art (he has, apparently, got her face tattooed on his forearm).

As Alan Hansen would no doubt concur, they are just words, perhaps. But they are words which encapsulate a time, a place and a history. These are the words that made a game.

Jim White

JULY 2014

ACKNOWLEDGEMENTS

THERE ARE A NUMBER OF PEOPLE without whom this book would never have seen the light of day. Not least Becci Sharpe at Head of Zeus, whose idea it was in the first place. Thanks too to Richard Milbank. The most encouraging and diligent of editors, Richard is a rare thing, someone who has made the process of producing the work a pleasure at every stage. Also to Peter Lewis for his generous and eagle-eyed copyediting, and to Cat Ledger for being a brilliant agent. And I owe a major debt to Ian Wylie and Sian Griffiths for their incredibly kind offer to let me use their place in France to break the back of the manuscript. Without their hospitality, frankly, I'd probably still be writing.

Thank you also to those I spoke to about the quotes in this book, who were so forthcoming with their insights, analysis and anecdotes. Alan Smith, Graham Taylor, Martin Tyler, Simon Bird, Hunter Davies, Melvyn Bragg, Mohamed Al-Fayed, Ron Atkinson, George Reynolds, Pete Molyneux, Andy Mitten, Keith Gillespie, Mark Ogden and Patrick Barclay: I owe you at least one drink. Not to mention those who I observed delivering some of the lines used herein, including José Mourinho, Alan Hansen, Gary Neville, Alex Ferguson and Eric Cantona: without you none of this would have been possible.

Thanks to Bols, as ever, for her patience, tolerance and support.

Finally, it would be utterly remiss of me not to state in print how grateful I am to Ivan Knapp for his wonderful research. Taking the idea and running with it, he came up with some fantastic stuff from the archives. So brilliant a job did he do, it is a fair bet to suggest that if there is anything you find interesting, intriguing or original in this book, it will largely be down to him. Everything else is just words...

PART I

KICKING OFF

1314–1916

1314

‘**...there is great noise in the** city caused by hustling over large balls from which many evils may arise which God forbid; we command and forbid, on behalf of the King, on pain of imprisonment, such game to be used in the city in the future.’

First recorded law against street football, issued by the Mayor of London, 13 April 1314.

Prince William likes a game of football. The Aston Villa-favouring second in line to the throne enjoys nothing more than a kickaround on the lawn of his gran's place, in his slightly too long shorts and his carefully mismatched socks. Which puts him at quite a distance from his predecessors. Throughout history, when not fomenting war or cavorting with ladies-in-waiting, the monarchy has spent much of its time trying to stamp out football.

Take Edward II, the first monarch to legislate against the beautiful game. Though in truth, early fourteenth-century football was more Dark Age thrash metal than a silky symphony of pass and move. This royal edict of 1314 was issued in response to the pleas of London merchants to clamp down on the medieval hooligans vandalising their shopfronts and scaring their clientele. Two more Edwards (Edward III in 1349 and Edward IV in 1477) would both use the law against the game, as would a Richard (Richard II, 1399), and two Henrys (Henry IV in 1401 and Henry VIII in 1540). Like their present-day descendant, history suggests that Williams, even when attached to Marys, were more tolerant of the game.

The primitive sport that these not-so-merry monarchs were endeavouring to suppress has changed out of all recognition in the intervening centuries. But a whiff of its exuberant, free-for-all flavour can still be had on Twelfth Night in the North Lincolnshire village of Haxey. Here, every 6 January, the clock is turned back to less complicated times. Televisions are switched off, tablets disconnected from the wi-fi, smart phones temporarily ignored as the entire population, plus much of that of the surrounding area, engages in what seems like an afternoon of prolonged public push-me-pull-you, followed by an evening of prolonged public drinking. Frankly, it appears that the locals are getting medieval on one another's hides.

Closer inspection of the mayhem seething across the wolds reveals that this is the annual playing of the Haxey Hood. It has been going on since the fourteenth century, more than 700 years of unbroken tradition represented in the heaving mass of humanity blundering through mud-filled fens, scrabbling and scrapping as they try to force a black leather tube back to their favoured pub, in competition with small armies of men and a few women representing three other local hostelries.

Watched from the sidelines, as the steam rises from the backs of the pushers and shovers, the Haxey Hood can resemble a scrummage without purpose, a rolling bundle of blokes splattering across the muddy countryside, fuelled by copious amounts of New Year ale, soundtracked by urgent cries of 'heave it boys!' and 'kill 'em!' A bit like the first day of the Harrods Sale, in fact.

But it turns out this is an event steeped in ritual and tradition. Despite every appearance, this isn't just a rural riot, there are dozens of arcane rules, lots of roles and positions, supervised by a sizeable hierarchy of officials. It may sound like it's been scripted by the League of Gentlemen, but when a bunch of portly farmers dressed like Morris dancers and calling themselves Boggins open proceedings by lighting a bonfire under a chap smeared in minstrel-style blackface paint in the village square, they have not turned feral. They are doing what has been done once a year on this spot for seven centuries: they are Smoking the Fool. And if you think being the Fool might not be the best thing to be at the Haxey Hood (that face paint alone is enough to warrant investigation by the Commission for Racial Equality), then obviously you are unaware of the tradition which entitles him to demand a kiss from any female he encounters during the day.

The Hood is one of those precursors of football that sprang up across the country in the Middle Ages. It may not look much like the modern game, with its gleaming stadia, pristine pitches and players signing contracts worth £300,000 a week. But what goes on in Haxey marks the start of an evolutionary process that led to the game of Ronaldo, Rooney and Roman Abramovich. This is where it all began.

Now almost entirely extinct, Haxey-like shenanigans were once a familiar sight, on high days and holidays, in every village, market town and city square across Britain. By the middle of the fifteenth century so many folk games had become established, the king's officers and local mayors were everywhere moved to intervene. This was not just a case of the ruling classes being spoilsports, out to stop the working man from enjoying his rare moments of leisure (although two centuries later the Puritans of Cromwell's Commonwealth *would* try to ban football simply because they didn't like it). Rather, as this decree dating from 1477 states, it was because games like the Hood distracted the populace from what the then powers-that-be regarded as its primary function:

> No person shall practise... football and such games, but every strong and able-bodied person shall practise with the bow for the reason that the national defence depends upon such bowmen.

Those few spare hours when young Englishmen were not toiling in field or workshop were not to be spent arsing about with ball, barrel or roundel of cheese, but in the manly pursuit of archery, honing their skills with the longbow that had won the day at Crécy and Agincourt. The reason Haxey's version of the game survived intact –

along with those of places like Ashbourne in Derbyshire and Alnwick in Northumberland – is probably because it was rural, and played under the protection of the local landowner. It was, after all, the wife of a fourteenth-century lord of the manor who had first sparked the anarchy when her hood blew off as she traversed the fens, sending her footmen off on a wild chase across the fields in its recovery. Or so Haxey legend has it.

In London, Canterbury and Edinburgh, however, the burghers were less tolerant of mobs of inebriated lads getting together annually to beat the living daylights out of each other while chasing an inflated pig's bladder down alleyway and up passage. For centuries the holiday bundles roaring down tight city streets earned the ire of the authorities. The football act issued by James I of Scotland in 1424 read: 'It is statut and the king forbiddis that na man play at the fut ball under the payne of iiij d.'

A fourpenny fine for playing fitba in an Edinburgh street was no small sum for the average medieval labourer. Some two hundred years later, in 1659, the Mayor of York went much further. He fined eleven

> It is statut and the king forbiddis that na man play at the fut ball.

players 20 shillings each when their game resulted in a smashed church window, at the time an astonishingly draconian fine. The prosecution provoked a violent protest, in which more than 100 men stormed the mayor's house and ransacked it.

By the early nineteenth century, though, local by-laws had done little to suppress the urge to play. So widespread were such games, and so fearful were the citizenry at what was unleashed, that a nationwide ban on street football was introduced in 1818. At about the same time, bored pupils in public schools started to develop their own versions of football, adapted to the wider green spaces of those elite institutions.

But in Haxey, they played on through ban and edict. Every Twelfth

Night the Boggins and the Fool cocked a snook at their urban contemporaries, stuck a couple of bowman's fingers up to their ruling masters and roared their way across field and brook. And the good thing was, even in defeat, the pub was always there. No matter what rules you play by, that has forever been the fundamental by-law of English football: win or lose there is always the booze.

1863 'The maximum length of the ground shall be 200 yards, the maximum breadth shall be 100 yards, the length and breadth shall be marked off with flags; and the goal shall be defined by two upright posts, eight yards apart, without any tape or bar across them.'

The First Law of Association Football, 8 December 1863.

These words may read like an extract from a DIY manual, but they were the cornerstone on which our national game was constructed. They record the very founding moment of what would become a shared obsession. These are the words that brought modern football into being.

Drawn up by Ebenezer Cobb Morley and a committee of university chaps across a series of meetings held in the Freemasons' Tavern in Great Queen Street, Covent Garden, this was the First Law of Association Football. Given the impact that its bland prose had on the world, it should have been delivered on tablets of stone rather than on the back of a beer mat.

Morley's initiative was to have a profound impact not just on society in Britain, but across the globe. So much so that his list of thirteen laws, published that year by the newly formed Football Association in pamphlet form, was selected by

> If people came back from 1862... they'd look around and think: 'what are these massive buildings?'

Melvyn Bragg, Baron Bragg of Wigton, as one of the *12 Books that Changed the World* for a 2006 television series. And when I spoke to him about it, His Lordship made a convincing case for its inclusion.

If people came back from 1862, the year before the laws were written, to now, they'd look around see our football stadiums and think: what are these massive buildings? What goes on in them? What is this thing that fills our newspapers with news? And it's not just here, it is massive everywhere. Then you find that 20 million women are playing, then you find it's worth billions of pounds a year and that the men who play it are iconic figures, they set the fashions like Beau Brummell used to. Yes, it did change the world.

Before that final meeting in the Freemasons', people played something resembling football across the country, but to no pattern. There were folk games in villages like Haxey, unruly tussles at Eastertide and Twelfth Night on heath and green; there were various arcane developments in England's public schools, all governed by obscure local regulations. Then Morley suggested that representatives from a group of clubs get together and try to produce a set of rules that would work for all. The urge to bureaucratise, after all, goes to the heart of what it means to be a Briton.

Delegates turned up at the pub from the following clubs: Forest (later to become Wanderers, the first winners of the FA Cup); NN

Kilburn (NN stands for No Names but the club was always known by its initials); Barnes; War Office; Crusaders; Perceval House (Blackheath); Crystal Palace; Kensington School; Blackheath; Surbiton; and Blackheath Proprietary School. In addition Charterhouse School sent an observer and several unattached footballers were present.

It was a lively meeting. The Blackheath contingent wanted the rules to embrace those of the game being played at Rugby School, with all its William Webb Ellis, pick-the-ball-up-and- run-with-it plot diversions. The rest did not. When Blackheath were defeated in a vote, they took their ball off in a huff and eight years later helped form the Rugby Football Union. But those who stayed constructed their thirteen rules. It was a moment the world seemed to have been waiting for.

'It absolutely stunned me when I realised,' Bragg told me. 'These guys met in a pub, knocked these rules together and from that moment it was a sensational success. There's been nothing like it. This was a game played by no more than a thousand young men in England. Even then, it was different games. Half-time was introduced so that university men could play Eton rules one half, Rugby rules the next. Then it was standardised and it went like a rocket. Not just round Britain, but British sailors took it round the world. They got off the boat and started playing it. Which is why the first teams in most countries – Le Havre in France, Genoa in Italy – were in ports.'

> These guys met in a pub, knocked these rules together and from that moment it was a sensational success.

And it was the rules that made the game. Perfectly coinciding with the rise in leisure, driven by adherents of muscular Christianity, who saw in its rhythms an unbeatable weapon in the battle against masturbation in the young and the bottle among the working class, Morley's way of doing things spread like a pandemic. Within ten years of the pub meeting, 30,000 people were watching matches played to his laws in Russia.

So what was it about the Freemasons' Tavern rule-book that made it so instantly accessible across classes, countries and creeds? What was it exactly that Morley unwittingly unleashed?

'Its beauty is its brevity,' reckoned Bragg. 'There were only thirteen rules. You could paste them up in the dressing room and say: look, that's how it works. And the thing was, until the book came out, nobody, anywhere, was playing the game like that.'

Plus there was its flexibility. Morley's was to be an ever-changing rule book, constantly adapting to circumstance. Here are a couple of the original laws, long since removed from the game's statutes.

1. The two sides change ends after each goal is won.

2. If a player makes a fair catch, he shall be entitled to a free kick, providing he claims it by making a mark with his heel at once; and in order to take such kick he may go back as far as he pleases, and no player on the opposite side shall advance beyond his mark until he has kicked.

Over the years new laws were added to replace those lost. In 1871 goalkeepers were introduced, followed in 1891 by penalty kicks, while in 1992 the back-pass rule was altered. At the start of the 2013–14 season, the glacially slow advance of technology finally bore fruit when cameras were brought in to alert the referee when the ball had crossed the goal line.

And none of them would have arrived were it not for Morley's first law. This is indeed the quotation that started it all.

1872 'The Scotch now came away with a great rush, Leckie and others dribbling the ball so smartly that the English lines were closely besieged and the ball was soon behind.'

Report from *The Scotsman* newspaper of the first officially sanctioned England v. Scotland international match, played at the West of Scotland Cricket Ground, Hamilton Crescent, Glasgow, 30 November 1872.

Demonstrating quite what a rampaging forest fire the spread of Association Football was, less than a decade after Ebenezer Cobb Morley and his pals had met in a London pub to decide on the laws of the game, St Andrew's Day 1872 saw the first official international between Scotland and England.

Not that those trudging through a grim, foggy Glasgow afternoon would have appreciated that they were witnessing a 'Eureka!' moment, the fountainhead of a new species of footballing contest that would spawn the World Cup and the European Championships, and the thrill, intensity and fervour of Brazil versus Argentina, Germany against Holland, or Croatia against Serbia. Around 3,500 people were reckoned to have made their way to the ground in Partick, each paying a shilling admission (the same amount as had been charged at the first FA Cup final in London that March). For that outlay, they were treated to what *The Scotsman*'s reporter suggested was a pretty stagnant, uninspiring 0–0 draw.

Yet, with the keen eye of hindsight, there were many hints of what was to come. The Scots were kitted out in dark blue shirts, with a thistle embroidered on the chest. And – in a manner that was to echo down the generations – neither side was able to field its best players. According to *The Scotsman*, 'the teams were got together with some difficulty, each side losing some of their best men almost at the last moment'. Roy Hodgson will know exactly how they felt.

The Scots, selected by the captain and goalkeeper Robert Gardner, had hoped to include in their team Arthur Kinnaird of Wanderers and Henry Renny-Tailyour of Royal Engineers, Scots who played their football in England, the original Anglos. But neither was available to travel north. So, with no more than ten clubs then established in the country, Gardner decided to stay close to home. He chose all eleven players from his own Queen's Park side. England's skipper Charles Alcock, meanwhile, found himself unable to play because of injury, and picked his eleven from nine different clubs, largely basing his selection on those who could afford to get themselves up to Glasgow.

The Scots did not gain much advantage from choosing a team whose players were familiar with each other's style of play. There is no evidence from *The Scotsman* report of a single pass being executed in the entire match. Although it was members of the Queen's Park club who twenty years later became the first to embrace the pass, in those early days the game was dominated by the dribble; players would simply run with the ball until they either put themselves in position to shoot at goal, or they lost it. As the newspaper's report has it: 'Kerr closed the match by the most brilliant run of the day, dribbling the ball past the whole field.'

Scotland had the advantage in the first half, England performed better in the second. But neither could land so much as a shot on target. It was not until the return game, played at the Kennington Oval the following May, that the first international goals were scored. Half a dozen of them, in fact, as Scotland won 4–2 and promptly established themselves as the de facto world champions of football. Just as they would do when they won at Wembley in 1967, the year after England had lifted the Jules Rimet trophy.

From fog-bound Partick, the idea of pitting nation against nation on the football pitch snowballed. By 1884, there was a fully-fledged annual home international programme, featuring England, Scotland, Wales and Ireland, an idea which lasted a century until its demise in 1984. Soon the French, the Italians, the Belgians and the Germans were all invited to take on the English and the Scots. And since that inauspicious Glaswegian afternoon, the original international football match between the old rivals has been replayed 111 times, more than any other such fixture. After a gap of fourteen years, its most recent staging was as part of the FA's 150th anniversary celebrations, when England beat Scotland 3–2 at Wembley on 14 August 2013. They may have been present at the most historic of footballing occasions, but how the fans dispersing from the Partick touchline back in 1872 would have welcomed a scoreline like that.

1883 'A northern horde of uncouth garb and strange oaths.'

Report in the *Pall Mall Gazette* on fans of Blackburn Olympic arriving in London for the FA Cup final, Kennington Oval, 31 March 1883.

It is difficult to know what the writer is objecting to most here: the visitors' fashion sense, their odd way of speaking, or the fact that they were – gulp – Northerners. Or perhaps he had identified something even more disturbing in the several hundred Blackburn supporters who spilled out of Euston station on that late Victorian weekend, sparking their clogs on the capital's gilded pavements: the fact that they were the harbingers of change.

The Football Association's finest creation – the FA Cup, the world's first formal football competition – had been instituted in 1872. And for the first decade, even as the number of teams entering increased year by year, its final reflected the social make-up of those who had gathered in the Freemasons' Tavern in 1863 to establish the organisation. These were public school and university types, well-bred fellows, the officer class, who saw the game as a physical expression of their core beliefs in chivalry, artistry and deference. As Old Etonians and Wanderers (a team made up of Oxbridge graduates) dominated the Cup in its early years, it was clear who this competition was designed for: good chaps.

But the beauty of football was that its very simplicity allowed anyone quickly to understand its processes. There was nothing exclusive about kicking a ball around. And soon, the game gained a foothold in the industrial North, where factory owners and priests alike saw in it a way for their workers and flock to occupy their leisure time in a more improving manner than the traditional method of getting bladdered. So it was that in 1882, Blackburn Rovers – working class, uncouth and unquestionably northern – became the first side from outside the circle of home counties' privilege to reach the final. They lost to the Old Etonians, but a year later their local rivals got there too. An invasion was now underway.

Olympic had only been in existence since 1878, formed by the amalgamation of two other Blackburn clubs, Black Star and James Street. Playing in a muddy field behind the Hole-in-t'-Wall pub, they did not look a particularly sophisticated or ambitious operation. But then Sydney Yates was invited to join their committee.

A local iron foundry owner, Yates was a nineteenth-century Jack Walker, a man who recognised that football was the perfect vehicle to promote the business virtues of his home town. He bankrolled the club, providing whatever cash was required to help improve performance (though ostensibly not, as this was against the rules, to pay players). And almost immediately his input propelled Olympic to prominence. In 1883 – only the fifth time they had entered the competition – Olympic beat Accrington, Lower Darwen, Darwen Ramblers, Church and the Druids (from Ruabon, near Wrexham) to reach the semi-final of the FA Cup. Here, for the first time, they encountered the Establishment: they were drawn against Old Carthusians, made up of former pupils of Charterhouse School. The assumption was that their first engagement with the representatives of the moneyed South would signal their departure from the competition. However, at a neutral venue in Whalley Range, Manchester, Olympic trounced the Surrey toffs 4–0, so setting up a final against the most vaunted opponents of all, the Old Etonians.

What they did next was to have profound ramifications for the game. Coached by their best player Jack Hunter, the team spent the week leading up to the final doing intensive training in Blackpool, pounding the beach. It was a revolutionary idea, involving unheard-of levels of physical preparation, which suggests that the *Pall Mall Gazette*'s sneeringly condescending view of the arrival of their boisterous fans actually disguised a hefty degree of trepidation. This was not just a bunch of northern oiks coming to town. This was a footballing revolution.

And so it proved. In front of the then biggest-ever Cup final crowd – 8000 lined the touchline at the Kennington Oval – Olympic won 2–1, their superior fitness running their opponents ragged in extra time. Taking the Cup north for the first time, the team were granted a civic reception. Addressing the delirious fans, the captain Albert Warburton proclaimed: 'The Cup is very welcome in Lancashire. It will have a very good home and it'll never go back to London.'

In London, meanwhile, the victory of the uncouth North signalled near rebellion in the FA. Fearing that the public-school grip on the trophy might be replaced by grubbier fingers, several clubs angrily demanded an inquiry into Olympic's finances. How could an organisation of such modest size – interlopers and arrivistes at that – afford to send its players to Blackpool for the week leading up to the final? And how did they manage to persuade Hunter to come over from Sheffield to play for them in the first place? Was it the case that the Blackburn players were in fact professionals, the despised antithesis of the gentleman amateur?

Warburton's comments turned out to be prophetic: the Cup remained in Lancashire for a further three years, albeit in the trophy cabinet of Olympic's local rivals Blackburn Rovers. And far from standing steadfast against the growing swell of professionalism pressing down from the North, the FA bowed to the inevitable and, in 1885, legalised payments to players.

Ironically, given the anger generated by their Cup win, it was professionalism that led to the demise of Olympic; Blackburn was simply too small a place to sustain two pro clubs. When Sydney Yates decided to back the bigger local side, Olympic did not have enough financial clout to compete for players with other Lancashire outfits. And when, in 1888, it was Rovers who were invited to join the newly formed Football League (only one club per city was to be admitted)

Olympic were doomed. The club whose followers so upset the sensibilities of the London press when it became the first non-public-school, working-class (and coincidentally the first wholly English) side to win the Cup in 1883, was wound up just six years later.

1909 'I waited for him to try to hurl me once more, and with a hip fling of the type only English footballers know, I gave him a good tumble worthy of poetics. He took five minutes to get back up, by which point he had been totally trampled, and then he abandoned the match, and football itself, forever.'

Herbert Kilpin, founder of AC Milan, describes a tackling manoeuvre popular at the time in a speech to mark the tenth anniversary of the club, 1909.

Kilpin was a lace maker from Nottingham who settled in Milan as the nineteenth century came to a close. Like many a Victorian traveller leaving home shores, even as he sought his fortune overseas, he preferred to pack in his trunk the British way of doing things. Not for him the warm embrace of Italian culture, with its pasta, cappuccino and red wine: no, he was more of a meat pie and warm ale man. When it came to sport, too, he gave the Palio di Siena a miss. All those teams in their garish satin outfits with names like the Caterpillars and the She-Wolves racing bareback around a dusty piazza: not real sport at all.

Football, on the other hand, now there was a pastime. Especially for a Nottingham man, brought up in the place that boasted the oldest surviving football club in the world – Notts County. And, just two decades after being introduced by British sailors to the port of Genoa in the wake of the FA's codification, by the close of the century football was making inroads into Italian life. In Milan, on a Saturday afternoon, there were pick-up matches regularly going on in the city parks.

If Kilpin's vivid account of one such fixture is to be believed, the locals were already adapting the laws to their own way of doing things. His depiction of a tussle with a Milanese rival suggests that the urge to impose sweeping national stereotypes on the game was evident even in its earliest days. Just as Germans are invariably typecast as organised, the Dutch as self-destructive and Brazilians as having the beat of the samba coursing through their veins, so even back then Kilpin thought the Italian approach to football mirrored wider national characteristics: in other words, it was cynical, underhand and not wholly within the spirit of the thing. And what was more, unlike the yeoman English way of playing the game, it was cowardly. If nothing else, Kilpin's depiction demonstrates that, in the early years of the new century, football remained a game of rough and tumble, in which a throw that would not look out of place in an all-in wrestling bout could be described as 'poetic'.

That was how the game should be played, Kilpin believed. And in an effort to promulgate its virtues, with a fellow Brit, a businessman called Alfred Edwards, he established a club in his adopted city. Showing characteristic disregard for local convention, the pair named it, in the English manner, The Milan Cricket and Football Club, with Edwards as its first chairman and Kilpin its founding captain. Thus it was that in 1899, the organisation which ninety years later was used by its owner Silvio Berlusconi as a shining symbol of Italian nationalism – the ideal platform from which to launch a substantial political career – began life as that most English of institutions: a cricket club. A cricket club, moreover, with the cross of St George incorporated in its crest as a reminder of its Englishness.

The cricketing side of the club withered away within a decade, as the Italians made clear their disdain for a game in which they might be obliged to stand around for days without proper resolution (that was what the coffee bar was invented for, after all). Seven European Cup wins, however, are testament to the manner in which football became embedded in the foundations of the grand old city. Edwards' and Kilpin's establishment is now the club that has won more official UEFA and FIFA titles than any other in Europe.

Throughout all that trophy accumulation, through the split in 1908 that spawned Italy's second-biggest club, Internazionale, through the dazzling playing days of Italian stalwarts like Gianni Rivera, Paolo Maldini, Franco Baresi and Andrea Pirlo, under the artful Italian leadership of Arrigo Sacchi, Fabio Capello and Carlo Ancelotti, the club has continued to maintain pride in the Anglicised name bequeathed by its founders. Not that everyone liked it.

> As any proper football hipster will tell you... the way to say it is 'Meee-lan'.

Mussolini in particular took offence, forcing the club to change its title to Milano in the 1930s. But the moment he was gone, they reverted back to Milan, the link to their British heritage restored (though they did retain the 'AC' element of Mussolini's Associazione Calcio Milano).

The pronunciation of the name, however, remains relentlessly Italian. As any proper football hipster will tell you, rolling the vowels around their mouth like a well-cellared Chianti, the way to say it is 'Meee-lan'. You can bet Kilpin never called it that.

1916 'Best of luck. Special love to my sweetheart Mary Jane. And best regards to the lads at the Orient.'

Last recorded words of William Jonas, the Orient inside-forward, before he went over the top at Delville Wood, on the Somme, 27 July 1916.

It might sound idyllic, with its name faintly reminiscent of dingle and dell, but, in the summer of 1916, Delville Wood was anything but. Right on the front line of the Battle of the Somme, sandwiched between the German and British positions, pockmarked by shell holes, its trees reduced to branchless stumps, it was aptly damned as Devil's Wood by the British forces fighting through it. It was not a place that many who entered came out of alive.

After somehow emerging unscathed through the first four weeks of carnage, as General Sir Douglas Haig's Somme offensive sank into inertia, Private Jonas found himself in the wood on the afternoon of 27 July 1916. He was in a forward trench alongside his Clapton [now Leyton] Orient team-mate Sergeant Major Richard McFadden. They had been sent there as part of a platoon charged with clearing out an advance guard of Germans. But they quickly came under heavy fire. With ordnance flying around their heads and the Germans seemingly everywhere, the two professional footballers were in a desperate position. So Jonas decided to make a run back to the main British positions. He did what he did at Brisbane Road every other Saturday; he just went for it.

He didn't get far. Along with those parting words above, in a letter back to Orient, McFadden recorded what happened next:

No sooner had he leapt up than my best friend of 20 years was killed before my eyes. Words cannot express my feelings at this time.

By the time the letter was passed round the dressing room at Orient a month later, McFadden was also dead, falling while leading another attack.

The pair had signed up for action on the night of 15 December 1914 when the FA held a meeting at Fulham Town Hall for footballers interested in enlisting. Such was the demand from young players misled into believing that what was taking place across the Channel was a game, the 17th Middlesex Football Battalion was founded that evening. McFadden and Jonas, both attacking inside-forwards at Orient, were among the first to sign up. They were joined that night by six professionals from Croydon Common (a club which did not survive the war), three each from Brighton, Chelsea and Watford, two apiece from Crystal Palace, Luton and Spurs, plus dozens of other players, amateur and professional. Yet it was Orient who provided easily the largest contingent from any English club: forty-one players and staff members were eventually to sign up.

During the four years of bloodshed, 900 men were lost from the 17th Middlesex, many of them professionals. Aston Villa's William Gerrish was one of the first to perish; the bodies of Oscar Linkson, the Manchester United full-back, and the Spurs hero Walter Tull were never recovered; Leeds City's Evelyn Lintott, an England international, was killed on the first day of the Somme offensive. Meanwhile, the dying words of Corporal Ben Butler of Queens Park Rangers as he succumbed to his injuries in a field hospital were recorded as 'no more football for me'.

no more football for me

Some, though, did survive and went on to resume their playing careers. Fred Keenor, the Cardiff City and Wales defender, was injured at the Somme but recovered and skippered the Bluebirds to FA Cup final victory in 1927. Bradford's Frank Buckley, the Football Battalion's commanding officer, went on to play for both Manchester clubs and eventually became manager of Wolverhampton Wanderers, where he nurtured the talents of Billy Wright.

But in London's East End there was to be no such regeneration. At the Somme alone, Orient lost George Scott as well as McFadden and Jonas. When news broke of their deaths, Arsenal published a tribute referring back to the great performances the trio had given against them: 'In civil life they were heroes and they proved themselves heroes on the battlefield.'

> In civil life they were heroes and they proved themselves heroes on the battlefield.

The *Daily Mail* published a poignant epitaph to the practice of many infantrymen, including those in the Football Battalion, of kicking a ball into no man's land at the start of advances during the Somme offensive. The piece was inspired by 'the football charge' of the East Surrey Regiment, led by one Billie Nevill.

On through the hail of slaughter,
Where gallant comrades fall,
Where blood is poured like water,
They drive the trickling ball.
The fear of death before them,
Is but an empty name;
True to the land that bore them,
The Surreys played the game.

Needless to say, Nevill lost his life in the ball-propelled attack.

PART II

EARLY DOORS

1923–58

1923 'To put it mildly, the whole thing was a bloody shambles.'

Terry Hickey, a spectator at the first FA Cup final to be staged at the Empire Stadium, Wembley, 28 April 1923.

Terry Hickey was reminiscing for a BBC documentary fifty years after the first match held at the location that became known as the home of the game, the 1923 FA Cup final between Bolton Wanderers and West Ham United. It was, he reflected, a miracle that no one was seriously injured or killed at Wembley that day, such was the hopelessness of the organisation. Contemporary records suggest Hickey was not alone in his assessment. The *Daily Mail* spoke of crowd control being 'useless'. The report in *The Times* was even more damning, describing the incompetence on display as 'lethally chaotic'.

As a crowd of some 300,000 descended upon a stadium designed to hold less than half that number, thousands of people, finding themselves with nowhere to go, poured on to the playing area. The fact that the event is not recalled today as the Wembley Stadium Disaster was not thanks to the stewards, policemen or turnstile operators on duty that afternoon. It was down to a horse called Billy. So efficient was he in restoring some sort of order to the proceedings that the event has gone down in history as the White Horse Final. Though even that description is not strictly accurate. Billy was in fact a grey.

Back in 1923, the FA's Challenge Cup committee had been for some time searching for a permanent home for its annual final. And when a stadium was proposed as the centrepiece of the British Empire Exhibition to be staged in Wembley in 1924 (albeit one that was originally intended to be demolished after the show was over), ears pricked up at the FA: this was surely the ideal venue.

Costing some £750,000 (or just over a fortnight's wages for Wayne Rooney) the building went up in less than a year. Its construction involved 25,000 tons of concrete, 1,500 tons of steel and half a million rivets. And nothing appeared to be left to chance. A few days before Wembley's first match, a battalion of infantry was ordered to mark time on the terraces for fifteen minutes to test whether they were substantial enough to withstand the pounding of a crowd. And with that, the FA blazers satisfied themselves that the new venue was as sturdy as it looked. With a tardiness that might have alarmed even the organisers of the 2014 World Cup in Brazil, Wembley Stadium was completed just four days before its opening game.

On the day of the final, tens of thousands of the committed and the merely curious made their way up the Metropolitan Line, through the newly opened Wembley Central station, and along Wembley Way to the grand new facility with its imposing twin-tower frontage. By 1 p.m. the swell of humanity was so substantial that Bolton had to abandon their team charabanc and make their way to the stadium on foot. By 2 p.m. the crowd had completely overwhelmed the turnstiles, forcing their way through the exit gates. With nowhere to go on the already rammed lower terraces, the fans spilled onto the pitch. By 3 p.m., when the game was due to kick off, there were so many people on the playing surface that it was impossible to spot a single blade of grass. Fearful of the consequences if they failed to start the game (no less a dignitary than King George V himself was there to present the trophy), the authorities attempted to clear the area. It soon became obvious that something approaching a miracle would be required.

The Times described the incompetence on display as 'lethally chaotic'.

As it happens, Billy was not scheduled to be on duty that day. But his rider, PC George Scorey, had heard of the growing problems of overcrowding at the stadium and had turned up on his mount to see if he could assist. He was immediately dispatched down onto the pitch.

There were other horses in the ensuing operation, but it was Billy who became forever associated with that day. Not only because his grey colouring stood out on the black-and-white cinema newsreels that carried footage of the drama across the world, but also because of the calm way in which he went about his work. Cool, controlled and gently persuasive, Billy soon cleared sufficient space for the game to go ahead. As PC Scorey told the BBC fifty years on: 'He seemed to understand what was required of him. He was very good, easing them back with his nose and his tail until we got the crowd back along one of the goal-lines.'

And there they stayed. Eventually, forty-five minutes after it was supposed to start, the game kicked off, albeit with the crowd still packing the touchlines. The circumstances were farcical. After no more than two minutes had elapsed, a West Ham player had to fight his way through the mass of spectators to retrieve a misplaced pass. As he did so, the ball was returned and play continued. And he was still scrambling to get back onto the pitch when Bolton took the lead through David Jack (who was later to become the first footballer to attract a £10,000 transfer fee when he moved to Arsenal; see page 30).

There was no chance of the players making it through the throng to the dressing rooms at half-time, so they stayed out on the pitch. And it was Bolton who took final advantage of the chaos when Jack Smith scored the decisive second goal. It became an article of West Ham folklore, however, that in the build-up to his strike, the ball had been kept in play by the unlawful intervention of a boot applied by one of the 126,047 people officially recorded as being present. Most estimates put it closer to 300,000, including that one over-enthusiastic Bolton fan.

> He was very good, easing them back with his nose and his tail...

Billy's part in the proceedings was immediately noted. He became celebrated after the newsreel footage hit the country's cinemas the following week. Eighty-seven years later, in 2010, he was accorded the belated honour of having a pedestrian bridge named after him when the old stadium was reconstructed. A public vote had been called to decide in whose name the bridge should be built and he beat off a string of eminent human candidates, including Sir Bobby Charlton, Sir Geoff Hurst and Sir Alf Ramsey. Malcolm Tarling, a leading supporter of the Back Billy's Bid campaign, said at the time: 'There can be no more fitting tribute to Wembley's first and probably only four-legged hero than this. Billy would have been very proud.'

Though Billy might have preferred it if history had managed to record his colouring properly.

1925 'Arsenal Football Club is open to receive applications for the position of Team Manager. He must be experienced and possess the highest qualifications for the post, both as to ability and personal character. Gentlemen whose sole ability to build up a good side depends on the payment of heavy and exorbitant transfer fees need not apply.'

Advertisement placed by Sir Henry Norris, Arsenal chairman, in *The Athletic News*, summer 1925.

Sir Henry could barely believe his good fortune when it turned out that one of those responding to his advert was a certain Herbert Chapman. The manager who had just led Huddersfield Town to two successive league championships was feeling a little disappointed that his achievements had not been materially recognised. So when

Arsenal offered him an impressive £2000 a year to come to Highbury – double his salary at the Yorkshire club – he was on the first train to King's Cross.

Over the next nine years until his sudden death in January 1934, Chapman changed everything at Arsenal. Instituting a five-year plan like some footballing Lenin, he turned the Gunners from a going-nowhere sort of club into the grand institution that lorded it from Highbury's marbled corridors. He presided over the club's first two league titles, in 1930–31 and 1932–3, plus their first FA Cup win, in 1930. In the process, he changed the whole way coaching was viewed. Though he had been no more than a journeyman as a player, he was a pioneer in recognising the importance of tactics, training, psychology and preparation. He understood how to get the most out of those with significantly more skill than he ever possessed. In short, he was the precursor of the professional career coach.

But as Chapman went about his transformative business, he never lost sight of the central requirement of his job as set out in Sir Henry's original advertisement. In a manner that brings him ever closer to his professorial successor Arsène Wenger, he did not like to spend his employer's money. Even when the pugnacious Sir Henry himself stepped down in disgrace following an illegal payments scandal, to be replaced by Samuel Hill-Wood, grandfather of the recent Arsenal chairman Peter (who retired in 2013), Chapman never stopped watching the pennies. As he brought in recruits who subsequently went on to be woven into Arsenal legend, players like Alex James and Cliff Bastin, he did so with one eye on his budget. He spent the club's cash like it was his own.

> He spent the club's cash like it was his own.

Take his approach to discussions in 1928 with Bolton Wanderers about the signing of David Jack, scorer in the White Horse Cup final (see page 26). Wanderers' officials had made it clear that in order to part with their best player they were looking for a fee of something approaching £13,500, almost twice the existing transfer record. Chapman had other ideas, and set his cunning to work. His assistant Bob Wall recounted his preparations for the negotiations in a Manchester hotel:

> We arrived at the hotel half-an-hour early. Chapman immediately went into the lounge bar. He called the waiter, placed two pound notes in his hand and said: 'George, this is Mr Wall, my assistant. He will drink whisky and dry ginger. I will drink gin and tonic. We shall be joined by guests. They will drink whatever they like. See that our guests are given double of everything, but Mr Wall's whisky and dry ginger will contain no whisky, and my gin and tonic will contain no gin.'

Over the ensuing couple of hours of discussions, encouraged by the waiter's generous hand, the Bolton directors got merrier than a Blackpool hen party, while Chapman and Wall remained stone-cold sober. The signatures on the subsequent registration document may have been somewhat wobbly, but they record that the Arsenal boss had neatly managed to secure Jack's services for just £10,800.

There was more to Chapman than mere financial nous, however. Unlike almost all of his English contemporaries, he was a student of the way the game was played in Europe, keen to absorb many of the trends current on the continent (he was in charge of England as well as Arsenal at the time of his sudden death in 1934). He insisted on taking responsibility for all aspects of team selection (up until then, line-ups had been picked by a committee of directors, together with the captain). Tactically he was way ahead of his contemporaries, his Arsenal passing their way to victory over bemused opponents. An advocate of the counter-attack, he was defensively astute, too, organising his back line in a way that denied space in the final third to opponents who liked to run with the ball. He came up with the WM formation – basically 3-4-3 – to counter a change in the offside law which reduced the number of opposition players that attackers needed between themselves and the goal-line from three to two. It was a system that utterly bamboozled most of the other teams in the league. Such was his team's proficiency at stopping others from scoring that they quickly earned the disparaging and enduring soubriquet 'Boring Arsenal'.

Boring, maybe, but deadly efficient. And victorious. Chapman died of pneumonia at the age of fifty-five in January 1934, but the patterns and procedures he had established would lead to three more titles in the pre-war decade. Thanks to Chapman, Arsenal, by now so reliable they had become known as 'The Bank of England Club', dominated the domestic game for ten years.

> ...they quickly earned the disparaging and enduring soubriquet 'Boring Arsenal'.

These days he is immortalised in bronze in a statue outside the Emirates Stadium. Dressed in plus-fours, the great moderniser forever surveys the stadium that he would have loved to work in. Appropriately enough, he has his hands clasped behind his back. After all, as the advertisement that first enticed him to North London intimated, he was never a man who liked to put his hand in his pocket.

1934 'Nearly everything possible had been done to spoil the game: the heavy financial interest; the absurd transfer and player-selling system; the lack of any birth or residential qualifications; the publicity given to every feature of it by the press; the monstrous partisanships of the crowds.'

J. B. Priestley, *English Journey*, published 1934.

These were the words of a man who loved his football. Or at least who had once loved the game. In 1929 the novelist, playwright and social observer J. B. Priestley set out his feelings in the novel that first made his name, *The Good Companions*. For him, football was the game which best expressed the values of the working class.

> To say that these men paid their shillings to watch twenty-two hirelings kick a ball is merely to say that a violin is wood and catgut, that Hamlet is so much paper and ink. For a shilling Bruddersford United AFC offered you conflict and art.*

This is how football had developed in the half-century since it was formally established. A sport first codified and organised by the wealthy and privileged, and invested by them with qualities of chivalry and gentility, had within fifty years become overwhelmingly the game of the working man. Its stadiums towered over the terraced houses of every northern town; its rhythms beat in time with the

* *Bruddersford United AFC* is the football club of the fictional Yorkshire town at the centre of the novel.

patterns of daily life. Children played makeshift games on the cobbles, young men dreamt of developing the ball skills that would free them from the grinding routine of factory and pit. And for thousands of inner-city dwellers, Saturday in the stands offered escape. Here was the place where local pride could be expressed, where frustrations could be vented, where, for ninety minutes, another world existed. For Priestley, football was no mere sport. It was the working man's ballet. And what's more, never mind its inherent element of competition, for him football was the perfect expression of socialism: team-work, togetherness, community; individualism subsumed into the common good.

Or so he once thought. By 1933, however, he was not so sure. His problem was not with the ideals of the game, but with what it had become in reality. As he set out on his *English Journey,* a rambling exploration of the nation's industrial and rural heartlands in which he provided an eyewitness account of a population suffering the devastating economic and social consequences of the Great Depression, he was no longer convinced that the game he loved was still underpinned by the communitarian values that had once so evidently been its bedrock.

> Priestley believed that football was being ruined by those in charge of it.

Priestley believed that football was being ruined by those in charge of it, who were turning it into little more than an ugly reflection of the ills of wider society. He saw the rich exploiting the game for their own ends, and the working class being seduced away from solidarity to selfishness. Modern football offered not a model social structure in which everyone worked together for the same ends, but the spectacle of a game – hijacked by the financial classes to fuel their own short-term ambitions – that was nothing more than a vehicle for division, exploitation and abuse.

Some things don't change, then...

1942 'FUSSBALL SPIEL REVANCHE!' ['Return Football Match']

Headline on a poster advertising a match between FC Flakelf and FC Start, Zenit Stadium, Kiev, 9 August 1942.

It is the football story that for nearly half a century paid vivid testament to the heroism of the Soviet people, the story that epitomised the tenacity of their wartime resistance, the story that, in its tragic dénouement, spoke of the true meaning of sporting endeavour. The name that the game was subsequently given – 'The Death Match' – hints at what unfolded. And the story is indeed an extraordinary one. But the version of the tale in general circulation since the end of the Second World War is almost entirely a myth constructed by the Soviet Communist state. The reality is rather more complex.

At the time of Hitler's invasion in 1941, the Soviet Union was in love with football. It was one of the few pastimes the ruling Communist party actually encouraged among the population. There was nothing bourgeois, decadent or reactionary about kicking a ball, the Politburo believed. For nearly a quarter of a century since the Russian Revolution, football had been the sport of the Soviet masses, a proper proletarian pastime which everyone was urged to watch or play (that is, when they were not busy trying to please their leader Joseph Stalin by attempting to break Comrade Alexei Stakhanov's record of cutting 102 tons of coal in a six-hour shift). And the Soviet people genuinely loved the game, seeing within it an opportunity to escape, for a few short hours, the iron grip of the ruling party. Not to mention the chance – through their choice of who to support – to cock a snook at those in power.

This was particularly true in Kiev, where Dynamo, the local football club founded in 1927, had been challenging the well-resourced, party-backed Moscow outfits for supremacy in the Soviet football leagues.

Indeed, when the competition was suspended as Hitler launched Operation Barbarossa in the summer of 1941 and huge swathes of Soviet territory fell to the advancing panzers, Dynamo were top of the league, flying a flag for Ukrainian initiative, much to the chagrin of many a Communist official in the capital.

As the German tanks rumbled into Kiev, Nikolai Trusevich, Dynamo's recently retired goalkeeper and a member of the Red Army, had to lie low. He found himself a job in a bakery, and recruited several of his former team-mates to work there. With life settling into something approaching a routine under their new Nazi masters that was not altogether different from life under their old Communist bosses, the bakery lads looked to football as a means to escape. They formed a team, which they called FC Start, and began playing pick-up fixtures around the occupied city. With four Dynamo stalwarts and three players from Lokomotiv Kiev in their ranks, they were pretty good. In fact, they were *very* good.

Word got round and the German commandant of the Luftwaffe base near the city, looking for decent opposition to challenge his regimental side called *Flakelf* (literally 'Flak-eleven', a team of anti-aircraft gunners), organised a game against them. He thought it would motivate the troops and boost their morale. The commandant's plan depended, of course, on a successful outcome: the Luftwaffe boys had to win in order to prove the racial superiority of the German occupiers over their Slavic opponents. It didn't go well. Start won the game, played on 6 August 1942, by five goals to one. So the commandant strengthened his team and organised a rematch. Posters went up around Kiev advertising the grudge game, to be played three days later.

Since history is written by the victors, after the war Soviet propagandists seized on the tale of the football team that took on the Germans. Two novels were written about the brave Kiev boys, and a film called *Third Time* played to packed houses in the USSR throughout the 1960s; two decades later the plot was purloined by Hollywood and became the basis of John Huston's cheesy Christmas television staple *Escape to Victory* (1981), in which a team of Allied POWs – comprising an unlikely line-up of Sylvester Stallone, Michael Caine, Pelé and Bobby Moore, supported by various Ipswich Town stalwarts – defeat a Nazi eleven in an exhibition match before escaping in the mayhem that follows the final whistle.

The story of the 'Death Match' became a familiar one in Soviet classrooms. Generations learned of the footballers who wore red shirts to symbolise their devotion to Communism, who played on a pitch surrounded by armed guards and snarling dogs, who were instructed before kick-off that their role was a simple one: they were there to lose.

The tale insisted that, as the game began, the Kiev resistors immediately demonstrated that they were not going to be cowed. Playing for the honour of the Soviet Union, they attacked the Germans with vim. Alarmed that the tide was against the invaders, the referee – an SS officer – flagrantly bent the rules, disallowing perfectly good Start goals and ignoring ugly fouls by the Germans. At half-time, the commandant addressed the Kiev players threatening them with dire consequences if they persisted in their attempts to win.

That was not enough to scare the Soviet boys, though. The threats merely encouraged them to go forward. Victory was all that mattered, getting one over the hated Germans,

> The Kiev lads barely had time to acknowledge their triumph before they were summarily executed.

showing that the only way was the Communist way. In the end, not even German cheating could deprive FC Start of victory: they won the return match 5–3. But their joy was shortlived. The Kiev lads barely had time to acknowledge their triumph against all the odds before they were summarily executed by the Germans, fuming at defeat, right there on the football pitch.

It was a tale that spoke of selfless courage and collective resolve, of group solidarity in the face of terrible danger. As such, it became one of the great moral fables to emerge from the Soviet experience of the 'Great Patriotic War', its purpose to inspire similar loyalty among the populace to the party and the motherland. And so it stood for forty-five years.

It was not until the fall of Communism that the embroidery around the story began to be unpicked. In 1992, the fiftieth anniversary of the game, the newly independent Kiev radio station commissioned an investigation into it. The producers spoke with Makar Honcharenko, the only FC Start player then still alive. Now the Communist bosses were no longer breathing down his neck, he could tell the truth. Which turned out to be horribly mundane, the banality of evil writ large.

Honcharenko claimed the only part of the old Soviet legend that adhered to historical veracity was the names of the participants and the scoreline. Start did indeed beat the Luftwaffe select XI in the revenge match. But there were no threats, no coercion, no immediate reprisal. The Germans were, in fact, relatively hospitable, as shown by the photograph taken after the game of the two teams chatting amiably to one another. They played to the rules; the referee was neither SS nor bent. Even the red tops the Start team wore were not symbolic; they were loaned to them by their hosts as they had turned up in the same colour shirts as the Germans. After the match, far from being shot where they stood, the Start players went back to the bakery and toasted their win long into the night in vodka. 'Nobody from the official administration blackmailed us into giving up the match,' he said.

And, according to Honcharenko, there was a different explanation for the subsequent deaths of the players from the one that was so frequently peddled. A week after the German game, Start hammered a rival Kiev team called Rukh 8–0. So humiliated was the Rukh trainer Georgi Shvetsov that he immediately told the Nazis that the bulk of the Start team – the lads working in the bakery – were Soviet spies who had used the game against the Luftwaffe as cover to gather information about the strength of the occupying forces. Acting on his malicious tip-off, the Gestapo rounded up six of the players in the bakery and sent them to labour camps. Two more joined them within a week, all of them brutally tortured. By the end of the war, five of the incarcerated players were dead. 'They died like many other Soviet people because the two totalitarian systems were fighting each other and they were destined to become victims of that grand-scale massacre,' Honcharenko explained.

And the tale has a grim postscript. Two of Honcharenko's team-mates who survived and made it to 1945 were – with breathtaking irony, given how their memory was later exploited to reinforce the Communist system – executed by Soviet forces as collaborators the moment Kiev was liberated from the Nazis. Their crime? Playing football with the enemy.

1948 'Everything I know about morality and the obligations of men, I owe it to football.'

Albert Camus, Racing Universitaire d'Alger student magazine, 1948.

Goalkeepers love the fact that the great Algerian-born French philosopher and novelist was one of their own. They love it that during his time at the Racing Universitaire d'Alger club, Albert Camus played for the college team not as centre-forward or tricksy winger but in goal. And the popular image is of him standing there, in the baking heat of an Algiers afternoon, sweat pooling beneath his knitted jersey, taking the moments when the ball was up the other end of the pitch to ponder the meaning of life. This was the existentialist keeper, apart, separate, not entirely one of the team. Think Neville Southall, but with a French accent. And a preference for books rather than beer and rubbish collection.

Despite the distraction of pondering the Earth, the universe and everything when his own team attacked, Camus wasn't half bad as a goalie, either. Contemporary records suggest he might well have had a chance of making it in the game, until he contracted TB as a seventeen-year-old and the disease put paid to his ambition to play professionally.

Instead, coughing and spluttering over his typewriter, a smouldering Gauloise permanently attached to his bottom lip like some angst-ridden Gallic Humphrey Bogart, he became a novelist and essay writer, an icon of postwar French literature. But it seems that the principal philosopher of the Absurd remained a man who loved his football. Camus' observation of 1948 – which appeared in an essay for his old university magazine that he wrote when he was an established literary figure – has long been taken to be an affirmation of the game's qualities, and more specifically of its educative potential. For instance, it might be said that by passing the ball, a player learns about selflessness. Or that it is through team-work that he discovers the joys of cooperation. Or that by giving his all until the final whistle, he understands the importance of resilience and fortitude. Printed across the front of one of their products, the quotation remains a bestseller for the clever chaps at the Philosophy Football T-shirt company.

Yet, one wonders, if football was such a significant influence on him, why are there so few references to the game in Camus' *oeuvre*? If it was standing in goal for the university team that taught the novelist all he knew about the joys of life, how come the hero of *The Outsider* finds no connection between the offside trap and his growing sense of alienation as he goes about his murderous spree on the beach? Why is there no analysis of the pros and cons of Vittorio Pozzo's *Metodo* formation in *The Plague*? More to the point, in his essay published in 1935 entitled *Christian Metaphysics and Neoplatonism*, in his railing against established religion, why doesn't the writer posit the view that the one true faith is, in fact, football?

Closer analysis of his piece for the university magazine, beyond that soaring opening sentence, suggests Camus was in fact being a touch ironic. Sure, standing there between the sticks gave him insight into *la condition humaine*. But it was not wholly affirmative. Take this paragraph: 'I learned... that a ball never arrives from the direction you expected it. That helped me in later life, especially in mainland France, where nobody plays straight.' And this, remember, was with a ball encased in leather. Imagine how he would feel if faced by a Brazuca World Cup ball of 2014, banana-swerving through the air after a Cristiano Ronaldo free kick. Now that really is untrustworthy.

> As every 'keeper will tell you... goalies really are a breed apart.

If you look again at the wording of Camus' apparent *homage* to *le foot*, you become aware that it contains a certain whiff of sarcasm. The truth is that what he was suggesting in his essay is that his time as a goalkeeper exposed him to some of the worst aspects of human nature: the unreliability of others; their propensity for cheating and deception. Useful things of which to be mindful, undoubtedly, but not exactly life-enhancing. It was not so much morality the game taught him as *im*morality. Particularly from the French. How he would have agreed with Andrea Pirlo's observation about the penalty shoot-out at the 2006 World Cup final. The great Italian midfielder admitted in his autobiography that he had offered up a prayer before he took his spot kick, certain in his mind that God could not be a Frenchman.

So it was that being a keeper in his college team had an undoubted effect on Camus: it made him more wary and less trusting of others, more alert to the possibility of deceit. It turned him, in short, into an outsider. But then, as every 'keeper will tell you – from 'Fatty' Foulkes to Jens Lehmann, via Bruce Grobbelaar, René Higuita and Fabien Barthez – goalies really are a breed apart.

1949 'The Preston Plumber and his ten drips.'

Description in *The Daily Express* of Tom Finney's Preston North End as they were relegated from Division One in May 1949.

Tom Finney, one of the finest players ever to pull on an England international jersey, was known throughout his career as 'The Preston Plumber'. This was not a subtle allusion to his ability to twist opposing full-backs into the shape of a U-bend. No, the nickname had a more prosaic origin. In truth, he was a plumber and he came from Preston.

Despite his teenaged son being relentlessly courted for his ball skills by his home town football club, Finney's father had insisted the diminutive young winger complete his apprenticeship in the arcane science of piping and water flow. Football, said Old Man Finney, was not a proper trade. A man needed a craft. So young Tom completed his plumbing qualifications, and continued to fit pipes and clear drains even when he was an established international player, bamboozling Italian and Portuguese defenders, and scoring thirty goals for his country. After Preston once earned a draw in an FA Cup tie and Finney was told the replay would be on the following Tuesday, he is reported to have said: 'I can't do Tuesday, I'm fitting a bathroom.'

And he needed to be out there with his monkey wrench. Finney's career spanned the era of the maximum wage in football, when the game's feudal practices insisted that the players – however many paying customers their skills might draw through the turnstiles – should not benefit financially from the game to the tune of more than £20 a week. And that was in the good times. After completing his

I can't do Tuesday, I'm fitting a bathroom.

wartime service, Finney began at Preston in 1946 on a mere £9 a week.

Risible as that return may have been, Finney never complained. The man who was never once booked in his entire career regarded playing football as a privilege. He adhered strictly to the belief that he and his fellow professionals had a duty to entertain a public left battered and exhausted by the impact of war and wartime austerity. Even when the Italian club Palermo made a bid to sign him in 1952, offering unheard-of rewards of a £10,000 signing-on fee, £130 a week wages, bonuses of up to £100 a game, plus a luxury car and free travel to and from Italy, Finney made no objection when Preston unilaterally turned down their approach.

Instead, he played on and on for his home-town club, despite never winning the First Division or the FA Cup. Though he came close – Preston were pipped to the title by Arsenal only on goal difference in 1953 – his sole trophy in more than fifteen years' stalwart service with the Lancashire side was the Second Division championship. Not for nothing did his name become a byword for the ultimate football loyalist.

Finney voiced no resentment or frustration at being the star asset in a team made up largely of journeymen. What got his goat was the sneering so often directed at the outfit he loved. There was a joke that did the rounds when Preston were relegated in 1949 (a season in which he was largely absent through injury) that 'Tom Finney should claim income-tax relief... for his ten dependents.' Even his official biographer Paul Agnew noted that 'when Finney didn't play, neither did North End'. The player himself, however, would have none of it. Such talk, he insisted, was disrespectful. 'A one-man team has never existed anywhere,' he countered.

But the suspicion still lingers that such a team did once exist, in a town in Lancashire in the late 1940s and 1950s. After Finney finally retired in 1960 to concentrate on his plumbing business (which did very well, at one point employing more than 150 people, earning the boss enough in dividends to drive a top-of-the-range Mercedes), his reputation as one of the game's decent types only grew. It was Bill Shankly who best summed up Finney's untarnished excellence. Fifteen years after his former Preston team-mate had kicked a ball for the final time, the Liverpool manager was asked whether he agreed with the proposition that his bubble-permed forward Kevin Keegan, the darling of 1970s football, was a better player even than Finney. 'Aye, you're probably right, he maybe is just that wee bit better than Tom,' Shankly said. 'But then remember Finney's nearly sixty.'

1950 'These Are The World Champions'

Front-page headline in the Rio de Janeiro daily newspaper *O Mundo*, 16 July 1950.

Hubris may have been invented by the ancient Greeks, but, on the morning of 16 July 1950, it was honed to shimmering perfection by the editorial staff of the Rio de Janeiro newspaper *O Mundo*. That day their national team was to take part in the final game of the World Cup against Uruguay. This was the big one, the one that was going to decide the destination of the World Cup trophy in the first staging of the competition since the Second World War. It was held, moreover, in Brazil, a country where football was woven into the fabric of daily life, running Roman Catholicism a close second as the national religion. And so certain were the newspapermen of home victory, they filled their front page with a photograph of the eleven gold-shirted Brazilians who were about to take to the field below that simple headline. For them there was no question, *These Are The World Champions*.

The thing was, at the time, nobody thought *O Mundo* was tempting fate. The whole of Brazil was united in the absolute conviction that Moacir Barbosa, Augusto da Costa, Juvenal Amarijo, José Carlos Bauer, Danilo Alvim, João 'Bigode' Ferreira, Albino Friaça, Thomaz 'Zizinho' Soares, Ademir Menezes, Jair da Rosa Pinto and Francisco 'Chico' Aramburu would win the cup for them. They were, after all, the most talented group of players ever assembled, ambassadors for their nation, the boys who would put Brazil where it deserved to be: at the top of the footballing world.

The Brazil team, moreover, had illuminated the tournament with the kind of football that melded strength, skill and athleticism. It was true that Europe provided little in the way of opposition. Germany were banned (it was too soon after the war for them to be readmitted); despite qualifying, Scotland withdrew from participation; Hungary and the Soviet Union refused to travel from behind the Iron Curtain (chiefly because their officials feared half the squads would defect). Argentina decided to boycott the tournament (largely out of pique that they had not been chosen to host it); France pulled out just before, complaining about the amount of travel required around the vast host country; and while England did turn up, for what was their first-ever outing at a World Cup, they crashed out after an infamous defeat in Belo Horizonte to the expatriate journeymen of the USA. Moreover, Yugoslavia, Mexico and Switzerland, Brazil's opponents in the first group stage, had been dispatched with the ease of a child swatting a fly, no doubt using a rolled-up copy of O Mundo.

For the only time in World Cup history, there was no knock-out phase, not even so much as a proper final: after the group stages came a final group stage, contested by the four winners of the first round – Uruguay, Sweden, Spain and Brazil. And after Brazil had hammered Spain 6–1 and Sweden 7–1, it was a fair

Gol do Uruguay?

assumption that their concluding game against their tiny neighbours Uruguay – who had drawn with Spain and scraped through 3–2 against Sweden – was but a technicality, nothing more than a coronation. In what was effectively the final, the striker Ademir, who had scored five goals in the first two games of the second group stage, was expected to tear them apart.

And so, on that shimmering July afternoon, 199,854 people crammed into the newly built Maracanã stadium in anticipation of a victory carnival. They heard the Mayor of Rio, in a pre-match speech, insist the Brazilian players had 'no rivals in the entire hemisphere' and claim that 'in less than a few hours' they would be 'hailed as champions by millions of compatriots'.

Instead came shame, despair and misery. Obdulio Varela, the Uruguayan captain, had taken a copy of that O Mundo front page into the dressing room ahead of the game and invited his team-mates to urinate on it. The Rio journalists had done his team talk for him. And Uruguay found the most compelling revenge for the printed presumptions of their hosts. After Friaça had put Brazil ahead and Juan Schiaffino had equalised for the Uruguayans, the unthinkable arrived with the shocking suddenness of a lightning strike. In the 79th minute, Alcides Ghiggia beat the Brazil 'keeper Barbosa at his near post to poke the ball goalwards. Barbosa should have saved it, the save really was routine. Instead, gripped with nerves, he let the ball squirm under his body. His mistake reduced the stadium to shocked silence, the only sound coming from the players in pale blue shirts as they shrieked out their celebratory delight. And from the Brazilian radio commentator Luiz Mendes who asked the seemingly baffled question 'Gol do Uruguay?' a dozen times. Uruguay, a nation with a population smaller than that of Rio, had taken the World Cup for the second time in the competition's short history. The much-vaunted Brazilians, who had participated in all four FIFA World Cup competitions since 1930 and not won any, had fluffed their chance to lift the trophy for the first time.

According to apocryphal tales which blossomed in the aftermath of the events of 16 July, so traumatised were certain of Rio's residents by the defeat of their national team that dozens of them trailed up to the statue of Christ the Redeemer overlooking the city and flung themselves to their deaths. History does not record, however, whether the Mystic Megs of the editorial staff of *O Mundo* were among their number.

1953 'Get the ball to Stanley, he'll win it for you.'

Joe Smith, manager of Blackpool, at half-time during the FA Cup final, Empire Stadium, Wembley, 2 May 1953.

Few footballers have been as cruelly served by footballing epithet as Stan Mortensen. In 1953 the Blackpool and England striker scored the only hat-trick ever recorded in an FA Cup Final at Wembley. In ninety years of trying, no one else has managed to put the ball in the net three times in the seasonal grand finale, as he did that sunlit afternoon. It is among the most glittering individual goalscoring achievements in the domestic game.

But it was not him, not that Stanley, to whom his manager was referring. Nor, in the roll-call of football heroes, has his name been forever associated with Blackpool's surging, nerve-jangling late, late win over their Lancashire rivals Bolton. Instead of being the central character in a unique footballing drama, the most prolific scorer in Cup final history has been pushed to its margins. Folk memory has subsequently consigned Mortensen to the role of just a bit-part player in what has been known ever since as 'The Matthews Final'.

Mind you, Stanley Matthews didn't play at all badly himself that afternoon. His virtuosity on the right wing electrified the nation. And how the nation was in need of a bit of electrifying. Eight years on from the end of the war, rationing still held sway, cities were still pockmarked by bomb sites, and austerity retained a deadening grip on life in Britain. At Wembley, however, there unfolded evidence that victory could still be seized from the apparent jaws of defeat. In front of the new monarch, just a month away from her official coronation, the game spoke of possibilities ahead, of the optimistic virtues of sticking with it, of playing to the final whistle.

And Matthews was a man built to keep going. Blessed with a

natural technique that enabled him to bamboozle defenders at the first dip of his shoulder, he allied it to the kind of fitness regime which was anathema in a game in which, back then, the standard physical preparation involved a pint, a chip butty and twenty Capstan Full Strength. Brought up by a boxing champion father, from the age of four the 'Wizard of the Dribble' was inculcated into a daily routine of press-ups and squat thrusts. And then there was the jogging: years before the country's streets were awash with lycra, he ran miles every morning. That was why he loved playing for Blackpool: he was invariably on the beach by 8 a.m., pounding the sand, filling his lungs with the sea air he considered therapeutic. Matthews was a man years ahead of his contemporaries in his physical preparation. The result of his efforts, his team-mate Jimmy Armfield recalls, was that he never saw him out of breath. Even aged 38, as he was in 1953, Matthews could keep going far longer than his younger adversaries.

Yet for all his accomplishments – largely by dint of his most productive years coinciding with the wartime cessation of footballing competition – Matthews had won nothing. He had been on the losing Blackpool side in the Cup finals of 1948 and 1951. When his team arrived at what was to be the first final broadcast live on television, there was a sense across the country that this was his last chance. The shared hope was that finally his time might arrive. No one, was the widespread consensus, deserved it more.

In the first half, it didn't look like fate was finally going to look kindly on the Wizard. In a game that had little of the feel of the epic it was shortly to become, Bolton were 2–1 up at half-time (Nat Lofthouse and Bobby Langton the scorers for Wanderers, Mortensen for Blackpool). Up till then, Matthews was largely anonymous, his magic neutralised by the opposition's insistent marking.

Even after Joe Smith had given his simple half-time instruction to get the ball to Stanley, there was no immediate change in circumstance. For those hoping for a romantic conclusion, there was a further setback ten minutes into the second half. There was a degree of comedy about Bolton's third goal, which suggested Providence was mocking Matthews. The Wanderers left-half Eric Bell had torn his hamstring soon after half-time. Before the days of substitutes, he was obliged to stay on the pitch. Now he was limping around doing not much more than trying not to get in the way. Somehow, however, he found himself in the Blackpool area at precisely the right time to get behind a cross and score what appeared to be the decisive third Bolton goal.

It was then, when everything seemed to be conspiring against him, that Matthews decided to take things into his own hands. Or rather his feet. The wingman seized full advantage of the space afforded him by Bell's hobbling incapacity. He tore down the now largely unoccupied right flank, exhausting the Bolton full-back Ralph Banks, pulling the Wanderers back line all over the pitch.

By now, every time he got the ball, the crowd hummed in expectation. Continually galloping to the byline, he swung over cross after delicious cross. Nat Lofthouse, Bolton's England centre-forward, was more than a little anxious about the way Matthews could manipulate the heavy leather ball with such precision.

'I was thinking beforehand whether our defence could cope with Stanley's accuracy,' Lofthouse recalled towards the end of his life. 'You never saw him place a cross in the six-yard box where the goalkeeper might reach it. It was always half a yard outside, tempting.'

And so it happened. With twenty-two minutes left, as if laser-guided, a Matthews cross landed perfectly on Mortensen's forehead to bring Blackpool back into the game. Then, at 3–2, Matthews cut inside, running at his retreating opponents yet again. In both the expensive seats and on the terraces the crowd was on its feet, thrilling to the sight of this grand old stalwart in full flow. The tormented Bolton defence hacked Matthews down. And Mortensen hammered the resulting free kick into the net for the equaliser, completing his hat-trick. According to Armfield, it was as powerful a free kick as he had ever seen, an absolute piledriver.

As the end hove into view, there were twenty-one players on the Wembley pitch, their legs already drained by the occasion, resigned to half an hour's extra time. Not Matthews, however. In the second minute of injury time, he feinted past poor Banks yet again, hared to the byline and pulled back another exquisitely inviting cross.

For once, it was not Mortensen's forehead it found. For once, the centre-forward had mistimed his run. He could only watch as the ball drifted behind him, that tempting half a yard beyond the 'keeper's reach. Fearing that he had blown the most glorious of invitations, Mortensen was thrilled to see his colleague, the South African Bill Perry, drift in from the other wing to meet Matthews's brilliant assist and score the winner. The most unlikely of turnarounds was complete, victory was Blackpool's.

> They'll probably call it The Matthews Funeral.

The winning manager made it immediately clear whom he held responsible for victory. Smith dashed from the bench to embrace his Wizard at the final whistle. As they made their lap of honour after receiving the trophy from Princess (soon to be Queen) Elizabeth, the Blackpool players hoisted up their hero and carried Matthews shoulder-high. Mortensen was delighted to join them in their act of homage.

For evermore this was to be immortalised as the Matthews Final, the perfect soubriquet to sum up the happy amalgam of wish-fulfilment and glorious achievement. Though it did mean that the scorer of the only Cup final hat-trick was to find himself permanently in the shadows, upstaged by his more celebrated colleague. When the news broke of Stan Mortensen's passing on 23 May 1991, sports writer Matthew Engel of *The Guardian* observed wryly: 'They'll probably call it the Matthews Funeral.'

1953 'Like a fire engine heading to the wrong fire.'

Geoffrey Green's description of Billy Wright's attempted tackle on Ferenc Puskás, in his report on England's defeat by Hungary, *The Times*, 26 November 1953.

Six months after their triumph in the FA Cup Final (see pages 47–50), the two Stans – Mortensen and Matthews – were back at Wembley. This time they were on England duty, lining up against the Olympic champions Hungary. And this time, far from leaving the pitch in a trail of delirium, they were to be given a humbling lesson in the art of football.

Managed by Walter Winterbottom, England went into this game certain of themselves and their way of playing football. The embarrassing defeat to the USA in the 1950 World Cup had been explained away as a consequence of being obliged to play in unsavoury foreign parts. Sure, their magnificent wingman Tom Finney was injured, but this evening the game was being played at Wembley, so there was no need to worry: in international history, England had only lost once on home soil – to their near neighbours Ireland in 1949 – and that was at Goodison Park, not Wembley.

It had to be admitted they didn't know much about Hungary, but then they didn't need to: they were England. So superior did they consider themselves that, as the two teams made their way out onto the pitch side by side, Billy Wright, England's captain, recalled mocking their opponents' attire:

I looked down and noticed that the Hungarians had on these strange, lightweight boots, cut away like slippers under the ankle bone. I turned to big Stan Mortensen and said, 'We should be alright here, Stan, they haven't got the proper kit.'

Just as the Hungarians' footwear was unfamiliar to the English, so their tactics would prove to be. England, as always, would play the WM formation as invented by Herbert Chapman twenty years earlier. The assumption, even as Wright engaged in the formalities of the coin toss, was that that would be good enough to beat a bunch of Commies in silly booties.

> We should be alright here, Stan, they haven't got the proper kit.

Within sixty seconds it was clear it wouldn't be. The England team were immediately baffled by Hungary's fluid, fast-flowing formation. Nándor Hidegkuti was wearing the number nine but didn't play where the England boys expected him to. The slippery Magyar played in midfield, attacking from deep, the original false nine. England's stolid defenders had no idea what to do, or who to mark. Instead of adapting to circumstance they looked befuddled, like a bunch of inebriates.

It wasn't just that the Hungarians scored goals – lots of them – it was the manner in which they did it. It was as if they were toying with England, taking the mickey. When Ferenc Puskás scored the third, dragging the ball back on the edge of the area, sending Wright sliding off in completely the wrong direction, up in the press box, Geoffrey Green of *The Times* shook his head and tapped out his telling description of England's captain looking like 'a fire engine heading to the wrong fire'.

As Hidegkuti completed his hat-trick, as Hungary notched up six goals to England's three, completely puncturing the home side's sense of innate superiority as they did so, the reports from the English press crew mixed awed appreciation of the opposition with ferocious criticism of the home team. Admiration for continental skill and know-how; exasperation at English technical inadequacy: thus was established what would become the default response for journalists covering England matches for most of the following six decades.

'They shot with the accuracy and speed of archers,' cooed Green's report of the Hungarian attacking threat. 'It was Agincourt in reverse.' According to Green, Puskás, with his constant soft-shoe shuffling, was responsible for 'sheer jugglery'. While England, he sarcastically added, 'could probably win against Scotland at Hampden Park next April'. But in world terms, coupled with the humiliation in Belo Horizonte, the defeat marked how far behind they had slipped. Pat Ward-Thomas in *The Guardian* agreed.

> On the evidence of this afternoon this standard will not long be good enough for England to retain her position in the high places of the football world. The essential difference lay in attack, where none of the English forwards except Matthews approached the speed, ball control, and positional play of the Hungarians, which were as near perfect as one could hope to see.

The Times summed up what was going on at Wembley in the headline printed above Green's report: it called the Hungarian approach 'A New Conception of Football'. And that is what it was: a thrilling tactical methodology that was copied by many a young coach in England. Starting with the Manchester City centre-forward, Don Revie, who persuaded his team-mates to adopt the Hungarian formation – with himself playing in the Hidegkuti role – English football began to adapt. Alf Ramsey was later to say that his evening chasing Puskás's shadow changed his entire attitude to the game. That was the moment, he later admitted, that England realised it had to grow up as a footballing nation.

The fortunes of the England side were not to be transformed overnight, however. Even as the likes of Revie and Ramsey were trying to modernise, the national team was to suffer even greater indignity in the return fixture the following summer. Despite a radical overhaul of playing resources – six members of the England side that November night in Wembley were never picked for their country again – they lost 7–1 to the now-renowned Magnificent Magyars in Budapest. Eighty-two years after they played the world's first official international match (see pages 10–12), this was not only England's heaviest-ever defeat, but by far the most chastening. Its haunting consequences would not be exorcised for more than a dozen years.

1954 'Tor für Deutschland! *Drei zu zwei führt Deutschland... Halten Sie mich für verrückt, halten Sie mich für übergeschnappt!'* ['Goal for Germany! Germany lead 3–2... Call me crazy, call me nuts!']

Radio commentator Herbert Zimmermann delivers the news that West Germany has won the World Cup final, Wankdorf Stadium, Bern, Switzerland, 4 July 1954.

It was meant to be a formality. It was meant to be the result that crowned as world champions the finest football team on the planet. But, for the second tournament in succession, the World Cup final failed to go to plan (see pages 43–6). And for the victors, the reward was all the more delicious for its utter unexpectedness. For the victorious West Germans this was, and will forever be remembered as, *Das Wunder von Bern* – 'the Miracle of Bern'.

Ever since they had humiliated England home and away the previous year, the widely held assumption was that Hungary would win the 1954 World Cup. They had everything: organisation, skill and tactics, plus – in Ferenc Puskás – the finest player the game had ever known. And when they cruised past Brazil (in a match that ended in a dressing-room brawl) and the holders Uruguay in the quarter- and semi-finals, it looked a racing certainty. Especially as they were due to play West Germany in the final, a side they had demolished 8–3 in the group stage.

The Germans, though, were a wily bunch. Propelled, as a subsequent inquiry was to allege, by liberal doses of amphetamines disguised as vitamin injections, they had defied expectation on their way to Bern. That earlier defeat to Hungary was all part of the plan: with qualification already secured, their coach Sepp Herberger had deliberately fielded a weakened side in order to instil an assumption of security in their opponents.

More pertinently, the Germans were driven by a sense of destiny. This was the first international sporting competition they had been allowed to enter after the war. The final was the first time the German national anthem (now with different, less belligerent, words) had been played outside Germany since 1945. For the German team what the competition represented was acceptance by the rest of the sporting world, a chance to demonstrate a healthy patriotism untainted by the foul excesses of Nazism.

Also, they had technology on their side. The day before the final, the Swiss heavens opened. And it continued raining throughout the game, turning an already soft Bern pitch into a quagmire. The Hungarians were unable to wear their usual lightweight boots with short studs (which had earned the misplaced scorn of Billy Wright the previous year; see page 51). To gain any traction in the conditions, they were obliged to turn out in heavier clod-hopping footwear which, together with the standing water on the pitch, hugely restricted their passing game. The Germans, however, were kitted out by the fledgling sports outfitter Adidas in a new type of boot fitted with detachable studs. As the rain fell, they merely screwed a longer stud into their normal footwear and were able to dance around their opponents.

Even so, the final began as if following the ordained script. The Hungarians were 2–0 up within ten minutes. But as the pitch deteriorated, the Germans took control, easing into a 3–2 lead. The sense that fate was on their side was reinforced when the English referee William Ling wrongly disallowed a Puskás equaliser for off-side in the eighty-ninth minute. Puskás was not amused. 'I couldn't believe it,' he seethed. 'I could have murdered him. To lose a World Cup on such a decision just isn't right.'

When Ling blew the final whistle, up in the radio commentary box, Herbert Zimmerman reflected the feelings of his homeland: like him, the country went duly bonkers. So thrilled were the West Germans by this victory, the name of the winning captain Fritz Walter, a former prisoner of war, became immortalised in common discourse. Even now, whenever it rains, someone in Germany will describe it as 'Walter weather'.

> Every nation has a founding legend. For modern Germany it is the 3–2 victory over Hungary in the 1954 World Cup.

'Every nation has a founding legend,' announced the news magazine *Der Spiegel* on the fiftieth anniversary of the match. 'For modern Germany it is the 3–2 victory over Hungary in the 1954 World Cup.'

Their famous and unexpected World Cup victory in Switzerland restored to postwar Germany a sense of self-confidence and self-worth. That feeling was amply reinforced when Sönke Wortmann's charming cinematic retelling of the story became the highest-grossing German-language movie of all time on its release in 2004. The film's title? *The Miracle of Bern*, of course.

1958 'The road back may be long and hard, but with the memory of those who died at Munich, of their stirring achievements and wonderful sportsmanship ever with us, Manchester United will rise again.'

Club chairman Harold Hardman's message to United supporters, 19 February 1958.

A hurried four pages, a hint of ink still drying on its cover, the programme for Manchester United's FA Cup tie with Sheffield Wednesday on 19 February 1958 may not be the rarest of items of footballing memorabilia (Google it and there are always at least half a dozen examples up for sale). But it is among the most moving. Just a fortnight after eight of Matt Busby's young team had perished on the slush-coated runway of Munich airport, the editor had no idea who might be turning out in the red shirts that evening. Every certainty had been removed. So he left empty the space that had only recently been occupied with such distinction by such names as Pegg, Whelan, Edwards and Byrne. The gaps were not there to serve as memorial to the lost Busby Babes, the Flowers of Manchester. They were simply to allow the fans to fill in the names of whoever could be rustled up to play for the Reds on that winter day.

Looking at those empty white boxes five and a bit decades on, what seems astonishing is that the game went ahead at all. Surely, this was the very definition of too soon. In retrospect, the anxiety to engage in competitive action less than fourteen days after the soul had been ripped from the club seems callous. Two of the players who had survived the crash were among the eleven picked that night, expected to carry on without any suggestion of counselling. United had wanted no favours from the footballing authorities, they brooked no thought of postponement or delay. There was a belief that the best form of therapy (though no one used that word back then) was to stiffen the upper lip, straighten the back and uncomplainingly re-engage as soon as possible with the organisation's core purpose. No time for grief, get out there and play was the only way to recover.

That is the message Harold Hardman was seeking to convey in his statement printed on the programme's cover: United will go on. Nothing – not even the crushing grief that follows hard on the heels of devastating loss – was to stand in the way of momentum. And with those words, Hardman provided United with a guiding philosophy that prevailed for another fifty years. No individual is bigger than the institution. All that matters is the club.

On the fiftieth anniversary of the crash, a BBC documentary crew filmed Harry Gregg, one of the few who emerged from the tangled wreckage of the club's chartered plane unscathed, walking through the old airport terminal. 'Because of what happened when we left this building,' he said as he picked his way through the dusty, long-disused hall, 'Manchester United changed from a football club into an institution.'

Gregg was only half right. While the disaster gave United a uniquely romantic backstory, it was how they responded to that horrific moment that made the club what it is today. Fans don't pledge their allegiance out of pity. In Singapore, Shanghai and Seoul the new generations of red-shirted enthusiasts don't choose to follow United's fortunes because of what happened to a bunch of blokes who died when their grandfathers were still in short trousers. It is because of what happened in the years after the crash. It was then that Hardman's words came to fruition.

There had been sporting tragedies before United's. Just under a decade earlier, in May 1949, the Italian champions Torino had lost their first team in a plane crash at Superga. Eighteen players had died when the chartered aircraft bringing them back from a friendly in Portugal crashed into a hilltop basilica in the suburbs of Turin. When this disaster occurred, there were still four games left in the league season. Torino's youth team stepped into the breach and the Italian FA, as a mark of respect, insisted that their opponents field weakened line-ups, gifting them the points to enable them to finish as champions. Despite the gesture, Torino, at the time of the crash the dominant force in Italian football ('Il Grande Torino' won five Serie A titles in the late 1940s), never recovered their potency. Since 1949 they have won just a single Serie A title, in 1976.

> Pick yourself up and start again was the prevailing philosophy.

Hardman's words set United on a different path. Not that there was anything particularly unusual about his tone, he was merely reflecting a national mood. Just thirteen years after the end of the war, when half a million young British men had returned from the charnel sands of North Africa, from watching their friends die on the killing fields of Normandy, or from near-starvation in Japanese labour camps, there was no mood for self-pity. There was no recognition of post-traumatic stress disorder back then. Pick yourself up and start again was the prevailing philosophy. You got on with it: that was the British way.

There are some who, looking back, reckon that the stoical, 'let's get on with it' approach provided a convenient smokescreen for not providing adequate compensation. Munich survivors like Albert Scanlon and Johnny Berry, the ones who, unlike Bobby Charlton and Bill Foulkes, never recovered their pre-crash prowess, took years to receive proper financial recompense for the horrors they suffered. The club, some believe, preferred to embrace rhetoric rather than acknowledge its proper responsibilities.

But what cannot be denied is that post-Munich, renewal became the central value at United, carved into the very superstructure of Old Trafford. Within ten years, Hardman's philosophy would bring extraordinary rewards. In 1968 Busby's third great side won the European Cup, the very trophy the Babes had perished pursuing. And, four decades on, Hardman's call to forward thinking became central to Alex Ferguson's reign at the club. For twenty-six years under the Scotsman's guidance, there was no looking back. Nothing stood in the way of progress. Nothing – not celebrity players, nor the efforts of rivals, nor Roy Keane's acid tongue – would be allowed to obstruct the club's constant need to refresh and rebuild. In those few well-chosen words in the aftermath of tragedy, Hardman could have been providing the script for the Ferguson years that lay ahead.

1958 'The scientific systems of the Soviet Union died a death right there. They put the first man in space, but they couldn't mark Garrincha.'

Luiz Mendes, Brazilian radio commentator, Ullevi stadium, Gothenburg, 15 June 1958.

Ask most Brazilians who they regard as the best player their country has ever produced – the finest indeed in football history – and the answer may come as a surprise. It is not Pelé. It is not Jairzinho or Rivelino or Socrates or Zico. It is not Romário, Ronaldinho or Ronaldo (the gap-toothed burger-loving one). It is not even Fred. No, the widespread belief across much of the nation is that the greatest footballer ever to don the golden shirt is Manuel Francisco dos Santos, the man who was so tiny as a child he was called Garrincha, 'the wren'. Though by the time he finished playing, others had more elevated nicknames for him. 'If Frank Sinatra was The Voice,' said the cooing Brazilian commentator Luiz Mendes of his sporting hero, 'Garrincha was The Dribble.'

Garrincha was not exactly dealt a winning hand in life. Born into abject poverty, the son of an alcoholic father, completely uneducated, he bore an odd deformity which meant one leg bowed outwards and the other inwards, rendering him simultaneously bow-legged and knock-kneed. But chuck a football at him, and from the earliest age he crackled and sparkled. The cheeky, carefree boy came alive. And here was the thing about him that so chimes with the romantic image Brazilians have of the game and their nation's connection with it: he was almost completely uncoached, not to say uncoachable. He did what he did on a football pitch not because of scientific analysis of his Prozone stats but because he wanted to. Garrincha was as close to a force of nature as has ever been unleashed on a football pitch. He just did what came to him. Not for nothing did he become known as *Anjo de Pernas Tortas* or 'the Angel with Bent Legs'.

> If Frank Sinatra was The Voice, Garrincha was The Dribble.

What Garrincha liked to do more than anything was dribble. He lived by the process of running at opponents with the ball and then beating them. He could feint, he could shimmy, he could use his unique physiology to huge advantage: no one knew which way his legs were going when he stood still, never mind when he ran at pace. And boy, how the fans loved to see him go full pelt.

It was when he was playing for his club Botafogo that a football crowd was first heard to use the bullfighting cry '*olé*' to applaud a moment of spectacular skill. His team were playing the Argentine champions River Plate in the winter of 1957 and Garrincha had spent the game doing what he liked best: tormenting his marker to the point of distraction. Poor Federico Vairo knew precisely what the winger was going to do: he was certain to feint one way and go the other. Yup, he knew that much. But there was a sizeable gap between knowing it and stopping him. During one dash down the wing, with the Argentinian hot on his heels, Garrincha deliberately left the ball behind and carried on sprinting. By now befuddled, Vairo followed him with all due urgency, even though the ball remained where Garrincha had left it. The only legitimate response to this Benny Hill moment was the roared '*olé*' which echoed round the stadium.

And the '*olés*' only grew louder in the 1958 World Cup Finals, held in Sweden. After picking up a knock in training, Garrincha made his first appearance in the tournament in Brazil's final group game against the Soviet Union. This pitched the relentlessly drilled, organised and resourced Soviets, the epitome of modern training methods, against the carefree, unschooled Brazilians. It was billed as science against nature. Though that analysis was a touch simplistic. The Brazilians had in fact gone to considerable lengths in their preparations to try ensure that the traumas of 1950 were not revisited. One precaution taken by the team management – knowing the womanising proclivities of players like Garrincha – was to ask the hotel accommodating them when they first arrived in Sweden temporarily to replace all their female staff with men. They didn't want the players distracted (not that it stopped the priapic winger: he was to father at least one Swedish child on tours of the country later in his career).

While the word 'natural' might not have been an accurate description of the wider Brazilian enterprise in 1958, it neatly summarised the twenty-five-year-old Garrincha. And he was brilliant against the Soviets, juggling, feinting and dribbling, ensuring the result was Nature 2, Science 0. The perfect prelude to Garrincha-inspired victory in the final in Stockholm which finally brought the Brazilians their long-awaited world title. In his 1995 history of football, *Soccer in Sun and Shadow*, the Uruguayan novelist Eduardo Galeano neatly summed up what Garrincha was all about: 'When he

> When he was out there... the match was a party invitation.

was out there, the pitch was a circus ring, the ball a tamed animal, the match a party invitation.'

The best party, though, was still to come. With Pelé injured, Garrincha carried the Brazil team to victory in the 1962 tournament, winning the Golden Boot in the process. No player – not even Maradona in 1986 – has been as instrumental in the delivery of the trophy as he was in '62 in Chile. He was simply astonishing, tearing the world of football apart with his natural skill.

Sadly, it was nature that ultimately undermined him. His oddly shaped legs put tremendous pressure on his knees and hips every time he galloped down the line. He needed endless operations, the last of which effectively finished him as a player in 1968.

And with that, he was largely finished as a man. While Pelé flourished in retirement, joining Brazil's footballing establishment, Garrincha went into a sad decline. Wretchedly ripped off for most of his playing career, he retired in penury. It would be wrong to say that nothing gave him as much pleasure as football; after all, he fathered at least fourteen children. And his family sued a journalist who wrote about his legendary size in the trouser department, saying it demeaned his memory; they lost the case, as the judge reckoned it was not a bad reputation for a man to have. But it was football that gave him a rationale, gave him legs. Without it, he drank himself to oblivion on *cachaça*, the local sugarcane spirit: the genius he had displayed in Stockholm and Santiago a fading memory; the body he had pushed to triumph over deformity now degenerating into physical ruin. Propped up in a *favela* bar, this was a national hero forgotten.

> His family sued a journalist who wrote about his legendary size in the trouser department.

Or so it appeared until, when he

died of alcoholic poisoning aged just fifty in 1983, his funeral unleashed an astonishing outpouring of emotion in his homeland. Millions lined the route of his cortège – more than for any other figure in the country's history – to mourn the lost hero of Brazilian football. His exalted place in the nation's history was confirmed when the new stadium in the capital Brasilia built for the 2014 World Cup was named after him, a belated acknowledgment that his countrymen had failed properly to celebrate Garrincha's achievement when he was still alive.

1950s 'There were plenty of fellas in the Fifties who would kick your bollocks off. At the end, they would shake your hand and help you look for them.'

Bolton centre-forward Nat Lofthouse, interviewed in the 1970s.

Then again, it wasn't his bollocks – severed or otherwise – Nat Lofthouse needed to worry about. It was another spherical object. During the 1950s in England there was one globe that was to have significant long-term consequences for him and many other footballers: the match ball. An object whose sheer weight caused permanent damage to those who spent their lives heading it.

English football – like much of English life – has long been gripped by nostalgia. Lofthouse, a fearsome striker for Bolton Wanderers, was by no means the last to hark back. For the football fan it has always been the case that things simply ain't what they used to be. How much better everything was back then, back in simpler times, back in the days when modern life hadn't spoiled it all.

Lofthouse was speaking in the 1970s, when football was a very different game from the one he played twenty years earlier. Surveying the skimpy shorts and bouffant facial fungus of players paid wages way beyond a level he could ever have dreamt of, Lofthouse looks back to make unflattering comparison. And in the process sounds as if he were scripted by Monty Python's Four Yorkshiremen. More than likely his misty-eyed reminiscence was sparked by some instance of contemporary footballers not respecting one another – maybe Francis Lee and Norman Hunter fighting on the pitch, or Kevin Keegan and Billy Bremner being sent off at Wembley for scrapping like schoolboys. His humorous vision was that when he played back then players were proper lads. Uncompromising maybe, tough enough certainly to conduct on-pitch surgery without the assistance of anaesthetic, but they were gentlemen too. Back then there were no hard feelings, just hard men.

Lofthouse had a point: football certainly *did* change at the end of the 1950s. But history suggests it changed for the better. Sure, players had become figures of wider popular culture, detached from their roots, no longer catching the bus to the ground with the fans before kick-off. But the revolution first unleashed by the Hungarians had swept away much of the archaic way the game was played, improving it beyond measure. Far greater emphasis was now placed on ball retention and control, on tactics and technique: sheer physicality was no longer enough.

Furthermore, the laws were changed, giving protection for the skilled from the licensed thuggery that was an integral part of the game in Lofthouse's day. By the 1970s, the kind of violence that Aston Villa's Peter McParland had used on Ray Wood, the Manchester United goalkeeper, in the 1957 FA Cup final – a bruising shoulder charge which, had it occurred on the street, might have resulted in arrest – had been outlawed.

But the feature of the game in the 1970s that had seen most

improvement from the 1950s was the balls (footballs, that is, not the severed male body parts of Lofthouse's nostalgia). Nowhere was technological advance more evident than in the object at the heart of the game. By the 1970s, now lighter, waterproof and infinitely more pliable, the ball was no longer the weighty weapon it had been in Lofthouse's day. When he was playing, the ball, encased in leather, would soak up water like a sponge in wet conditions, becoming so heavy it might as well have been hewn from granite. Some unscrupulous coaches would dunk the match ball in a bucket of water before kick-off in order to undermine the skills of the opposition. For a centre-forward like Lofthouse, who was expected to get his head on the ball continuously as it was lumped upfield, the consequences of its design were debilitating. He was not the only player to suffer from persistent headaches, blackouts and

> He was not the only player to suffer from persistent headaches, blackouts and memory loss in later life.

memory loss in later life. West Brom's Jeff Astle died in 2001 of brain damage brought on by a lifetime of heading the ball. Never mind having their bollocks kicked off, back in the 1950s these guys had their brains mashed. And it would have taken some search party to help them look for their lost memories after the game.

PART III

INTO THE FIRST HALF

1961–89

1961 'Five times your wages: was it that that tempted you?'

Denis Law is quizzed by reporters after he signed for Torino, July 1961.

Denis Law should not have been the first British footballer to be the subject of a £100,000 transfer. That accolade should have gone to Jimmy Greaves, a year earlier. But Tottenham's manager Bill Nicholson had a moral problem about authorising that sort of spend on a mere sportsman. He steadfastly refused to cross that fiscal threshold, so paid out £99,999 to buy Greaves from AC Milan.

Others were less reticent. Law, who had started at Huddersfield Town under Bill Shankly's management, had only been at Manchester City for a season before he became Britain's first six-figure man. When the offer was made, it was not a hard decision for him to go to Italy. The maximum wage had only just been abolished in English football after Fulham's Jimmy Hill had threatened to lead the players out on strike in January 1961, and Law's remuneration at Maine Road remained the most allowed under the former strictures. He was on £20 a week, the equivalent of £377 in today's money. When Torino offered him more than £100 a week, Law was on the first plane to Lombardy.

Torino may have been breaking records, but this was some player they were getting for their money. The little Scottish forward was wily, crafty and not remotely shy about getting his retaliation in first. He appeared to be perfectly attuned to the physical and technical requirements of the game in Italy. So much so, he was subject to an extended tug of love between Italian clubs. Internazionale insisted he had made a pre-contractual agreement with them to head to Milan, not Turin. Law was adamant he hadn't signed any pre-nup, and Inter's claim was only dropped at the last, to enable him to make his debut for Torino at the start of the 1961–2 season.

Nervous about what to expect in Italy (he had suffered from

homesickness for several years after coming to England from Scotland as a fifteen-year-old), Law was initially rather pleased with what he found. Torino's pre-season training took place at a luxury hotel complex in the Alps, a world away from City's Moss Side base. This was the life. But, once the action turned serious, it quickly became apparent to the slim, sharp-boned fisherman's son from Aberdeen that things were not quite as advertised. That £100 a week Law was promised, for instance, was largely a chimera. Most of his earnings turned out to be performance-related. It *was* possible for him to pick up that sort of money, but only if he was part of a team that won every week. And at Torino, winning seemed to be well down the list of tactical priorities. As Law recalled: 'Everything about the place was lovely but the football was awful.

> Everything about the place was lovely but the football was awful.

Every result was basically 0–0. Every team just defended.'

In the days of *catenaccio*, the Italian defensive system in which the principal aim was to lock out opponents, there was little reward for a swashbuckler like Law. Generally stationed up front on his own, starved of service and attention, he was so shunned by his team-mates that he began to worry about the state of his personal hygiene.

By April 1962, chastened and disillusioned, Law was looking for a way out. During an international break with Scotland, he met up with Matt Busby and told the Manchester United manager of his unhappiness. Busby told him that if he put in a transfer request, United would make a bid for his services. On his return to Turin, Law did just that. The demand was ignored. His relationship with his employers then deteriorated beyond repair when he was sent off against Napoli towards the end of a season in which he had scored ten goals in twenty-nine appearances. After the match, he learned that Torino's coach, Beniamino Santos, had instructed the referee to send him off because he was angry at Law for taking a throw-in.

Throw-ins, he was informed, were not part of his remit.

Such petty acts of authoritarianism infuriated the non-conformist Law and he responded by walking out of the club. He was told by letter that he was to be transferred across town to Juventus. He responded by flying home to Aberdeen. After a lengthy stand-off, he learned that Busby had been true to his word and he had been signed for United. On 10 July 1962, Law set another new British record transfer fee of £115,000. For the second time in a year, he had crashed through the international transfer ceiling. This time, the record stood for a further four seasons, until the £150,000 paid by Leicester to Fulham for Allan Clarke in June 1968.

The move back to Manchester was the making of Law. At Old Trafford he immediately found his feet. His goals won his club the title in 1963 and he was voted European Footballer of the Year in 1964. Of the gilded attacking trinity he forged with Bobby Charlton and George Best (see pages 86–90), Law was always the fans' favourite, heralded as the King of the Stretford End, his habit of celebrating goals by pulling his sleeve over his knuckles and thrusting his right arm skyward to celebrate his 171 goals in 309 appearances copied in a thousand school playgrounds. His regal reputation lingers still: he is the only figure in United history to be granted not one, but two statues at Old Trafford.

And it wasn't just in England that he was held in the highest renown. When the great Dutch international Dennis Bergkamp joined Arsenal in 1995, he revealed that he was named after Law. His parents had wanted his Christian name to share the same spelling as their hero. But the Dutch authorities had insisted on the insertion of an extra 'N'. Apparently the lowland bureaucrats felt that just the one would make it confusingly similar to Denise. And that was a girl's name.

1964 'I've heard of selling dummies, but this club keeps buying them.'

Len Shackleton on his former club Newcastle United in 1964.

Len Shackleton was a footballer born before his time. Not in the way he played the game: he was a fine but not historically exceptional wingman in the days when England was blessed with the talents of Tom Finney and Stanley Matthews. It was more the way he talked about football that set him apart. With his sarky quips, his irreverent observations and his anti-establishment jibes, he would have made a fortune as a pundit in today's media. This was Roy Keane with a sense of humour, Eamon Dunphy with a sense of proportion, Robbie Savage with a plausible haircut. Had social media existed in the 1950s, Shackleton's Twitter following would have reached seven figures. He would have today's television viewers cackling endlessly. This was a man who knew how to time a gag.

Lighting up the wing for Newcastle (he scored six on his debut for the club, a 13–0 thrashing of Newport County) and then – for a record fee of £20,800 – Sunderland, even when he played he was forever making light of his profession. 'Newcastle have been unlucky with injuries,' he once said. 'Their players keep recovering.'

On the pitch Shackleton was just as keen to entertain. His favourite trick was to bounce the ball off the corner flag to bamboozle defenders. If he didn't like his centre-forward (and he held a particular antipathy for Sunderland's Trevor Ford) he would put a devilish spin on the ball when he passed it, to make control almost impossible. On one occasion he dribbled past several defenders and played the ball invitingly to an unmarked Ford with a loud and sarky 'don't say I don't ever pass to you'. But the pass was weighted with wicked backspin, and Ford missed the chance.

Not for nothing was Shackleton known as 'The Clown Prince of Soccer', a nickname he employed in 1956 as the title of his autobiography. This was not Alan Shearer revealing the joys of creosoting his fence: Shackleton's book was a belter. One chapter heading became infamous. It was called 'The Average Director's Knowledge of Football', and consisted of a single blank page.

Observations like that did not endear him to the establishment. His attitude meant he was reckoned by some not have the necessary gravitas, not to take the game with sufficient seriousness. He played just five times for England, his only goal a delightful chip over the goalkeeper in a match against the then world champions West Germany in December 1954. Even that finish did not help his selection. On being asked by a reporter why Shackleton had again been overlooked for international recognition, an FA committee member once angrily retorted: 'It's because we play at Wembley. Not the London Palladium.'

> It's because we play at Wembley. Not the London Palladium.

Shackleton didn't appear to mind. For him, everything was a source of laughs. He even turned the announcement in 1957 of his premature retirement from the game, precipitated by a nagging knee injury, into a joke. Standing in front of waiting pressmen, he said he had something important to say. He then proceeded to flick a penny in the air, catch it on the toe of his shoe and kick it up again into the breast pocket of his jacket. At which he turned on his heel and walked off.

A showman such as Shackleton was not long out of the limelight. He soon got a job as a journalist for the *Newcastle Chronicle*, working the northeastern football patch for the next twenty-five years. Over the years his acuity never faltered. In 1964 he turned his attentions to those in charge of his former club with that devastating put-down about dummies. He seemed to reserve particular venom for those at

St James' Park, as evidenced by another quip: 'I'm not biased when it comes to Newcastle. I don't care who beats them.'

Shackleton's acidic observations have retained their relevance on Tyneside over the decades. In fact, if anything, it might be argued that things have latterly got even worse. When Joe Kinnear departed as Director of Football in February 2014, it brought to an end his eighteen months in charge of the club's player recruitment department. In that time, he did not actually manage to recruit a single player. No one was signed. Not even a dummy. If only Len Shackleton had been available to pass comment on that record of achievement. But, sadly, he died in 2000, probably still smiling.

I'm not biased when it comes to Newcastle. I don't care who beats them.

1966 'Some people are on the pitch. They think it's all over... it is now.'

Kenneth Wolstenholme, commentary on the World Cup final for the BBC, Empire Stadium, Wembley, 30 July 1966.

Kenneth Wolstenholme's now legendary words, spoken as Geoff Hurst's piledriver shot bulged the West German net in the last minute of extra time in the 1966 World Cup final, were bang on the money. Though not perhaps in quite the way that the modest, gentlemanly Wolstenholme – Second World War bomber pilot turned BBC commentator – might have imagined. The moment the whistle sounded on England's victory, and a gaggle of over-enthusiastic supporters started their celebratory pitch invasion, and when Nobby Stiles began his giddy little jig down by the corner flag, it really was all over. England's time as a force in world football *was* finished, done, terminated. Like Monty Python's parrot, it was no more.

Since that warm July afternoon, when Bobby Moore wiped his palms down the front of his shorts so as not to soil the queen's pristine white gloves as they shook hands before the trophy presentation, ten nations have won either the World Cup or the European Championship (and four have won both): Brazil, Germany, Argentina, Italy, France, Spain, Czechoslovakia, Holland, Denmark and Greece. The closest England have come to employing the engravers is losing two semi-finals. They missed out altogether on the World Cup Finals in 1974, 1978 and 1994 and on the European championships in 1976 and 2008. In international terms, almost from the moment Geoff Hurst's hat-trick (with a little bit of help from Tofiq Bahramov, the myopic Azerbaijani linesman) secured the world title, England have reverted to type. They have become international also-rans; their standard level of achievement is to lose in the quarter-finals. Generally on penalties. And along the way there have been some memorably painful stuffings at the hands of cannier, more skilful opponents: a 3–1 Marco van Basten-inspired drubbing from the Netherlands in the 1988 European Championship, a 4–1 humiliation at the hands of Germany in the 2010 World Cup, not to mention the shambolic early departure from Brazil in 2014, stand out amid a plethora of grisly post-1966 low points.

How did it come to this? How did the country beaming in self-congratulatory triumph on the top of the pile in July 1966 fall so far from grace? How did a succession of players, coaches and chief executives fail to come close to replicating that sun-dappled victory? How did England turn into a byword for international underachievement?

'When I played I always loved to go out against English teams because they always gave the ball back to you when you lost it,' said Johan Cruyff in 1998. It is a common sneer of the continental sophisticate. English players are reckoned to possess much heart but little brain, believed to wield a bludgeon while others stab with a rapier. Difficult to beat, for sure. But very hard to lose against. And the reason why Cruyff's cruel jibe could not be gainsaid by statistics can be traced back to that moment Wolstenholme summarised.

It was not so much who made up the England team that afternoon that gives us a clue as to what happened next. It was who was left out. Sir Alf Ramsey found no room in his side for probably his most gifted player. Jimmy Greaves, the mercurial Spurs forward, was not picked. In those days before substitutes, he was obliged to watch the action dressed in his suit from the tunnel, his disappointment later to be expressed in a decade-long drinking binge. Ramsey didn't trust the skilled and slippery Greaves. He could find no room to amalgamate his sublime finishing into his team, preferring the more robust approach of Hurst and Liverpool's Roger Hunt. And his distrust set the tone for the near five decades of hurt (and counting) that lay ahead.

> When I played I always loved to go out against English teams because they always gave the ball back to you when you lost it.

It is a commonplace to suggest that had Greaves been Brazilian the team would have been built around his abilities. But English football, like much of English society, was then split between the cavalier and the roundhead. And when Ramsey won the World Cup, the roundhead way gained the upper hand. Of all the things that Ramsey could be remembered for representing – strangulated pronunciation, wingless wonders, a visceral loathing of the media – a love of individualists would not be high on the list.

With that victory, Ramsey's embrace of the pragmatic became enshrined at the heart of the English game. Why do things any other way, when Ramsey had demonstrated that efficiency could prevail? The man himself may not have survived a failure to qualify for the 1974 World Cup, but his philosophy remained intact and central, channelled through a coach called Charles Hughes who became the

FA's technical director in the late 1970s. Hughes had studied football and came to the conclusion that possession was mere self-indulgence. He had worked out that goals were usually scored after no more than three touches of the ball. He believed in something called 'Positions of Maximum Opportunity', and encouraged his teams to get the ball into POMOs as quickly as possible. This meant not passing your way from the back, but hoofing it forward at every opportunity. He wrote the manual on which the English coaching tradition was based for two decades. He ensured that one of his protégés – Graham Taylor – became England coach. That's the same Graham Taylor who said this in 1992:

> Possession and patience are myths. It's anathema to people in the game to say this, but goals come from mistakes, not from possession.

And the same Graham Taylor whose England failed to qualify for the World Cup in 1994.

During the 1970s, English clubs produced such creative players as Rodney Marsh, Tony Currie, Alan Hudson, Stan Bowles, Duncan McKenzie, Charlie George and Frank Worthington. Between them, they gained fewer international caps than Liverpool's industrious full-back Phil Neal. They may not have represented the apex of the work ethic, but these were players blessed with the kind of ability to unpick a defence that would – if properly applied – have elevated the England team. Marsh dined out for years on a story which summarised the philosophical gap at the heart of the English game.

> Sir Alf said to me before an England game that he'd be watching me for the first 45 minutes and if I didn't work hard enough he'd pull me off at half-time. So I said: 'Blimey, at Man City all we get is an orange and a cup of tea!' It didn't go down well.

Hughes's philosophy held sway in the national system, most perniciously in coaching development. The long ball was embedded in the English way in a manner eschewed by the other major international traditions. No one in Spain

> Sir Alf said... if I didn't work hard enough he'd pull me off at half-time.

was encouraged to get it in the mixer, no one in Holland was coached to get rid, no defender in Germany was told just to hoof it into Row Z. As for the Brazilians – and as for Brian Clough, the man whom the English footballing establishment was terrified to embrace – they had the perverse idea that the game should be played on grass, rather than in the air.

Hughes's prehistoric methodology was eventually exposed for what it always had been: nonsense. These days FA coaches are taught to encourage possession in their charges, to play from the back, to embrace the ball, rather than view it as a soldier might a hand-grenade. But the damage Hughes and his acolytes wrought has had lasting consequences. When the Premier League arrived and money came cascading into the domestic game, much of it was spent on bringing in the foreign players capable of electrifying the crowd, to the growing detriment of undernourished home-grown talent.

Wolstenholme was not to know it, but his choice of words could not have been more prophetic. The triumph of the Ramsey way that summer's afternoon in 1966 was to maroon much of English football in the Dark Ages just as the rest of the football world was emerging into the light.

1967 'We are going to attack as we never have before.'

Jock Stein, manager of Celtic FC, ahead of their European Cup final against Internazionale, Lisbon, 25 May 1967.

There has never been a European Cup-winning side as representative of their community as Celtic were in 1967. All but one of the players who turned out for Jock Stein that season was born within a thirty-mile radius of Parkhead. These were lads who had grown up and learned the game within the shadows of the Celtic floodlights. The fans knew them as friends, neighbours or relatives. They went to the same schools as them, caught the same buses, attended the same places of worship (every one of the Celtic team went to church on the morning of the European Cup final; it was, after all, staged on Ascension Day). He may not have been plying his trade in one of the grand leagues of Europe, or had at his disposal the kind of money available to his rivals in Spain, Italy or for that matter England, but when Jock Stein inherited this group of players as manager in 1965, he saw within them a collective determination to reflect and augment Glaswegian pride. He was at pains to express this *esprit de corps* in his pre-match press conference:

> Cups are not won by individuals, they are won by men in a team, men who put their club before personal prestige. I am lucky, I have the players who do just that for Celtic.

Driven by their loyalty to the institution, these were players who had already achieved unprecedented feats that season. They had won the Scottish FA Cup, the Scottish League Championship and the Scottish League Cup before arriving in Lisbon to take on Internazionale in the biggest of all club competitions. If theirs had been a relatively easy route to the European Cup final – Zurich, Nantes, FK Vojvodina and

Dukla Prague hardly represent the most elevated of opposition – their opponents in the final were of the highest order. Guided by Helenio Herrera, at the time the best-paid coach in world football, 'Grande Inter' were regarded as the apex of football modernism. They were winners of the European Cup twice in the previous three seasons. The assumption was – such was their mastery of the defensive arts of *catenaccio*, as practised by Giacinto Facchetti and Tarcisio Burgnich – that any side which fell a goal behind them was finished.

The cunning Stein played on such assumptions ahead of the game. When he discovered that the Italian team were going to watch his side's final practice session in Lisbon's Estádio Nacional, he instructed his players not to take it too seriously, to horse around. He deliberately kept things as undisciplined as possible. The Celtic players remember seeing their Italian counterparts up in the stands laughing at the apparently shambolic amateurism of the session. As a piece of subterfuge it worked brilliantly, lulling their opponents into a false sense of superiority; they went into the game thinking that the side from football's back of beyond were a hapless set of chancers.

> Cups are not won by individuals, they are won by men in a team, men who put their club before personal prestige.

And so it appeared when the two teams lined up in the tunnel. Billy McNeill, Stein's galloping midfielder, recalls that the *Nerazzurri* players looked fantastic in their blue and black striped shirts and tight black shorts. In contrast, Celtic's players didn't even have numbers on their backs, club tradition dictating they carried numbers solely on their white shorts. Still, they managed to spook their lofty opponents by singing 'The Celtic Song' in unison as they lined up ahead of walking out. There was something appropriate about them chanting like fans as they made their way out onto the pitch. These were Celtic lads to a man.

But this was more than just a community club. As it happened, Stein's sacrifice of his final training session belied an attention to detail that was almost forensic. He had won every tournament he had entered that season by shrewd analysis of every opponent, from Elgin City (beaten 7–0 in the second round of the Scottish Cup), to Rangers (defeated 1–0 in the final of the Scottish League Cup). Knowing the Italian team favoured man-for-man marking, Stein instructed his forwards to move into wide areas in the expectation that the defenders would follow. Then he told his full-backs to exploit the space opened up by such movement. That is what he meant by 'attack as we never have before': virtually every player on his side, bar the goalkeeper, would be expected to get forward when the opportunity arose.

The plan, though, did not seem to be working in the opening exchanges. Inter took the lead within the first ten minutes, when Jim Craig clumsily upended Renato Cappellini and Sandro Mazzola scored from the penalty spot. Up in the stands many of the 12,000 Celtic fans who had made their way to the stadium worried that this was but the start of the humiliation.

There had never been an exodus out of Glasgow to match the one that occurred in that last week of May 1967. Stories were legion of how supporters had begged, borrowed, stolen and, in the case of one man, even sold the family home in order to rustle up the cash to be there. This was not just a football match they were attending, this was the culmination of a sporting dream, the moment when the glories of the Glasgow way – or at least the East End, Catholic, Celtic way – would be made manifest. These weren't just footballers they'd come to cheer on, these were the upholders of a tradition.

Though it took a while for that tradition to exert itself. Inter, falling back on the habits of *catenaccio* defence drilled into them on the training field in Appiano, in the Alpine foothills outside Milan, blocked their every incursion. The more Celtic dashed about, the more Inter smothered. In the stands, nerves were being shredded.

But then, in the sixty-third minute, Craig made amends for his penalty blunder by setting up Tommy Gemmell for the equaliser that many thought would never come. And when, in the eighty-fourth minute, Stevie Chalmers deflected in Bobby Murdoch's long-range shot with a deft flick he had practised in every training session that season, the visitors from Glasgow went collectively bonkers in the stands.

At the final whistle, there was a pitch invasion by delirious Celtic fans seeking to celebrate the moment by stripping the players of every item of kit. McNeill recalls having to dive back into the throng in order to retrieve the goalkeeper Ronnie Simpson's cap from the back of the goal. Simpson, who kept his false teeth in the cap, had forgotten his headgear in the excitement of victory and was anxious not to look gummy in the celebratory pictures. Astonishingly, no one had taken it, missing out on the most intimate of victory souvenirs. Such was the mayhem, the police prevented McNeill from climbing the steps to the royal box to receive the trophy: it was presented to him amid chaotic scenes on the pitch.

There followed one hell of a ceilidh. At the airport over the next few days, the Portuguese authorities had a table laid out with British passports that had been lost by delirious Celtic supporters who had been entirely denuded of their possessions. Tales are told to this day of Scottish supporters who never made it home at all, choosing instead to spend a lifetime in Lisbon.

> Tales are told to this day of supporters who never made it home at all.

McNeill remembers celebrating with the fans long into the night and the next morning. He recalls Bill Shankly being there in the midst of the jubilation, telling him repeatedly what a genius Jock Stein was. But the thing was, McNeill, the leader of the team that became known for evermore as the Lisbon Lions, didn't need telling. He already knew.

1968 'Of course I didn't take my wife to watch Rochdale as an anniversary present. It was her birthday. Would I have got married in the football season? Besides, it wasn't Rochdale. It was Rochdale reserves.'

Bill Shankly.

Never mind a book, you could build an entire *library* of Shanks quotations. And you could get David Peace, the man who wrote *Red or Dead* (2013), a 700-page door-stop of a novel based on the great Liverpool manager's sayings, to curate it.

There was a deep seam for Peace to mine when he constructed his monumental shrine to the Shankly wit: this was a man as verbally dextrous as any in the history of the game. His pugnacious Scots delivery allied to a stand-up's sense of timing meant that his every press statement sparkled with gems. When he opened his mouth, notebooks were filled. He didn't just write their headlines, he gave football reporters their first paragraph and their last paragraph, and usually the thirty or so in between.

It was an ability of which he was acutely aware. Shankly was not an educated man but he nonetheless instinctively understood the power of words. And though he used plenty, few were wasted. Everything he said carried a simple message: his Liverpool side were the best not just in English football but in the world.

A lot of football success is in the mind. You must believe that you are the best and then make sure that you are. In my time at Liverpool we always said we had the best two teams on Merseyside, Liverpool and Liverpool reserves.

One of the first to recognise and exploit the burgeoning power of the media, Shankly expended much of his vocal energy on bigging up his own. This was not mere boastfulness, it was shrewd man-management. The theory was simple: if he used every opportunity to talk up their prowess, his players would surely start to believe in themselves. So for Shankly there was no false modesty: Liverpool were everything; Liverpool were it. Everybody else was scrapping for second place. He was the Muhammad Ali of football management. Thus it was that in August 1966 he greeted World Cup winner Alan Ball's arrival on Merseyside to play for Everton with the words: 'Never mind Alan, at least you'll be able to play next to a great team.'

Even in defeat, there was no recognition of rivals' prowess. The only thing that ever beat his Liverpool was ill fortune. 'They're nothing but rubbish,' he insisted to reporters after a 3–0 defeat by Internazionale in the 1965 European Cup semi-final. 'Three breakaways, that's all they got.' But there was method in Shankly's serial disrespect of opponents. In the British game, he was among the first to appreciate that a quote could be dropped like an aural hand-grenade. A sarky word about his opponents ahead of a Merseyside derby ('if Everton were playing at the bottom of my garden, I'd draw the curtains') was intended to undermine and distract. You never know: it might – just might – weaken the opposition's resolve.

> In my time at Liverpool we always said we had the best two teams on Merseyside, Liverpool and Liverpool reserves.

'Always make them think.' José Mourinho, a student of the Shankly way, said some four decades later of his own approach to the pre-match sparring and verbal jousting. And that's what Shankly did: he always made them think. There was more, though, to Shankly's portfolio of neatly honed phrases than just upsetting the neighbours. Taking his lead from such US philosopher-coaches as Vince Lombardi (legendary top man at the Green Bay Packers in the 1960s), he saw his sport as a metaphor for life. In its rhythms, he believed, could be found the answer to everything. Mind you, that was in part because for him football *was* everything. As his sad post-retirement twilight revealed, there was nothing else in his life. When he gave up at Liverpool in 1974 there was no Alex Ferguson-style triumphal tour, no autobiography, no wine dealing or piano lessons or celebrity appearances on *Who Wants to Be a Millionaire?* His demise was punctuated by visits to Tranmere Rovers, watching Rochdale reserves and turning up at Liverpool training sessions. Or at least he did that until he was quietly asked not to stand there on the touchline gawping. His presence, he was told, was distracting.

His approach to football is summed up in his most famous quotation, the one that would undoubtedly be carved into the stonework above the entrance to the Peace-run library: 'Some people think football is a matter of life and death. I'm very disappointed with that attitude. It's much more important than that.'

> Some people think football is a matter of life and death. I'm very disappointed with that attitude. It's much more important than that.

There is little wonder he thought like that. In Glenbuck, the tiny Ayrshire colliery village where Shankly was born, football was the be-all and end-all, the guiding principle of a man's life. Only 1,000 people resided within the community's boundaries, but between its founding in 1871 and its demise in 1931, the local team – wistfully named the Glenbuck Cherrypickers after the process of selecting the best bits of coal from the pit conveyor belt – produced no fewer than fifty professional footballers and seven Scottish internationals. Where Shankly came from, football could change a man's life, could lift him from back-breaking toil and give him a platform of national prominence. As he so often suggested, football brought light and hope to the working man.

Unlike all four of his brothers, including Bob, a fellow Scotland international, Shankly never played for the Cherrypickers first team. As an eighteen-year-old, he was about to make his debut when the pit – the only source of local employment – was closed and the football club soon followed. After the Cherrypickers' demise, the whole village went into a spiral of decline. Now it is gone; these days, no trace remains of this once-vibrant source of sporting talent; the last few buildings left standing were demolished in the 1990s to make way for large-scale open-cast mining. The village pitch – the place that transformed the existence of the Shankly clan – is invisible now, buried somewhere under a slagheap.

While football clearly did matter a very great deal to Shankly, his throwaway line about taking his wife to some meaningless match suggests his tongue was never far from his cheek. But self-awareness does not rule out the commission of acts of obsessive behaviour on Shankly's part. He may have laughed about it, but you suspect that for Nessie Shankly a trip to watch Rochdale reserves probably *was* her husband's annual acknowledgement of her birthday.

1969 'In 1969 I gave up alcohol and women. It was the worst twenty minutes of my life.'

George Best.

George Best enjoyed a far longer career making lucrative capital out of telling people how he buggered things up than he ever did as a top-flight player. The stage shows, the drunken chat-show appearances, the endless autobiographies: for more than twenty-five years there was a rich seam to be mined in his tale of squandered opportunity.

And his refrain was always the same: there were no regrets, no tears, nothing to provoke the loss of a moment's sleep. He was who he was; he did what he did. And that was that. No point wondering what might have happened, no point trying to alter the course of history. It was summed up in the story he retold endlessly of the waiter bringing a bottle of champagne to his hotel room and seeing a semi-naked Miss World on the bed, surrounded by thousands of pounds in casino winnings, and asking him: 'George, where did it all go wrong?' The fact that, as he later admitted, that episode never happened, that he invented it to play on popular perceptions, is indicative of a man who really didn't care what the rest of us thought. 'I spent a lot of money on booze, birds and fast cars,' he often said of himself. 'The rest I just squandered.'

But even as his decline began, there were millions who wished that he would change the drinking habits of a lifetime and sort himself out. The sadness about the decline and fall of George Best was its horrible, unstoppable inevitability. In 1969 the demons that would eventually consume him had already revealed themselves: the whole world could see exactly what was coming – and the whole world would watch, powerless, as he slowly, relentlessly and with chilling self-awareness, drank himself to death.

From the moment he made his debut in Manchester United's first team as a slim, floppy-locked seventeen-year-old on 14 September 1963, it was clear that the East Belfast-born Bestie was something special, that he had everything required not just to thrive in the professional game but to bestride it like a footballing colossus. From the moment he first appeared, just to witness him in all his elegance – a symphony of balance, bravery and bravura – was to be blessed. The West Bromwich Albion full-back Gordon Williams, who marked Best on his debut, provided a hint of the impact on the game made by the teenaged Northern Irishman when he recalled meeting the winger several years after their first encounter at Old Trafford:

I asked George to stand in front of me so I could see his face. He asked me why and I said, well, that day all I saw was your arse disappearing down the touchline.

The most gifted footballer ever born in the United Kingdom, Bestie made it look easy. Blessed with an abundance of pace, control, skill and daring, coupled, in his youth, with a Stakhanovite appetite for self-improvement (an early magazine profile from the mid-1960s records him as going home to early nights in his Manchester digs after a hard day's training, fuelled only by a glass of lemonade), he electrified the United team. In 1968, as he was approaching what many at the time thought would be a decade at the top, he led the side to the heights of glory. His second goal in the European Cup final, tricking and slipping his way through the Benfica defence and round the goalkeeper, was a perfect distillation of his genius.

He made the rest of life look easy too. Women melted in his presence; his departure from a room would invariably coincide with that of the best-looking female in it. He was the first pop-star footballer, the first to exploit the ever-increasing media demand for photogenic pop-cultural heroes. He did so with gusto. He loved it when the Portuguese media dubbed him 'the Fifth Beatle' (after he scored two goals against Benfica in a European Cup quarter-final in March 1966), was thrilled by the idea that he was helping the Sixties swing, relished the opportunities that came with being acknowledged as the sexiest man in shorts. He opened boutiques, he fronted nightclubs, he even appeared in commercials for sausages: this really was the man who could sell anything.

But, like many a pioneer, George Best trod new territory alone. Even by the mid-1960s the football establishment was effectively still stuck in the 1950s: this remained a game of patriarchs and old-school values. Sir Matt Busby, Best's boss at Old Trafford, who was approaching the end of his time in management, had not the faintest idea how to support his shooting star of a winger. Busby understood a world of deference, of the maximum wage, of players turning middle-aged before they were twenty-five. He didn't understand Georgie Best. The young Northern Irishman epitomised youthful revolution; he was a one-man wrecking ball to convention. Even among his contemporaries in the dressing room, he was an oddity, a one-off. It meant, as he circumnavigated Planet Fame, that Bestie did so without a guiding hand to steady his orbit.

> I spent a lot of money on booze, birds and fast cars. The rest I just squandered.

And by 1969 his life was already spinning out of control, a circus without a ringmaster. Just a year on from that Best-inspired European triumph at Wembley, Busby had retired, leaving his finest player, at twenty-three years of age, the centre of a fading institution, the flawed prince of a rapidly crumbling kingdom. He was obliged to carry United over the next couple of seasons, the one remaining world-class component of a team on the slide, increasingly surrounded by the mundane. A naturally intelligent man, Best found his position ridiculous. He tried his best – scoring forty-five goals in the 1968–9 and 1969–70 seasons. But he hated the responsibility. To escape the pressure of expectation he took to the bottle, discovering in alcohol an invaluable mechanism for blocking out the nonsense.

Despite the amount he was necking, the booze took its time in impairing his physical performance. He was, after all, naturally fitter than a butcher's dog. But it almost immediately started to cloud his judgment. By the start of the 1970s, as he began to express his disaffection through a serial lack of reliability, his story began to be told in a hundred tabloid front pages. He was forever running away, walking out of relationships and his club, chased by the paparazzi. On one occasion he was cornered in a mews house in Chelsea, where he was holed up with the actress Sinéad Cusack. On another he was discovered in Majorca, and was filmed on a hotel balcony playing keepy-uppy with a glass of something comforting in his hand. He constantly threatened retirement, only to be persuaded back by a United hierarchy desperately in need of his skills to paper over the cracks in their team-building.

But increasingly, when he did come back, he was cruising on empty, relying on the deposits of dedication he had made as a young man. He had no real desire, either, to change. Everything, even any attempt to battle with self-destruction, was dismissed with a shrug. 'I might go to Alcoholics Anonymous,' he said in 1980. 'But I think it would be difficult for me to be anonymous.' On another occasion he joked: 'I've stopped drinking. But only while I'm asleep.'

> I've stopped drinking. But only while I'm asleep.

The world knew this couldn't go on. And the world was right. Even with talent as electrifying as his, he had no hope of marrying his career to his lifestyle. Less than five years after that first, failed, attempt to compromise on his excess in 1969, George Best walked out of Old Trafford for the last time. Sure, there were brief flourishes – in the USA, at Fulham, even once at Stockport County – but he was effectively finished as a proper footballer the moment he departed the scene of his greatest triumphs. When he left, he was only twenty-seven – the same age Eric Cantona was when he first walked into Manchester United.

In the end, the drink finished him as a player. And he spent the next twenty-five years in an odd state of limbo, forever failing to find direction or purpose or anchor, a life lived in airport transit lounges and hotel rooms. Bestie seemed to be a spectator to his own decline, watching himself follow his mother, who drank herself to death in the wake of his fame, as if he were incapable of intervening. He couldn't even put aside the booze when he had a liver transplant, so precipitating his death at the tragically early age of fifty-nine. But even as he sank towards the inevitable, he never expressed any regret.

Bestie may never have mourned what was squandered in those lost years, what was thrown away by his wilful inability to steer clear of booze for more than twenty minutes. But the rest of us sure did.

1969 'There should be a law against him. He knows what's happening twenty minutes before anyone else.'

Celtic manager Jock Stein on Bobby Moore, 1969.

When the only English captain to lift the World Cup died in 1993, he had recently been employed as a football correspondent for *The Daily Sport*. The greatest defender this country has ever produced, working for a semi-pornographic comedy tabloid? There can be no more damning example of the English game's ingrained ability to squander its resources. Because, as Jock Stein's agonised compliment suggests, Moore really was something special.

The Scots might have hated what he achieved but they recognised what he represented. He made defending an art, a thing of beauty. Graham Taylor, the former England manager, reckons him the best player ever to wear the white of England. It is hard to argue. To check out the footage of his performance in the 1970 Mexico World Cup match against Brazil is to witness a masterclass. Sure, he wasn't quick. But, as Stein suggested a year before that game was played, such was his spatial intelligence he was always at least one step ahead of his opponents – opponents as vaunted as that Brazil side. His legendary tackle on the flying winger Jairzinho – clinical, uncompromising, sliding in and then coming away with the ball to instigate an attack in one fluid movement – was just a tiny part of his game that day in Guadalajara. Eschewing any hint of panic, he looks a man in control, a man who knew his hour had come. As he intercepts, heads and passes without ever ceding possession, it quickly becomes evident that Moore would stroll into the current England team. No wonder Pelé sought him out at the final whistle to offer warm congratulation and swap shirts: he recognised this was a man out of his time.

Moore played like that – as if transported from a future era – from the moment he appeared, fully formed, in the West Ham first team in September 1958. Not for him the attempt to kick the bollocks off an opponent that epitomised the defender's art throughout the 1950s. He saw his role as the fountainhead of collective creativity, the start of it all. His job was to pass, pass and pass again. Never mind the twenty minutes in advance of things that Stein saw in him; from the off he was years ahead of the rest.

> No wonder Pelé sought him out at the final whistle to swap shirts.

As a player it cannot be denied he reaped the reward and recognition he deserved. Despite the several contractual disputes he had with West Ham, he won the FA Cup and Cup Winners' Cup with the club and he lifted the World Cup with his country, achievements that would have been impossible without his substantial contribution. He gained, too, the sort of monetary return for his efforts that was beyond the dreams of the previous generation of professionals. By the standards of the time, he was comfortably well off.

But it was what happened to him after he retired that scars English football history. While Franz Beckenbauer, his direct rival for the epithet of the world's finest defender, became a leading light in German football administration; while Michel Platini went on to run UEFA; while Johan Cruyff managed his national team; Moore found advancement in the game impossible. He had a brief and unsuccessful foray as a manager, first at Oxford City (where his only claim to fame was giving the assistant manager's job to a young Harry Redknapp) and then Southend. Otherwise his talents were ignored. He didn't coach, he didn't administer, he didn't manage. His enormous football intelligence was squandered.

His statue now stands in pride of place outside the new Wembley and his widow Stephanie is frequently guest of honour at FA functions. But when he was alive he was rarely invited by the powers that be to offer his opinion, or asked to stand on a committee, or given the opportunity to influence things and demonstrate that his reading of the game was not restricted to the playing of it.

In part, he was unlucky that his retirement came at a time when English football was at a low point internationally, when looking back to the golden age he represented would have put the present into too stark a perspective. Indeed, Geoff Hurst and the other members of the 1966 team only began to benefit financially from their part in history when the football nostalgia business boomed around Euro 96, several years after Moore's death.

But there was something else about Moore that troubled the blazers. He was seen as a little too Dagenham for the snobby masters of the game. His financial dealings – the failed attempt to turn an Essex stately home into a country club, the East End pub which burned down the night before it was due to open as 'Mooro's', not to mention that business with the bracelet in Bogotá when he had to be bailed out of the nick on a trip to Colombia ahead of the 1970 World Cup – worried the establishment. Though there was never any genuine grounds for concern, there were always rumours about the company he kept. Moore's mates: in the FA they knew what that meant.

> He was seen as a little too Dagenham for the snobby masters of the game.

The story of an approach by Watford in the 1970s is indicative of his less-than-exalted standing within the game. Elton John had just bought the club, and interviewed Moore about becoming manager. The two men got on famously, and Moore was convinced he had landed the job. But, after promising he would be in touch immediately, John never got back to him. Something, it seemed, had caused the singer to change his mind.

The only conclusion we can draw is that Moore – England's golden boy of 1966 – was a victim of false assumptions. At the FA, he was treated as if he were nothing more than the hired help. Thus it was that the man who should have been the Football Association's grandest ambassador was instead at his death hacking around as a pundit for a local radio station.

The last time the public saw him was in October 1993, when England were playing San Marino in a World Cup qualifier at Wembley. At the scene of his finest triumph, where he had lifted the twelve-inch trophy that proclaimed England were on top of the world, instead of being at the centre of things, offering advice and inspiration to the next generation, Moore was on the periphery, spotted up in the press box, his gaunt, frail face swamped in a pair of headphones. The cancer that was to take him at the tragically early age of fifty-one had reduced him to a spectral figure. He was the golden ghost of English football.

1970 'At times it appeared that Mr Jennings would give a free-kick only on production of a death certificate.'

From Hugh McIlvanney's match report on the FA Cup final between Leeds United and Chelsea, *The Observer*, 12 April 1970.

Eric Jennings was not a referee who liked to interfere. When the forty-seven-year-old from Stourbridge took charge of the 1970 FA Cup final – commonly regarded, along with its replay, as the most violent exhibition of football ever staged in England – he preferred to keep his opinion to himself. Never mind that a whole series of Ron Harris fouls effectively crippled Eddie Gray, forget that Jack Charlton kneed and headbutted Peter Osgood, ignore the fact that Norman Hunter and Ian Hutchinson traded punches, so what if Eddie McCreadie flattened Billy Bremner with the kind of flying assault that even Bruce Lee might consider a tad excessive – come what may, Mr Jennings was going to let the game flow.

Twenty-seven years after the event, the referee David Elleray reviewed the two games on tape and offered the opinion that, had they taken place in the modern era, he would have issued six red cards and as many as twenty yellows. But Mr Jennings was not one for such fuss. He booked only one player – Chelsea's Hutchinson. We can only assume that in order to attract such censure, he must have committed murder.

The violence of the game seemed to stem from more than just the heat of the moment. It looked as if Chelsea and Leeds really didn't like each other: this was personal. As the two clubs jostled for supremacy at the top of the old First Division, they were not mere rivals, they appeared to be representatives of entirely separate traditions. Flash cockney poseurs against dour, humourless Yorkshiremen: what was being played out on the turf of Wembley and Old Trafford was a reflection of an ancient schism that had long cut across English society.

Chelsea may have been under the stewardship of the undemonstrative Dave Sexton, but his team reflected the flamboyant character of the man who was largely responsible for putting it together, his managerial predecessor Tommy Docherty. All sharp suits, suede shoes and Raquel Welch in the directors box, they were decidedly King's Road, still patrolling the vanguard of the Swinging Sixties, even as that psychedelic decade slipped into the monochrome 1970s. Leeds, on the other hand, were cut from very different cloth. Marshalled by the self-important Don Revie, they were brusque, efficient and pragmatic, accumulating trophies with a ruthlessness that was the very opposite of romantic (see pages 108–111).

Such generalisations do not tell the whole story. In players like Johnny Giles and Eddie Gray, Leeds were blessed with sublimely skilled entertainers, while Chelsea, in the barrow-boy presence of Dave Webb and Ron Harris, were no effete bunch of southern softie pushovers. Harris did not earn the nickname 'Chopper' merely for what was going on in his shorts. Such subtleties notwithstanding, however, whenever Leeds and Chelsea collided back then it was like a sporting re-run of the English Civil War; it was Revie's roundheads against Sexton's cavaliers. So when they were scheduled to meet in the first FA Cup final of the new decade, the footballing world braced itself for trouble. The blue touchpaper had been lit.

Played on a pitch churned up by the Horse of the Year Show, which had been staged in the stadium a week earlier, the final could not be mistaken for an exhibition of skill. Pockmarked by errors, its flow endlessly disrupted by the inadequacies of the playing surface, its brief outbreaks of football rarely disturbed the violence. Despite, or maybe precisely because of, the evident lawlessness, the game nonetheless provided compelling drama. Across ninety minutes, plus half an hour's extra time, even as the players hacked at one another's shins, it was impossible for the watching crowd to take their eyes off the action for a moment. At the whistle, the sides could not be separated, finishing up with a 2–2 draw.

Given the condition of the pitch, the FA scheduled the replay for Old Trafford on 29 April. Reinforcing the proposition that nothing sells quite like excess, 28 million viewers – the second highest audience for a televised sporting event in British broadcasting history – tuned in to watch the resumption of hostilities. Again they were not to be disappointed. Once more, Mr Jennings behaved like an old lady ignoring a street brawl by passing by on the other side of the road. Given licence by officialdom, the twenty-two players demonstrated quite how much they loathed each other

> Despite the evident lawlessness the game provided compelling drama.

by indulging in 120 minutes of unfettered aggression. But what a game it produced, a pulsating, unyielding scrap made all the more compelling because it evidently mattered so much to its participants.

Eventually Chelsea emerged as victors, winning 2–1 when Webb bundled home Hutchinson's howitzer throw-in in extra time. And, as their exhausted players gathered ahead of the presentation of the Cup, McIlvanney was not alone in wondering whether, rather than a medal, they might be given a boxing-style title belt.

1972 'All that was missing to have made it a really smart 1972 middle-class party would have been a few reefers, but footballers wouldn't touch such things. Some footballers might have moved into the middle classes but there are two things they won't have at their parties – drugs and homosexuals.'

Extract from *The Glory Game*, Hunter Davies's inside account of a season with Tottenham Hotspur, published in September 1972.

It was Mike England's party. Known to his team-mates – behind his back – as Brains, England was a most unusual footballer for the time. He was educated, alert, interested in the world around him. Unlike team-mates who preferred an executive cul-de-sac, he lived in an architect-designed house. And when he threw a party, he didn't invite the sort of guests normally seen at a footballers' gathering in the early 1970s – a couple of boxers and a sprinkling of ticket touts – he asked Olivia Newton-John. He also invited Hunter Davies, who, as was his way, took notes assiduously.

That season Davies, then a columnist on *The Sunday Times*, had been commissioned to write a book about Tottenham Hotspur, a behind-the-scenes, access-all-areas account of the workings of a football club in the manner of his acclaimed Beatles biography, published in 1968. This was not to be a book just about football, it would be an account of a cultural phenomenon.

Davies never received official backing from the club for his project. 'They never said yes, but they didn't say no,' he explains, forty-two years on. 'I'd written to both the chairman and manager asking their permission, and when neither replied, I wickedly gave the impression that the other one had said it was OK. So I sort of wormed my way in from there.' He told the players, meanwhile, in an attempt to gain their cooperation, that he would share the publishers' advance with them. 'There were fifteen members of first-team pool plus Bill Nick [the manager Bill Nicholson],' he recalls. 'That's 50 per cent of bugger all split sixteen ways.'

Aided and abetted by his friend Joe Kinnear, the Tottenham full-back ('I used to buy my clothes from the boutique he owned in Hampstead') Davies became the fly on the wall of the Tottenham dressing room. He went everywhere with the team: he was there at the training ground to report on the passions and scraps, he was there on the bus on the way back from tricky away fixtures, he was there sometimes sitting alongside the manager on the bench. And the result was a book which, dripping with insight, remains one of the finest ever written about the game.

Perhaps the most entertaining section is the appendix, in which Davies gives us the results of a survey he conducted into the players' private lives. As a picture of a time and a place it provides an incomparable historical record. Davies – who has made a career out of being a professional nosy parker – asked them everything from how they voted, to what paper they read to how much they contributed around the house. The answers to these questions were: largely Tory, *The Sun* and not very much. J. B. Priestley must have been turning in his grave. 'I never help in the house. I couldn't change a nappy. I've never washed a dish,' was goalkeeper Pat Jennings's approach to housework.

When the book came out, Spurs suddenly became aware of what they had acquiesced to. A serialisation in *The Sunday People* filleted the text for its most sensational revelations. And there were plenty, from Alan Gilzean's formidable drinking to the coach Eddie Baily's racist language – which was shocking even for the unreconstructed context of a 1970s football dressing room. The Tottenham board reacted with fury. Davies received a letter from Lord Goodman, then the country's leading libel lawyer, who was advising the club, demanding that the book be withdrawn. The author responded by sending the lawyer the two copies of the manuscript he had shown the chairman and manager before publication, on which they had both marked corrections, which he had made. It rather suggested they knew what was coming. That was the last he heard of the matter.

And the book remains in print. Not simply because it is brilliantly written, nor simply because of the fascinating snapshot it gives of the times, but largely because no one has managed to repeat the trick since. Despite numerous efforts to do a modern version, there has only ever been one *Glory Game*. 'I guess I muddied the waters for everyone,' says Davies. 'But there is no way you could get the kind of access I got back then these days. Not a hope.'

Everything has changed since Davies gave us his account of the inside workings of a leading football institution. Goodness, back then Spurs didn't even allow advertising hoardings inside the stadium. Forty years on, clubs have become far more commercially savvy, not to mention more controlling of their image. Everything has become far more formalised. In 1972, Nicholson never held a press conference, reporters gleaned information through a word dropped here and there, in the car park, on the bus, at the training ground. The idea of anyone today doing what Davies did then – actually sitting on the bench next to the manager during a game – is unthinkable. Not least because these days there are about twenty coaches, physios and fitness consultants crowding the dug-out.

> They never said yes, but they didn't say no.

Then there are the layers of management surrounding the players, which would make it a logistical impossibility for a writer to visit every member the squad at home to run through a questionnaire. Imagine the permissions that would now have to be sought and obtained.

'Not one of that Spurs team had an agent,' Davies recalls. 'When I did Wayne Rooney's book [some thirty-eight years later], the first time I met him was at his agent's office. In the room there were his agent, his personal manager, his lawyer, his accountant, his brand manager and, standing at the door, his be-suited bodyguard.'

In short, Davies claims, there were almost as many people in that room as there were at Mike England's party.

1973 'The goalkeeper's a clown.'

Brian Clough on Poland's Jan Tomaszewski, Wembley Stadium, 17 October 1973.

When England were drawn to play Poland and Wales in the qualifying group for the 1974 World Cup, few observers foresaw problems. This may have been the first time in more than a decade that the country was obliged to earn its passage to the tournament (as hosts in 1966 and holders in 1970, the invitation was automatic) but the Polish and Welsh were surely not obstacles likely to detain a side as accomplished as Alf Ramsey's.

However, after a bunch of performances that can be best described as shambolic, including a 2–0 defeat in Warsaw, Ramsey arrived at his final qualifying fixture knowing that only a win over the Poles would be sufficient to take him to West Germany for the finals.

Whatever the tension surrounding the game, the assumption was that England would do it. That was undoubtedly the feeling of the panel of experts gathered by ITV to pass comment on the game as it was beamed live into the nation's living rooms. In the Wembley studio, as he sat alongside Derek Dougan and the host Brian Moore, Brian Clough was unequivocal. The great motormouth had won the

First Division championship with Derby County in 1972 and latterly guided his team to the semi-finals of the European Cup, so his opinion – always readily offered – was much valued. And in his opinion, there was no doubt where the opposition's principal weakness lay. In the goalkeeper Jan Tomaszewski, whom Cloughie thought belonged in a circus, not on a football pitch.

Never one fully to embrace the concept of hard evidence, Clough had little to justify his claim. This Polish team had won the Olympic title in Munich the year before, they were shrewd, efficient and well-coached. And Tomaszewski was an experienced, athletic, brave shot-stopper. No one who had seen him play would confuse him with a large-shoed big-top performer with a collapsible car.

But then Clough was less interested in the accuracy of his analysis than in its effect. As he sat in the ITV studio he had an agenda. He recognised that if England faltered, Ramsey's position would become untenable. Already unpopular within the FA, the national manager was teetering on the brink of redundancy. And Clough wanted to be the man to take over. But he appreciated his candidacy would be tarnished if he made an overt public attack on Ramsey. So, his statement about the Polish goalkeeper was not intended as a legitimate critique of the player's stature. It was a pointed challenge to the man blocking his way: if you can't beat this lot, with Coco's younger brother between the sticks, then you have no right to remain as England manager.

As it transpired, Clough's glib character assassination could not have been more wrong. Tomaszewski had an inspired game. An England team including Colin Bell, Tony Currie, Martin Peters, Martin Chivers, Allan Clarke and Mike Channon could find no way past him. In the first half, continuously, heroically and acrobatically, he dealt with everything that came his way.

It was not enough, however, to change Clough's mind. At the half-time break – with England trailing by a single goal – he continued to press home his veiled assault on Ramsey. Dougan disagreed, angrily chiding his colleague for bad-mouthing the player, pointing out that if anyone was playing like a clown, it was England's Peter Shilton, who was at fault for Poland's goal. Brian Moore, meanwhile, looked increasingly worried that Clough's refusal to retract could only have karmic consequences. He was surely tempting fate.

And so he was. Throughout the second half, as England hurled everything at Poland short of the kitchen sink, Tomaszewski remained infuriatingly solid. Not even an Allan Clark penalty by way of an equaliser could ruffle his demeanour. As England fretted and thrashed around in search of a winner that would not arrive, as the substitute Kevin Hector – who played his club football under Clough at Derby – missed from close range, so the Pole continued to make save after save. Ultimately it was his heroics that carried his team to the finals, where they would finish a more than creditable third.

> Sport is sport but to admit his mistake of a wrong judgment was the feature of a great man.

Subsequently Tomaszewski became the bogeyman of English football, a constant reminder of the perils of World Cup qualification. Over the next four decades, every time England met Poland, his performance would be referenced, the clown who broke a nation's hearts. And the surprising thing is, the man himself – who in 2001 was elected to the Polish parliament as MP for the city of Łódź representing the conservative Law and Justice party – held no grudges about the disparaging treatment he received from the most outspoken figure in English football.

'I met Brian Clough on television a couple of years later and he told me he was wrong to judge me so harshly. We shook hands,' he said the last time England and Poland met in competitive action in 2013. 'Sport is sport but to admit his mistake of a wrong judgment was the feature of a great man.'

1974 'I go much faster than those who run without thinking.'

Edson Arantes do Nascimento, aka Pelé, 1974.

Inherent in our love of football is an urgent need to categorise. This is a game, after all, in which results are everything, in which a club's final position in the league table provides the best evidence of its true prowess. It is no surprise, then, that when it comes to the analysis of individuals it is not enough for the fan simply to remember a fine pass or cracking goal. Rather, we are forever seeking to impose objective criteria on what is essentially subjective. We want rankings and league tables. We want Cristiano Ronaldo sobbing as he is presented with the Ballon d'Or award as the world player of the year. But most of all, we have a collective urge to know the answer to the following question: who is the greatest footballer of all time?

As it turns out, it is not a question long in the answering. Beyond one particularly chaotic household in Buenos Aires, there is little debate about it. In fact, even there, Diego Maradona is beginning to soften about the question. 'My mother says it was me and Pelé's mother says it was him,' the great Argentine, unarguably among the world's best two, said in October 2010.

Actually, not just Pelé's mother. The thing is, no one, not even Mrs M, could argue with this statistic: Pelé is the only footballer in history to have three World Cup winner's medals in his trophy cabinet. No one else, not Xavi or Iniesta, not Zidane or Beckenbauer, not Ronaldo or the other Ronaldo, not even Carlton Palmer can match that. That alone puts the great Brazilian in a category of one. With just a single gong from his astonishing virtuoso performance in the 1986 World Cup, Maradona is not even close.

Legend suggests Edson Arantes do Nascimento owes his nickname to an Irish priest. The father, working as a missionary in the São

Paulo *favelas* of the 1950s, referred to the preternaturally talented youngster as '*piele*', an Irish term for football. Thus it was that from an early age he became synonymous with the game.

Pelé was only seventeen when he scored in the 1958 World Cup final in Stockholm and by the time Brazil successfully defended the trophy in Chile four years later (he was injured in the group stages and missed the final), the Brazilian president Jânio Quadros had declared him a national treasure, pushing through a government edict preventing him from moving abroad. He stayed with his home club Santos for most of his playing career, making 638 appearances. While the European game was denied the chance to see Pelé's skills deployed in any of its galáctico-hungry national leagues (and how Real Madrid tried, offering to make him the richest man in Spain if he donned the club's white shirt), every four years in the World Cup his talent eclipsed anything Italy, Germany, Argentina, Holland or England had to offer.

Mexico 1970 was the ultimate flowering not just of Pelé's talent, but of Brazilian football. Their gold shirts shimmering in what were the first colour television pictures of a World Cup, the Brazilians played the game to a different level. And Pelé was at the heart of their endeavours. As sportsmanlike and dignified as he was devastating in his finishing, he redefined what was possible on a football field.

In his career, he scored an astonishing 1281 goals in 1363 games. Part striker, part playmaker, the ultimate number ten, his ability was easy to recognise but hard to define. Johan Cruyff didn't even try. 'Pelé was the only footballer who surpassed the boundaries of logic,' the Dutchman once said.

And boy was he quick. It is a fair suggestion that he was so speedy on the pitch not just because he appeared to have rockets attached to his heels, but because he read the game better than anyone before and most since. In his suggestion that the physical works best when it is combined with the cerebral, he was speaking for everyone who views football as something more than a game of kick and rush.

His instinctive sense of geometry allowed him to find space or pick out passes which no one else could see. When he moved it was always for a purpose. Nowhere is his ability better illustrated than in Brazil's fourth goal against Italy in the 1970 World Cup final in Mexico City. Receiving the ball – crossed by Jairzinho – on the edge of the Italian penalty area, Pelé holds it up before playing it out to the right-hand flank, which for a split second appears to be entirely unoccupied. Watching it, even now you think: who's that to? What a waste. And then, running in from beyond the frame of the television picture, the full-back and captain Carlos Alberto comes dashing onto the ball to hammer it into the Italian net. Far from being a waste of possession, an aimless dink into space, it was the perfect assist, a pass that no one apart from the man who executed it could see.

> Pelé was the only footballer who surpassed the boundaries of logic.

Eventually Pelé's prowess found a market value beyond the boundaries of his homeland. In 1975, New York Cosmos paid a king's ransom to his club Santos to take him to the nascent North American Soccer League (see pages 120–23). He was identified as the man who could break the game in its last uncharted territory. For his two-year contract he was paid $3 million, a sum which at the time made him the highest-paid sportsman in history.

Despite the monetary investment, his first game in the United States was on a park pitch in New Jersey. Alarmed what the visiting media might make of what was little more than a mudbath, the Cosmos management had the surface painted in green emulsion. All went well – nobody even noticed the decorative subterfuge – until Pelé took his boots off at the end of the game. From the shower came a horrible scream. The emulsion had penetrated the great man's socks and turned the soles of his feet green. Terrified that he had

▶ The oldest rivalry in international football was first sparked in Glasgow in 1872, when Scotland took on England at what appeared to be competitive fancy dress.

DRIBBLING

▼ The packed stand at the Oval in 1883 where fans watched in shock as the flat-capped oiks of Blackburn Olympic seized the FA Cup and took in northwards for the first time.

THE HON: A: F: KINNAIRD:

CAPTAIN OF THE OLD ETONIANS

THE ENCLOSURE

S: A: WARBURTON.

CAPTAIN OF THE BLACKBURN OLYMPIC

CROSSLEY KICKING THE DECISIVE GOAL,

THE PRESIDENT PRESENTING THE CUP

YOUNG MEN OF BRITAIN !!
THE GERMANS SAID YOU WERE NOT IN EARNEST

Extract from Frankfurter Zeitung :–
"The young Britons prefer to exercise their long limbs on the football ground, rather than to expose them to any sort of risk in the service of their country."

"We knew you'd come –

and **GIVE THEM THE LIE !"**
PLAY *the* **GREATER GAME** *and* **JOIN** *the* **FOOTBALL BATTALION**

▲ Encouraged by posters like this, hundreds of young men joined the Football Battalion in December 1914 under the impression what was going on in Flanders was an extension of the game. It wasn't: Bradford City alone lost nine first-team players in the trenches.

◥ (opposite top) Billy the police horse eases back the crowd at the first FA Cup final to be played at Wembley, 28 April 1923. According to one eye-witness, the organisation at the event was 'a bloody shambles'.

▼ Arsenal's inimitable Herbert Chapman, the first modern manager, in typical pose: when it came to transfer business, this was a football boss who liked to keep his hands in his pockets.

▼ A poster advertising a match between a side picked from the occupying Luftwaffe and a local team in Kiev, August 1941. It was this game that inspired the film *Escape to Victory*, not to mention a Soviet myth that lasted five decades.

IV CAMPEONATO
MUNDIAL DE
FUTEBOL
·TAÇA JULES RIMET·

JUNHO DE 1950
BRASIL

◁ No hint of what was to come in this poster advertising the 1950 World Cup Finals in Brazil. What lay ahead was defeat by Uruguay in the Maracanã stadium, the most seismic shock in Brazilian footballing history. Or at least it was until 8 July 2014, when the country was witness to utter humiliation at the feet of Germany.

▽ A man who made his living out of handling water, the 'peerless plumber' Tom Finney negotiates his way through what appears to be a burst main while playing for Preston.

▲ Stan the Man: dipping his shoulder and employing his body swerve, Blackpool's Stanley Matthews bamboozles a Bolton defender on his way to giving his name to the 1953 FA Cup final.

▲ Unaware of the footballing lesson about to be unleashed, a confident Billy Wright leads out England ahead of their game with Hungary at Wembley in 1953. Mind, seeing the waistline of his opposite number Ferenc Puskás is enough to make anyone feel smug.

▶ The day a team died.

DAILY SKETCH
THE PAPER WITH AN EXTRA EVERY DAY
FRIDAY, FEBRUARY 7, 1958

2½d

21 DEAD
7 MANCHESTER UTD PLAYERS PERISH
HERO! IN AIR CRASH

By MICHAEL BORISSOW, Munich, 3 a.m.

SEVEN of "Busby's Babes," the best-known football team in Britain, died yesterday in the twisted wreckage of their chartered airliner. Matt Busby, the man who made them famous, was critically injured.

Manchester United's Elizabethan airliner crashed at 3.4 p.m. while trying to take off in a snowstorm at Munich.

Of the 44 passengers and crew aboard, 20 died in the crash. Frank Swift, former England and Manchester City goalkeeper—died later in hospital.

Among the dead were well-known British sports writers returning with the team from Belgrade where United had drawn with the Red Star team and qualified for the semi-final of the European Cup for the second year running.

Skipper is a victim

The seven "Babes" who died included team captain Roger Byrne, 28-year-old English international left-back.

The other six were: right-half Eddie Colman, aged 21; centre-half Mark Jones, 23; centre-forward Tommy Taylor, 25; inside-forward Billy Whelan, 24; outside-left David Pegg, 22; and left-back Geoff Bent, 19.

Taylor also played for England. Whelan was an Eire international. Tom Curric, United's trainer, Bert Whalley, the team coach, Mr. W. Crickmer, the team secretary, and Mr. W. Satinoff, Manchester businessman and race-horse owner who expected to join the club board, were also killed.

Manager Busby has severe chest injuries, a broken foot, cuts and burns. A doctor at Munich's Isar Hospital said early to-day: "He has little chance. His condition is worsening."

Mr. Busby was given blood transfusions.

A nurse conducted him: "Mr. Busby, your friends will soon be ➤ **Back Page**

HERO of the disaster was goalie Harry Gregg—pictured in hospital. After escaping from the wreck he heard a little girl cry. The plane might have blown up. But he went back to rescue her. Full story, Page 2.

Exceptional Dress in Pure Botany Wool Jersey

87/6
97/6

Dorothy Ward Ltd
601 LONDON ROAD HADLEIGH, ESSEX

▲ Garrincha, Brazil's bendy-legged genius at the 1962 World Cup in Chile, a competition he made his own.

▲ Denis Law, with his manager Matt Busby, on the day he was brought back from the briefest of exiles in Italy, August 1962.

▼ Wembley stadium, 30 July 1966. Some might describe this as England's finest hour. Others that it marked the very moment it all started to go wrong.

▲ Bill Shankly (left) and other members of the Liverpool Boot Room, the finest coaching collective in English football history.

▲ Apart from the money, the fame and those eyes, it's very hard to see what half the world's female population saw in George Best in his prime.

▶ Respect: Pelé and Bobby Moore, Guadalajara, Mexico, 7 June 1970.

▲ A humbled, crestfallen, shattered England team, brought low by a Polish clown, Wembley, 17 October 1973.

◄ Meet the new boss: a sheepish Brian Clough leads out the Leeds United team at the Charity Shield against Liverpool, Wembley, 10 August 1974.

contracted some ghastly American podiatric condition, he tried to flee straight home to São Paulo. Eventually, after a pot of paint and a brush had been held up as evidence, he was talked into staying.

After he stopped playing, some of his commercial decisions didn't display quite the same unimpeachable brilliance he had in his playing days. He starred alongside Michael Caine, Sylvester Stallone, Mike Summerbee and John Wark in the film *Escape to Victory* (1981), perhaps the darkest blot on the CV of the legendary director John Huston. Then he signed up to a long-running series of commercials for Viagra. Pelé? The legendary 'black pearl' and 'king of football'? The scorer of seventy-seven goals for his country in ninety-three matches? The greatest footballer ever to pull on a shirt, cast as spokesman for – *the erectile dysfunction community*? That must surely have been the one and only run the great man made without thinking.

1974 'Gentlemen, the first thing you can do for me is throw your medals and your pots and pans in the dustbin because you've never won anything fairly. You've done it by cheating.'

Brian Clough to the Leeds players on his first day in charge at Elland Road, 31 July 1974.

As introductory remarks go, none in the history of football can have been quite as provocative as those uttered by the new manager of Leeds United in the summer of 1974. These were the champions of England he was addressing, internationals to a man, weighed down by the trophies they had accumulated together. And here was their new manager reducing their sterling efforts to a collection of kitchen utensils. Eschewing formality, the moment the sarcastic 'gentlemen' was out of his mouth, Brian Clough switched his rudeness dial right up to 11.

For a coach who would subsequently fill a book with his motivational quips, the way he traduced his team of champions that morning was also one of the most counter-productive moments of public speaking ever. Such words, aimed squarely at achievements in which they justifiably took pride, could have but one effect on the Leeds United squad: to sow in them the seeds of alienation, anger and resentment. Reading his comments forty years on, you can only wonder what a man as intuitively intelligent as Brian Clough was thinking. Though whatever it was, when it came to Leeds United Old Big 'Ed rarely thought straight.

Clough loathed Leeds. Or rather he loathed his long-serving predecessor as Leeds manager, Don Revie. The pair may have shared a background growing up in Middlesbrough, but Clough bridled at everything Revie stood for. Revie, he insisted, was cold, while he was warm; Revie was cynical, while he was an idealist; Revie believed in victory, while he believed in glory. Revie was the past, while he was very much the future. As Clough wrote in his first autobiography:

> Leeds had been the dirtiest and most cynical team in the country in the late Sixties and early Seventies, and from my soap-box as manager of Derby and the best pundit on television I had said so on numerous occasions.

The animus hung in the air like a poisoned cloud whenever the pair appeared on television together. As Clough's distaste for his fellow manager seeped down the camera lens and Revie responded with crushing condescension, television producers grinned in delight at the entertainment value of the clash of the two Tees-side titans, a welcome deviation from the bland conventions of the post-match interview. Given their evident animosity, it was all the more astonishing that, when Revie took over from the fired Alf Ramsey as England boss in the summer of 1974, it was Clough who filled his place in the Leeds dug-out. None among the Leeds first team could believe that the man who had so often attacked the club was now seeking to organise its victories.

But the truth was, at the time, Clough needed the job. He had flounced out of Derby County in October 1973 at the height of his powers and decamped to Brighton. He had soon tired of Third Division football on the South Coast, though, and longed for a return to the big time. After the Football Association turned to Revie rather than him to shape England's post-Ramsey future, he was devastated. So when Manny Cussins contacted him with a view to taking over from his despised rival, he snapped at the chance, convincing the Leeds chairman that his very hatred of the previous boss would drive him – and in consequence the club – to greater things. He wouldn't, he insisted, sleep a wink until his success was so great that 'that bloody name' was no longer mentioned around Elland Road. Now was his chance to show how it should be done. Tellingly Peter Taylor, the assistant manager who had acted as Clough's sanity valve at Derby and would later undertake a similar role at Nottingham Forest, preferred to stay at Brighton in the interim, turning down the chance to join his old partner in Yorkshire. 'I am not equipped to manage without Peter Taylor,' Clough once said, 'I am the shop window and he is the goods round the back.'

So Clough arrived at Leeds without the leavening influence that would prove a vital ingredient in his future triumphs. Driven by a venomous sense of revenge – not to mention a sizeable slug of Dutch courage – he went snarling into his first encounter with the players like a dog without a muzzle.

And what a disaster his words proved. Having insulted the Leeds squad collectively, he went on to deliver a pointed analysis of their individual shortcomings. He told the oft-injured Eddie Gray, for instance, that if he were a horse he 'would have been shot long ago'. He suggested that the elegant midfield schemer John Giles (who had turned down the manager's job before it was offered to Clough) should apply his undoubted skills a bit more and his studs a bit less.

It was a spectacularly ill-judged performance, from which there was to be no way back. Those players initially prepared to give Clough the benefit of the doubt instantly changed their minds. The manager's every intervention was subsequently greeted with a scowl, his tactical innovations with open dissent. To a man the Leeds players let Clough know what they thought of him. And it wasn't a lot.

To study the picture of the new boss leading the team out for the first time is to see this deep rift between manager and players etched in their body language. It was the 1974 FA Charity Shield played at Wembley on 10 August, and at the head of the Leeds line, Clough looks a tad sheepish. Behind him, the captain Billy Bremner, carrying the Championship trophy, one of those baubles Clough had told him to chuck in the bin, can barely suppress his scowl. There is no banter, no good cheer, no communication. The entire team looks as if they would rather be anywhere than in the same frame as their new boss.

It was the image David Peace used for the front cover of his coruscating imagined account of Clough's time at Leeds, *The Damned United* (2006). And Peace had some material to work with. Across the late summer of 1974 the stories poured out of Elland Road of rows, argument and dismay. By mid-September, with the club sinking to the bottom of the First Division table and the senior players in open revolt, Cussins called an end to the experiment. Clough had lasted just forty-four days.

Even then, as he retreated to his home in the Midlands, cushioned by the then biggest pay-off in English football history (reckoned to be over £100,000), ready to steel himself for revenge with another employer, Clough did not blame himself. Never mind those opening remarks, it was, he insisted, Revie's fault for poisoning the minds of the Leeds players against him at the outset; it was Revie who turned a dressing room into a cult, a coven, a *cosa nostra*.

John Giles, now a football pundit on RTÉ, takes a rather different view. After he had successfully sued Peace's publishers for the suggestion that he was conspirator-in-chief, plotting to oust the manager, the Irishman said this of Clough's unhappy reign:

I didn't get on with Brian – I found him rude and arrogant. But Brian was a highly intelligent guy who, in my opinion, was a genius. What happened at Leeds, happened. But at Derby County and Nottingham Forest, he was a genius.

1977 'This is the second time I've beaten the Germans here. The first time was in 1944. I drove into the city when it was liberated on a tank.'

Bob Paisley, manager of Liverpool FC, the day after his team had beaten Borussia Mönchengladbach in the European Cup final in Rome, 25 May 1977.

He may have been speaking more than thirty-two years after the end of the Second World War, but for the erstwhile tank trooper Bob Paisley those were still the days, the ones that every other aspect of postwar life had to measure up to. And in his reminiscences about his previous trip to the Eternal City, he reflected what was a common attitude in those days. The 1970s was the era of *Dad's Army*, of *Colditz* and *Secret Army*, of Basil Fawlty desperately trying not to mention the war even as he goose-stepped around the German guests unlucky enough to book into his Torquay hotel. Three decades on, the conflict remained deeply ingrained in British culture, constantly alluded to in comedy, comics and movies alike.

Football was no different. Reared on the war stories of their parents (and managers), for the hundreds of young Liverpool fans pouring across the Channel, Europe was a place to be tamed and conquered, full of dodgy food and cheap wine. Here was the chance to fight the war by another means. And Bob Paisley's Liverpool was a formidable fighting force. For almost a decade, thanks to their domestic dominance, his club was involved consistently in European competition. As the graffiti of the time put it, when it came to Europe, Liverpool ruled OK.

Though he was born in County Durham, Paisley was a Liverpool man to his bootstraps. He joined the club as a player immediately after his war service, making 253 appearances as left-half. He qualified as a physiotherapist, was made Bill Shankly's assistant in 1959 and then, when the great man suddenly retired in 1974, he took on the main role. What an appointment he proved to be. Schooled in the Liverpool way, he won twenty trophies in nine years in charge at Anfield, including six league titles and three European Cups.

Not a demonstrative man, unable to match Shankly's soaring feats of oratory, somebody who, despite his achievements, has yet to be the subject of a definitive biography, his genius lay in the simplicity of his instructions. 'If you're in the penalty area and don't know what to do with the ball', he once said, 'put it in the net and we'll discuss the options later.' Paisley's Liverpool players thrived on his lack of complication, his rejection of jargon and flannel. Not that saying the right thing was his only virtue. This was a manager with few equals in his ability to construct teams. Better still, he managed to maintain Liverpool's hegemony even as he continuously restructured its personnel; there was no such thing as a period of transition under Paisley, only an era of

> I've been here through the bad times here as well. One year we came second.

utter domination. As he once wryly put it: 'Mind you, I've been here through the bad times here as well. One year we came second.'

So smooth was the progression, there appeared to be something natural about it, something organic. But – as was demonstrated pointedly after his retirement – it was not happenstance that raised Liverpool to their pre-eminent position during the Paisley era. He maintained it through the pursuit of constant improvement. For such an apparently genial man, he had no room for sentiment: when time was up for a player, he moved him on with breathtaking speed. And invariably, he made the side more effective with every change. When Kevin Keegan left Merseyside to seek his fortune in Germany (his last Liverpool outing was the 1977 European Cup final), Paisley replaced his creative wellspring with the superior Kenny Dalglish.

When Tommy Smith's knees finally gave way, in came Alan Hansen and Mark Lawrenson. When Jimmy Case's energy began to dip, he promoted Graeme Souness. Better, better and always better.

And in Europe, Paisley's Liverpool were peerless. Tactically the manager invariably got it right. Away from home, through shrewd use of the back pass, his sides shut up shop, squeezing the space and denying their opponents possession. Then in the home leg, playing into the intimidating wall of sound thrown up by the Kop, they would attack, attack and attack again, scaring the living daylights out of their guests.

Paisley won his first European trophy in 1976, defeating Bruges in the final of the UEFA Cup. The next season, after Liverpool had won the 1975–6 First Division title, he was able to test his managerial philosophy in the European Cup for the first time (this was long before four Champions League places were up for grabs in the Premier League, a time when only the best – the league title holders – were invited into the big one). In Rome, his Liverpool, just crowned domestic champions yet again, displayed their wider dominance. Never mind any psychological trauma that might have afflicted them after they had been denied an historic first treble by Manchester United in the FA Cup final just five days earlier, they brushed aside the Germans 3–1. The manager's tactical initiative once again proved unmatchable: his deployment of Ian Callaghan as a roving additional midfielder completely wrong-footed his German opponents. In defeating Mönchengladbach, Paisley's men recorded the first win in the competition by an English side in nearly a decade. It was not to be the last.

> If you don't know what to do with the ball, put it in the net and we'll discuss the options later.

Indeed, it is one of the ironies of English football in the 1970s that as the national side stuttered and faltered, failing to qualify for the World Cup Finals in both 1974 and 1978, so the nation's clubs lorded it in Europe. After the win in Rome, Liverpool retained the trophy the next year against Bruges at Wembley. Then Brian Clough's Nottingham Forest won it twice in 1979 and 1980, before Paisley's Liverpool picked it up for a third time, beating Real Madrid in Paris in 1981. The very next season Aston Villa overcame Bayern Munich in the final before Liverpool returned to Rome in 1984 to overwhelm Roma's home advantage and win it for the fourth time, though on that occasion under Joe Fagan's rather than Paisley's stewardship. Seven times in eight years, the biggest of all trophies found its way across the Channel, back to England.

It was Paisley who established the pattern, who showed how it should be done. Whatever the growing embrace of hit and hope, as advocated by the antediluvian forces at the FA (see pages 73–7), he knew how to produce winning football teams. He had helped shape Shankly's philosophy of simplicity, of pass and move. Now he honed it to its logical conclusion. Through endless practice on the five-a-side pitch, his Liverpool out-passed all comers. 'It's not about the long ball or the short ball,' he once said of approach to the game. 'It's about the right ball.'

Under Bob Paisley, the modest wartime private who finally retired in 1983, Liverpool invariably played the right ball. It sounds simple enough. But few have managed to do it subsequently with such undemonstrative efficiency.

1978 'You can mark down 25 June 1978 as the day Scottish football conquers the world.'

Scotland manager Ally MacLeod, as his team set out for the World Cup Finals in Argentina.

When compiling their dictionary, the editors at the Oxford University Press need not expend too many words in the attempt to define the phrase 'blind optimism'. All they need is a picture of Alistair Reid MacLeod. Big Ally was the Scotland manager who raised levels of tartan expectation to heights not witnessed since the English were sent homeward tae think again from the Battle of Bannockburn in 1314. So over-excited was MacLeod in June 1978, such were his soaring levels of confidence, that he appeared to be a man on the brink of self-combustion.

He had become manager of Scotland in the autumn of 1977, taking over from Willie Ormond. His infectious enthusiasm was already legendary. As he managed first Ayr United and then Aberdeen, stories abounded of his absolute insistence that his team was destined for victory in every game. One yarn recalled him and his assistant studying the freshly published fixture list ahead of a new season. MacLeod went through it, saying 'we'll win that, we'll win that' to every game until he arrived at the fixture against Rangers. 'Well that's two points in the bank,' he said. At which his assistant, alarmed at MacLeod's wilful tempting of fate, interjected: 'But Ally, that's the champions you're talking about.' 'Champions or no,' came back the response, 'they'll not relish coming to the home of the undefeated league leaders.'

And so it proved with Scotland: his optimism moved up through the gears. As he steered the team through the latter stages of a tricky qualification group including the European champions Czechoslovakia to the World Cup finals in Argentina, so he became ever more elevated in his ambition. If it were not sufficient cause for celebration that Scotland had qualified while England – for the second tournament in succession – had faltered, MacLeod appeared convinced that his team could become the first European country to win the big prize in South America.

For sure, he had at his disposal the finest array of Scottish talent ever assembled, including Kenny Dalglish, Alan Hansen, Joe Jordan, Graeme Souness and Archie Gemmill. They were good all right. Though not, by any rational analysis, potential world champions. And certainly not, as in Ally's assessment, the greatest team the world had ever seen.

This was not some sort of psychological ploy, either. Even as saner observers in Scotland cautioned against his galloping certainty, it was clear that MacLeod was a true believer in his vision of Scotland's footballing destiny. He really did think he was about to lead a wee nation of some five and a half million souls to global football domination.

In Scotland, the expectation grew daily that MacLeod would indeed be returning to Prestwick airport on 26 June clutching the World Cup. In the build-up to the competition, the papers were filled with tales of the ingenuity of Scottish fans determined to be there to witness history at first hand (one bunch of intrepid kilt-wearers were reported to be planning to charter a submarine). The Top 20 reverberated

> We'll really shake 'em up when we win the World Cup.

to the sound of the comedian Andy Cameron's terrace chant 'Ally's Tartan Army,' with its insistent chorus 'We'll really shake 'em up when we win the World Cup'. Not if, note, but when.

Meanwhile, 25,000 people turned up to watch the players do a lap of honour around Hampden Park before they had even set off. 'What will you do if you win the World Cup?' the young Trevor McDonald, reporting for ITN, asked him that afternoon as he basked in the excitement flooding from the terraces. MacLeod, straight-faced, replied: 'Retain it.' MacLeod's boundless optimism sparked a vivid upswing in nationalistic fervour north of the border: many were as convinced as the manager that it was simply a matter of turning up and the cup would be theirs. And this was where MacLeod's problems lay. Let's put it this way: he was not a manager for whom detail was important. So certain was he that Scotland were going to win, he didn't worry about things like scouting the opposition. So it was that when his side arrived in Argentina, they were quickly undone.

There was a hint of what was to come when the bus taking them from the airport to their hotel broke down. Talk about symbolic. They lost their first game to Peru, a side on whom MacLeod had done no homework. Indeed he told a television interviewer before the match that Juan Carlos Oblitas, Peru's flying winger, would present no problem to his left-back Martin Buchan; there was just one problem with this analysis: Oblitas was a left winger, playing on the other side of the pitch from Buchan. With Scotland trailing, his half-time team talk consisted of the sole tactical instruction, issued to his goalkeeper, to 'hoof it long'.

Worse was to follow that 3–1 opening defeat. After the winger Willie Johnston was sent home for failing a drugs test (he claimed to have taken a cold cure which contained a proscribed substance) Scotland could only draw 1–1 with Iran. Downbeat and beleaguered, MacLeod sounded increasingly desperate as he told the media that the blame lay with the hotel pool: there was no water in it, so the players had been unable to take their mind off the football with a relaxing swim. By now his room for manoeuvre had been squeezed down to this: in their final group game, his Scotland had to beat the much-admired Dutch by three clear goals to progress.

It was then, finally released from the shackles of expectation and returning to their default position of underdogs, that the Scots showed their true potential. Archie Gemmill's goal, in which he waltzed through the Dutch defence as if they were training-ground cones, put Scotland 3–1 ahead. For a moment it appeared MacLeod's ludicrous assumptions might be about to be fulfilled; one more goal and they were through. It was a fleeting possibility that became etched into the nation's psyche, its glories revisited in the movie of Irvine Welsh's *Trainspotting*, in which footage of Gemmill's goal acted as a visual metaphor for orgasm.

However, as students of hubris knew would happen, the inevitable soon arrived. The Dutch scored a second goal to confine all Scottish discussion to what might have been. And while the Holland team went on to the final, where they lost to the hosts, MacLeod returned home to ignominy. Instead of the thousands of delirious admirers he had anticipated thronging the airport, he faced just a couple of dozen angry fans, berating him for letting them down.

MacLeod had no answer for the grumbly supporters; he simply stared at his shoes and shuffled to the waiting bus. This, however, was nothing compared to the backlash unleashed in the nation's media. 'Home By The Back Door,' was *The Daily Record's* sarky headline. He was publicly lambasted not so much for his side's failure as for his pre-tournament inflation of their prospects. He had talked

> With a bit of luck in the World Cup I might have been knighted... Now I'll probably be beheaded.

them up, and now, after they had come down, he had to face the hangover. And it was a stinker. 'With a bit of luck in the World Cup I might have been knighted,' he said. 'Now I'll probably be beheaded.'

Initially, the Scottish FA stood by him, acknowledging the lift he had given to the prominence of the national side. But – chastened and damaged by his experience – he lasted only one more game in charge, resigning in the autumn of 1978. In his autobiography, *The Ally MacLeod Story*, a more sober narrator looked back on the World Cup campaign and wondered whether he had 'generated just too much excitement. Had I raised the level of national optimism just too high?' It was a legitimate question which, with characteristic bravura, MacLeod dismissed with a breezy: 'Maybe. But would the Scottish fans have tolerated anything less from me than whole-hearted conviction?'

While it may not have been the legacy he anticipated, of this we can be sure: nobody in football has ever done whole-hearted conviction quite like Ally MacLeod did in the summer of 1978.

1979 'Tell the Kraut to get his ass up front. We don't pay a million for a guy to hang around in defence.'

Unidentified New York Cosmos executive on Franz Beckenbauer, 1979.

It was never going to be easy, introducing God's own sport into a godless sporting landscape. The rest of the world may have quickly fallen under the spell of association football, but America chose to grow its own sports and to stick with them. Football played under FA rules took a few faltering steps in the USA in the late 1860s and early 1870s, but was quickly overwhelmed as US college students began to do their own thing. Pursuing a separate line of evolution from the global sporting mainstream, baseball, basketball and the oval-ball sport of American football – or gridiron – came to define US life. Americans saw in the very rhythms of these sports an expression of American exceptionalism, of the distinctiveness of their national culture. For generations, it was an unspoken entry requirement for any immigrant arriving in New York that they cast off their former sporting loyalties and devote themselves to the American way. Football was a foreign game, a relic of the old world, to be ditched at Ellis Island.

So it was that while association football conquered first Europe, then South America, Africa and Asia, the USA remained steadfastly, doggedly aloof. Occasional moments of footballing glory – most notably the 1950 World Cup win over England – barely registered in wider American

> Americans think that any guy who runs around in shorts kicking a ball rather than catching it has to be a Commie or a fairy.

consciousness. Driven by scepticism in the press, football – or 'soccer' as Americans called it to differentiate it from their own sport of heft and grunt, helmets, shoulder pads and institutionalised brain damage – was dismissed as something degenerate, something impure, a foreign contagion to be resisted at all costs. Or as Clive Toye put it in 1976: 'Americans think that any guy who runs around in shorts kicking a ball rather than catching it has to be a Commie or a fairy.'

Toye was a former sportswriter for the *Daily Express* who emigrated to the US in the 1960s. Far from leaving his old religion at the border, whatever the sneery resistance of the media, he regarded his new homeland as territory ripe for conversion to the true faith. As general manager of the New York Cosmos he was there when the first significant effort was made to spread the word. In characteristically American fashion, that effort was driven by the liberal application of large amounts of cash.

The North American Soccer League came into being in 1968, its aim being to bring regular competitive professional football to the masses. But it was the arrival of Toye's Cosmos in December 1970 that first floated the idea that if you spend it they will come.

Toye's was the shop-window approach to sporting evangelism. Bring the best players in the world to America and they will provide the fuel to spark the revolution. Pelé, acquired in 1975, was his greatest signing. Franz Beckenbauer was not far behind. The German had lifted the World Cup in 1974 and had few peers when it came to the art of defence. Although, as the remarks quoted here from one of Toye's executive colleagues might suggest, it could be argued that the elegant sweeper's qualities were a little lost on a virgin market.

Toye's revolution, however, more than piqued interest. Crowds flocked to see his stars. Soccer did indeed begin to spread as players such as Johan Cruyff, George Best and Rodney Marsh bolstered their pensions in Los Angeles and Miami. The growing success of the NASL made the old guard even more vocal in their resistance to the sporting interloper from the Old World. One indicator of the emergence of soccer in America was the way football-related gags became a staple of the US comedy circuit. 'Soccer will never take over from baseball. Baseball is the only chance we blacks get to wave a bat at a white man without starting a riot,' chortled Eddie Murphy in his stand-up routine.

Ultimately celebrity was not enough to sustain the NASL. It folded along with the Cosmos in 1984. But, however much its US critics may have wished it to, football did not follow suit. It did not disappear. Though what gave the sport real traction in the US was the opposite of the Toye approach. It was not top-down but bottom-up growth. What stimulated the sport's development was not money but litigation.

The reality was, as the personal-injury market spiralled in the US, gridiron became too dangerous for writ-wary schools and clubs to pursue. Insurance became prohibitive. And soccer – wholesome, easy to understand and safe to play – stepped eagerly into the gap. A major constitutional ruling in 1972 that girls should be offered the same team school sport opportunities as boys further fuelled its growth. Soon, every kid in the country – driven to practise by the new demographic group of aspirant middle-class women voters dubbed 'soccer moms' – was exposed to its charms from an early age. Players like Tim Howard, Brad Friedel and Clint Dempsey grew up through the burgeoning school and college system to make careers in the Premier League. The US became a fixture in World Cups, qualifying regularly and – with much promotional push from commercial partners – hosting the tournament in 1994. Though that prospect did not seem to excite a columnist in the *National* paper called Frank Deptford, who wrote: 'They're going to bring this thing to the US and charge people money to watch it? If this thing were a Broadway show it would close overnight.'

Such formidable scepticism did not stop the onward march of the game, however. By the start of the twenty-first century, millions followed the Premier League and La Liga on US television networks. Thousands followed their team to Brazil for the 2014 World Cup. America had been finally won over by the grassroots. To the point where, four decades on from that New York Cosmos executive's remark about Beckenbauer, many an American enthusiast would have a deep appreciation of the skills of the great German. And – were they watching that game in 1979 – would suggest they might be best applied by keeping his ass in defence.

1981 'Lord Nelson, Lord Beaverbrook, Sir Winston Churchill, Sir Anthony Eden, Clement Attlee, Henry Cooper, Lady Diana. *Vi har slått dem alle sammen, vi har slått dem alle sammen* [we have beaten them all, we have beaten them all]... Maggie Thatcher, can you hear me? Maggie Thatcher... Maggie Thatcher... *som de sier på ditt språk i boksebarene rundt Madison Square Garden* [as you say in your language in the boxing bars around Madison Square Garden]: Your boys took a hell of a beating! Your boys took a hell of a beating!'

Norwegian commentator Bjørge Lillelien after Norway beat England 2–1 in a World Cup qualifier, Oslo, 9 September 1981.

When the snowboarder Jenny Jones won Britain's first ever Winter Olympic medal on snow in February 2014, the occupants of the BBC commentary box got a bit excited. There were shrieks of delight, much squealing, a torrent of tears. So thrilled were they that many viewers wondered what the emotional repercussions might have been had Jones won a gold medal rather than the bronze.

The morning after their celebratory broadcast many a newspaper columnist, reflecting on the commentary, thought that it was all a little undignified: 'hog-whimperingly awful' was how the *Daily Telegraph*'s Oliver Brown described it. This was the British Broadcasting

Corporation, after all. It wasn't Norway's broadcasting service.

The Norwegians are not renowned for their over-exuberance. Or at least they weren't until Ron Greenwood's England team turned up in Oslo for a World Cup qualifier in the autumn of 1981 and lost. At which point a nation went certifiably doolally. And they were led in their march to delirium by the radio veteran Bjørge Lillelien. When his finest hour arrived, he had been working for the Norwegian state broadcaster since 1957. Football was not his first love. He preferred to commentate on cross-country skiing. But boy did he enjoy himself that night, producing on the final whistle a football commentary classic, a stream-of-consciousness monologue that became instantly celebrated for its euphoric lack of inhibition.

It may have sounded comical to jaded British ears (and how quickly we got to hear it; it was broadcast on the BBC news the following day), but Lillelien was doing what any commentator should do in the circumstances: he was reflecting the feelings of his audience. For Norwegians, beating the English at their own game really meant that much. This was a nation brought up on the English way. Most young Norwegians followed English clubs. *Match of the Day* had long been a staple of their television schedules. Many a Norwegian footballer who would subsequently come to ply their trade in the English leagues learned the language through hearing managers and players deliver their platitudes every Saturday night. That was why Ronny Johnsen, John Arne Riise and the rest were immediately comfortable with describing their mood as 'sick as a parrot' or 'over the moon': they had grown up with such phrases. And now to beat the motherland of the game, the country they had all learned to admire: this was something special.

Which was why Lillelien's unhinged rant seemed so appropriate.

> Here were the great imperialists brought low: their boys really had taken a hell of a beating.

He was more than aware that most of his audience would be able to follow him as he switched seamlessly from Norwegian to English. More to the point, his list of British heroes of yesteryear chimed perfectly with the sense of catastrophic decline that had attended English football since the early 1970s. After failing to qualify for the previous two World Cups, after this defeat another campaign looked to be heading for ignominy. Here were the great imperialists brought low: their boys really had taken a hell of a beating.

As it turned out, with victory a couple of months later over Hungary, it was Ron Greenwood's England that made it to Spain for the 1982 World Cup finals rather than Norway, allowing the English audience to embrace Lillelien with rather more magnanimity than would have been the case had England lost out. He became a cult hero in Britain, his magnificently mad minute of improvisation reckoned by the *Observer* newspaper twenty years later to be the finest piece of sports commentary ever. It quickly found its place in sporting discourse, its central taunting conceit frequently borrowed. As when *The Guardian*'s cricket correspondent Mike Selvey somewhat sarcastically eulogised England's consolation win in a dead final Test in the 2003 Ashes with:

John Howard, Sir Donald Bradman, Banjo Patterson, Rolf Harris, Richie Benaud, Dawn Fraser, Malcolm Conn, Kerry Packer, Dame Edna Everidge, your boys took one hell of a beating.

Perhaps the sharpest parody came in the Manchester University student newspaper after their team had beaten Pembroke College, Cambridge to win the 2012 *University Challenge* trophy. 'Rab Butler, Clive James, Ted Hughes, William Pitt the Younger, Eric Idle, Peter Cook, Bill Oddie. Bill Oddie? Bill Oddie can you hear me? Your boys took a hell of a beating.'

As it transpired, Lillelien was never able to better his masterpiece.

Stricken by cancer, he died only six years after his finest moment. Thus he was unable to comment on the careers of the four Norwegians who subsequently became managers in English football. Because of this there can be no doubt, as the four of them suffered from a cascade of poor results in the promised land, there is only one apposite observation to summarise their careers in the English leagues: 'Egil Olsen, Henning Berg, Ståle Solbakken, Ole Gunnar Solskjaer: in England you boys took a hell of a beating.'*

1984 'The kicking went on. And on and on and on, that terrible soft sound, with the boy saying nothing, only wriggling on the ground.'

Bill Buford reporting on a local being attacked by visiting fans during Manchester United's European Cup Winners' Cup semi-final against Juventus, Turin, 25 April 1984.

There was a notable downside to the domination of European competition by English clubs in the 1970s and early 1980s: the fans came too. And for cities across France, Italy, Belgium and Germany these were visitors the locals could do without.

For many a young Englishman, football offered an unmissable opportunity to run with the pack, to loose the shackles of convention, to escape the constraints of the working week by wallowing in the adrenalin rush of the terrace brawl. When Saturday came, the time was right for fighting in the street. In the 1970s and 1980s, every club

---

* Egil Olsen oversaw Wimbledon's demotion from the Premier League in 2000; Henning Berg spent fifty-seven days as Blackburn manager in 2012, winning just once; Ståle Solbakken was sacked by Wolverhampton Wanderers in 2013 after his side was eliminated from the FA Cup by non-League Luton Town; while Ole Gunnar Solskjaer, Manchester United's baby-faced, last-minute hero of the 1999 Champions League final, presided over the relegation of Cardiff City from the Premier League in May 2014.

had its hooligan element, the lads who chanted out support for their local team from the terraces and then engaged in alcohol-fuelled defence of their patch. Almost every big match was accompanied by disturbance. Almost everywhere it kicked off. More often than not it was little more than a bunch of blokes shouting and running around. But sometimes there were explosions of really brutal violence that were terrifying for those unwittingly caught up in them. In 1974 English football violence crossed a grim Rubicon when a Blackpool fan was stabbed to death at a match with Bolton Wanderers, the first murder at a British football ground.

The pursuit of violence by urban youth in the country's town centres caused the establishment endless hand-wringing consternation. With every escalation of Saturday afternoon anarchy, newspaper editorials thundered and politicians rumbled. After every outbreak of trouble, chief constables were instructed by their political masters to sort this out. Those in charge at the FA and Football League, meanwhile, washed their hands of responsibility, insisting this was not football's problem, but a wider malaise of society.

As the police were obliged to become ever more resourceful in their search for methods of containing the problem, as the frisking and segregation and barriers became routine, so the hooligans became ever more sophisticated in their search for excitement. Organised meets were established between rival 'firms', like West Ham's Inter-City Firm or the Chelsea Headhunters. Gangs were corralled along military lines, with generals dishing out orders to their foot soldiers. They needed to be, just to keep one step ahead of the cops.

And that was why Europe offered such potential: it was virgin territory to be exploited by English fans long schooled in the push and shove of the domestic game. What European competitions offered was the chance to export trouble to exotic new locations, to face up to new opponents, to follow in their forefathers' footsteps in sweeping across the continent. This was the new British Expeditionary Force, blagging their way through foreign lands, their role not to stand and hold the trenches of Flanders but to bring mayhem to the town squares and piazzas of peaceful postwar Western Europe.

And then there were the shoplifting opportunities. As Liverpool dominated continental competition, it wasn't just European football trophies that were brought back to Merseyside. Squads of young Scousers would descend on the shopping centres of European cities as they followed their team, helping themselves to fancy goods. Casual fashion trends were set by the lads coming home with their liberated booty of tracksuits, labelled shirts and swanky trainers.

> This was not football's problem, but a wider malaise of society.

Best of all from their point of view, generally the English hoolie got away with continental misdemeanours. European shopkeepers were taken by surprise, the police caught flat-footed. Their inclination was not to convict but to get the light-fingered visitors and their heavy-drinking, vandalising compatriots out of town as quickly as possible.

All of which meant that, by 1984, when the hapless inhabitants of Bruges, St Etienne or Milan found their local team drawn against an English side, they had come to expect a whirlwind of trouble. City-centre bar owners appreciated the upturn in sales, but everyone else came to associate a visit from the English with the unleashing of anarchy. Apart, that is, from the local lads, who saw in the aggressive, disreputable tourists the role models for their own Ultra gangs.

That year the American writer Bill Buford, then the editor of the literary magazine *Granta*, decided that the phenomenon of football hooliganism would make a compelling study. In the mid-1980s, the educated elite had no interest in football as a competitive sport; they were unmoved by who won the FA Cup last year. But they saw in football's animalistic rituals a subject worthy of anthropological inspection. What fascinated them was the very thing that so alarmed the establishment: the game's violent parasites.

Buford was commissioned to write a book and, for research purposes, he attached himself to Manchester United's following. At the time, United's supporters were among the most feared in the English game, their reputation for violent disorder reaching its peak when the club was relegated for just one year to the Second Division in 1974, opening up many a sleepy English market town to a visit from the Red Army. And by the time Buford joined up with them, as FA Cup holders, they were enjoying the delights of a continental run in the European Cup Winners' Cup.

Not that Buford concerned himself with the niceties of the competition. He wasn't interested in how the team of Bryan Robson, Paul McGrath and Norman Whiteside, self-confidently managed by the ebullient Ron Atkinson, fared. What he wanted to do was to follow Sammy the Red Army general, to study at close quarters his stormtroopers as they unleashed anarchy in Europe. And in Turin, after the second leg of the Cup Winners' Cup semi-final, as the United firm sought revenge for their side's elimination, he was able to witness it in all its galloping, bone-crunching, vicariously thrilling intensity. While several of those who attended the match insist his was an exaggerated recollection, nonetheless it provides a vivid first-hand account, the rhythm of the prose pulsing with the stomach-churning vigour of a head bouncing off the pavement.

The very brutality of it all seemed to shock Buford into inertia. It took him more than six years after that night in Turin to complete his book, which he titled *Among the Thugs*. Six years in which, when it came to football and hooliganism, everything changed.

1985 'I was asked if I'd play a football manager in a television drama. I asked how long it would take. They said about ten days. I said that's par for the course.'

Tommy Docherty, 1985.

High-wire walker, bomb-disposal officer, lion-tamer, freshly commissioned officer on the Western Front? Few careers can match football management for precariousness and brevity of tenure. In a job that requires time to get things right, a manager is lucky if he is employed for more than a year. Players' egos, fans' expectations and the capricious nature of club owners are but three in the long list of reasons why – at the first hint of problems at a football club – it is the manager who is asked to leave. Sometimes things don't even have to be going that badly wrong for them to be jettisoned. Just ask Malky Mackay. Or Michael Laudrup.

Few managers in the history of football have been more experienced in the process of being shown the door than Tommy Docherty. Full of patter and acerbic observation, the quick-fire Scot turned his inability to hold down a job for long into a comedy act. For years after he gave up the game (or rather after the game gave *him* up) he toured theatres and nightclubs talking about his time, his routine crackling with anecdote and opinion, a tour de force of sending up of the absurdities of football's managerial hiring and firing.

One of his favourite lines in his stage show was the one about him having had more clubs than the golfer Jack Nicklaus. It turns out, as with much of the Doc's approach to life, that the gag does not adhere to the strictest definitions of accuracy. While Nicklaus carried fourteen clubs in his bag into major tournaments, the Doc managed only twelve different football clubs. Though he did have two spells at both Queens Park Rangers and Sydney Olympic and was Scotland's national manager. And in truth, watching him on stage recounting his career, it felt like a lot more.

The fact is, the Doc and a job in football were never destined to form a lasting relationship. A man rippling with nervous energy, he did not easily settle. By far his longest stay in a managerial post was his first. He survived for six years at Chelsea in the 1960s, revitalising the place, introducing a swathe of young players known as Docherty's Diamonds, including Terry Venables, Bobby Tambling and Peter Bonetti, leading them to the FA Cup final in 1967 before resigning over a lack of transfer funds. His shortest stay was at Queens Park Rangers a year later, where he lasted no more than twenty-eight days before flouncing out.

Docherty left jobs for many reasons: he was fired for bad results, he resigned when deprived of expected transfer revenues, or he simply fell out with his chairman. And chairmen were not a species for which the Doc had much time. Take his assessment of Jim Gregory, his late and not-much-lamented chairman at QPR, who, despite an obvious personal antipathy, employed him twice:

> When you shook hands with him, you counted your fingers. He was a crook. He spent all his time at a health farm in Tring. You couldn't call him, but he could call you. The day he sacked me, he gave me a bottle of champagne to celebrate our tremendous start to the season and then decided to get rid of me.

At Manchester United, the job that he felt he was destined for, and where he survived for what was for him a near-eternity of four-and-a-half seasons, the Doc came up with a new and original way of getting the sack. He was unceremoniously removed from his position weeks after winning the FA Cup in 1977 when it was revealed in a tabloid newspaper that he was sleeping with the club physiotherapist's wife (to whom he remains happily married to this day). A decade later, he finally retired from football management

> When you shook hands with him you counted your fingers.

when he left Altrincham in 1988, his last job. Though with Docherty 'retired' is a flexible term. In his case it simply meant being sacked for the final time.

Many aspects of professional football have changed since the Doc hung up his tracksuit and took to the stage: players' salaries have skyrocketed; English players in the top flight are rare as snow in June; the prawn sandwich coexists with the meat pie. But when it comes to managerial life expectancy, time has stood still. In the middle of the 2013–14 season it was revealed that every single club in the English league except Arsenal, had changed its manager at least once in the previous five years. At the time of writing the average length of employment for bosses in the Premier League has slipped to just thirteen months. Though you have to think, if the Doc was still aboard the managerial merry-go-round, quipping and chivvying, he would doubtless have pushed that average even lower.

Still, even the Doc cannot match the former Fulham, QPR and West Ham United striker Leroy Rosenior, who holds the ignominious record for the shortest managerial reign in English football history. He had just signed his contract at Torquay in the summer of 2007 – his second spell of managing the club – when he was informed that the place had been sold to a new owner, who wanted their own man. He was promptly sacked. Rosenior had been in charge for just ten minutes.

1985 'If this is what football is to become, let it die.'

Editorial in *L'Équipe* following the Heysel stadium disaster, 30 May 1985.

The European Champions Club Cup was an idea born in the summer of 1955 in the offices of the French daily sports newspaper, *L'Équipe,* dreamed up by its football correspondent Gabriel Hanot and his colleague Jacques Ferran. Yet here was Robert Parienté, the paper's editor, no more than twenty-nine years after the first triumphant flowering of his predecessors' brainchild, suggesting that not only the competition but the game itself should be allowed to expire. Football, he declared, had reached the end of its life cycle. You can sense this was a man who had seen enough. Exasperation and defeat oozed from his typewriter; world-weariness dripped from his prose.

And at the time it was not hard to share Parienté's disillusion. He was writing on the night of the worst disaster in the tournament's history. On the evening of 29 May 1985, thirty-nine Italian fans perished ahead of the European Cup final, their lives lost in the twisted masonry of the Heysel stadium in Brussels. What was so awful about their deaths was that every single one of them was utterly, wholly and completely avoidable. This was not an accident. This was culpable manslaughter.

The European Cup final of 1985 was to be Liverpool's fifth. The magnificent Merseyside club, bristling with authority and experience, was due to face the Italian champions Juventus. However, the moment he arrived at the Heysel stadium, Phil Neal, the Liverpool captain, had an uneasy feeling about the place. This was not like the grand venues in which he had previously played in European finals, it did not seem to him a fitting stage for a match of this significance. It was crumbling and past-it, an arena showing its age. Indeed, when they had visited the place on a fact-finding tour ahead of the final,

Liverpool officials had complained about its dilapidated condition to the organising body, UEFA. With its cracked terracing, broken barriers and shabby stands, it looked to them wholly inadequate. Their worries were ignored.

Before he had even walked out to conduct the pre-match formalities, Neal's fears were becoming reality. Liverpool fans, who had been drinking all day in the Grand Place in Brussels, arrived at the ground in provocative mood. Some were looking for revenge on Italian fans after a number of Liverpool supporters had been attacked by Roma followers at the European Cup final the previous year in Rome. Filtered into the section of terrace reserved for them, they discovered they were separated from the Juve supporters by only a flimsy fence, with just the thinnest of police lines to keep order. As the noisy chant and counter-chant crossed the divide, missiles were soon flying in both directions; the terraces themselves crumbled easily under a heel and hard core was ripped up and thrown. As lumps of concrete flew through the air, the mood became more heated. Then the Liverpool fans did something that English fans had been doing for two decades: they charged their rivals. What they did that evening was no more anarchic than many a Saturday in the Football League. The trouble was, as they embarked on their drunken rampage, the dividing fence separating them from the Juve followers crumpled as if made of papier-mâché, the police line melted and the panicked Italian supporters tried to flee their onrushing counterparts. As they did so, a wall collapsed and thirty-nine of them died in the ensuing crush, their lives ebbing away under the gaze of the camera. Their deaths were witnessed by 100 million television viewers across the globe.

Just a month after fifty-six people had perished when the main stand at Bradford's Valley Parade ground had been consumed in flames, this appeared to be football's nadir. For many an English supporter watching back home, there was a horrible inevitability about what unfolded. Two decades of habitual hooliganism had been building up to this ghastly moment. As Nick Hornby put it in his book *Fever Pitch*:

> The kids' stuff that proved murderous in Brussels belonged firmly and clearly on a continuum of apparently harmless but obviously threatening acts – violent chants, wanker signs, the whole, petty hard-act works – in which a very large minority of fans had been indulging for nearly 20 years. In short Heysel was an organic part of a culture that many of us, myself included, had contributed towards.

Within the British political establishment, the reaction to the disaster was much the same as in the offices of *L'Équipe*. Prime Minister Margaret Thatcher had no enthusiasm for sport of any kind. She had long railed against the impotence of the authorities in the face of football hooligans. Now she sprang into action.

'Football used to be our national game. It was renowned for its sportsmanship. There are some people who are upsetting the whole thing. It's the thugs that are destroying football,' she told a hastily arranged press conference. She had already summoned Bert Millichip and Ted Croker of the FA to Number Ten, where she instructed them immediately to withdraw English teams from all European competition. They did so, then agreed to UEFA's angry demand that the self-imposed exile be extended to five years, with Liverpool serving an additional year. 'We have to get the game cleaned up from this hooliganism at home and then perhaps we shall be able to go overseas again,' Mrs Thatcher added.

> Football used to be our national game. It was renowned for its sportsmanship. There are some people who are upsetting the whole thing.

Even as she spoke, the sense of shame was widespread. Embarrassment at English culpability was everywhere. The game was derided as an oozing, fetid sore on society. *The Sunday Times* summed up the prevailing attitude when it described football thus: 'A slum game played in slum stadiums watched by slum people.'

For those within the game, especially those at Anfield, the guilt was tangible. 'It felt as if Liverpool had let English football down, when for twenty years they had been its finest ambassador,' Phil Neal recalls. 'That's what really turned our stomachs, the feeling that the club's impeccable record over two decades in Europe had ended in something so horrific.'

For sure, without the Liverpool fans' drunken charge, those thirty-nine people would not have lost their lives. For sure, the English embrace of hooligan excess had delivered murderous consequences. For sure, the fourteen Liverpool fans who served time for involuntary manslaughter deserved their sentences. Yet the ready ease with which culpability was identified allowed the Belgian authorities and UEFA to escape without any scrutiny being directed at other significant failings that night in Brussels. 'Only the English fans were responsible,' UEFA's official observer, Gunter Schneider, reported. Of that there was no doubt.

Bolstered by that conviction, there was no judicial inquiry into the causes of the horrors. No one was brought to account for the shambolic organisation, inadequate policing or incompetent staging. No one questioned why a stadium that was on the verge of being demolished (it was rebuilt in 1994) was considered appropriate to host such a significant occasion. No one even bothered to ask why UEFA had shown such lack of respect for the dead they had insisted the game go ahead on the night, even as thirty-nine bodies lay in a makeshift morgue below the stands. Instead everyone agreed it was just an act of mindless violence, solely Liverpool's fault.

And so football blundered on, oblivious to its wider responsibilities.

The British government and the FA acquiesced in an act of 'mea culpa' by agreeing to banishment from Europe, but failed – with tragic consequences at Hillsborough four years later (see page xv) – to heed the warnings about English football's own crumbling infrastructure. After Heysel, nothing was properly addressed, nothing done to make the game safe to watch, none of its creaking inadequacies resolved. Nothing was about to get better. In the spring of 1985 there was not a lot to be jovial about in football. No wonder *L'Équipe*, the very progenitor of football's grandest club competition, was in despair.

1986 'A little with the head of Maradona and a little with the hand of God.'

Diego Maradona in the post-match press conference in the Estadio Azteca, Mexico City, 22 June 1986.

With these words, used to describe his first goal in Argentina's 2–1 victory over England in the 1986 World Cup quarter-final, the little genius did more than deliver one of football's most enduring one-liners: he created the epithet that came to define his career. Neat, amused, knowing: it said it all. There was only one minor problem with it. However many times you watch his opening goal again, it is impossible to detect any physical contribution from the head of Maradona. From every angle the only human body part involved in putting the ball in the net is the diminutive striker's podgy little hand.

Maradona, however, was not alone in reckoning that he got away with it because of supernatural intervention. Across Argentina the nation was united in its belief that what had unfolded in Mexico City that day was the working of divine providence. Sure, Maradona's actions might not have been strictly within the rules of the game, but the fact that their talisman got away with it suggested to his countrymen that someone up there was smiling down on them and their football team.

England's quarter-final clash with Argentina took place only four years after the end of the Falklands War. For the Argentines, the 1982 conflict ended in humiliation, as their forces were routed by British paratroopers at Goose Green and Mount Tumbledown, but their conviction of the legitimacy of their claim to the islands they called the Malvinas remained absolute.

For Maradona and his team-mates, from the moment it became clear they were to face England in the World Cup quarter-final, the possibilities of revenge for that wretched military defeat began to form in the mind. Publicly they let slip no intimation of their feelings. Diplomacy, convention and etiquette were adhered to absolutely. Before kick-off, they shook hands and exchanged pennants with their opponents. But privately they knew what this meant. As Maradona admitted in his autobiography *El Diego*: 'In the pre-match interviews we had all said that football and politics shouldn't be confused, but that was a lie. We did nothing but think about that. Bollocks was it just another match.'

On their way to the quarter-final, Argentina had sailed through their group, beating Bulgaria and South Korea and drawing with Italy, before dismissing Uruguay in the first knock-out round. England, by contrast, had initially stuttered, losing to Portugal and drawing with Morocco before Gary Lin-

> In the pre-match interviews we had all said that football and politics shouldn't be confused, but that was a lie.

eker's storming hat-trick had seen them through at the expense of Poland. In the last-sixteen phase, however, they had defeated Paraguay with aplomb, 3–0, with Lineker scoring another two. Back home, belief in manager Bobby Robson's side was growing.

For the first half of the game, there was nothing to choose between the teams; England matched their opponents stride for stride, tackle for tackle. Argentina could not find a way past Terry Butcher's obdurate defence. Then, early in the second half, Maradona made his first move. Running fast at the English back line, he played the ball out to Jorge Valdano, and carried on his sprint into the box. However, England's Steve Hodge, working like a Trojan as he tracked back, got in ahead of the intended recipient of the pass and flicked the ball back over his head towards his goalkeeper, the perennial Peter Shilton. As the 'keeper rose to punch clear, Maradona whipped in and slapped the ball, volleyball-style, off his wrist into the net. Not looking over his shoulder to check what the linesman thought, he ran to the halfway line in celebration. Despite vociferous English protestations led by a clearly apoplectic Steve Fenwick, Ali Bin Nasser, the Tunisian referee, awarded the goal.

After the ridiculous came the sublime. A few moments later, Maradona, buoyed by the success of his trickery, gathered the ball in his own half and began a purposeful run straight through the England defence. The Azteca Stadium is sited 7,200 ft above sea level and the air seemed thin indeed as Peter Reid, Butcher and Fenwick panted in the great striker's wash. After arriving in the area, Maradona artfully slipped the ball past Shilton to record one of the greatest strikes ever recorded in the World Cup. 'A brilliant goal,' admitted Robson after the game. 'I didn't like it but I had to admire it.'

Even then, England almost came back. Lineker scored with a header from a John Barnes cross, then put an equalising chance just wide. There was no disgrace in England being defeated by an Argentinian side graced by a sublimely gifted footballer – and this was, after all, a team that would go on to lift the World Cup. But back in Blighty the talk was not of Maradona's genius but of his bare-faced deceit.

'Maradona finds the knock-out punch,' ran the next day's headline in *The Guardian*. The consensus was, England had been cheated out of their rightful place in the semi-final. And the pain did not quickly diminish. Bobby Robson wrote of the incident in his autobiography: 'It wasn't the Hand of God. It was the hand of a rascal. God had nothing to do with it... That day, Maradona was diminished in my eyes forever.'

In Buenos Aires, it would have been hard to find anyone who agreed. There, huge crowds gathered at the final whistle. The celebrations were unfettered. The Union Flag was burned, Prime Minister Margaret Thatcher's name publicly cursed. The sense of what this meant was clear. The mass-circulation newspaper *Cronica* had as its front-page headline: 'Malvinas 2 England 1.' The paper's report was unequivocal: 'We beat the pirates with Maradona and a little hand... God save Argentina. He who robs a thief has a hundred years of pardon.'

It always seemed to be like this in games between England and Argentina. At the time of writing there have been just fourteen meetings between the two countries, but most seemed to boil with controversy. There was the 1966 World Cup quarter-final, when the Argentine captain Antonio Rattín was sent off for 'violence of the tongue' and Alf Ramsey prevented his players from swapping shirts with opponents he described as 'animals'. There was the 1998 match in which David Beckham was sent off for a retaliatory kick at Diego Simeone. Despite the fact that the Argentinian players Osvaldo Ardiles, Ricky Villa, Sergio Agüero and Pablo Zabaleta have been much admired for their performances for English clubs, internationally there is no intercontinental rivalry to match England v. Argentina for rancour and poison. As Maradona suggested, this is a contest in which sport and politics are forever intertwined.

1987 'A true football fan is one who knows the nationality of every player in the Republic of Ireland team.'

Musician Ken Bolam, 1987.

There was more than a degree of truth in a joke that did the rounds in the mid-1980s. It went: 'How do you confuse a footballer turning out for the Republic of Ireland team? Answer: play him the Irish national anthem and ask him to hum along.'

Andy Townsend was not the only one who was caught out by the strains of 'A Soldier's Song' playing out on the public-address system ahead of an international. Despite playing seventy times for the Irish team, latterly as captain, the personable Aston Villa and Chelsea midfielder-turned-television pundit never got to grips with the lyrics. He always looked embarrassed when the song was played, occasionally caught on camera attempting to move his lips in vague approximation to the words, a footballing John Redwood. But then he was born in Maidstone. And in the Kent schools where he learned the game there was not much call to commit 'A Soldier's Song' to memory.

The fact that Townsend turned out with such distinction in a green jersey was entirely due to Article 18 of the FIFA constitution, which became known, somewhat pejoratively, as the 'Granny Rule'. Though in Townsend's case it was apt: he was entitled to play for Ireland because his grandmother was Irish. Until the rule was passed in 1976, qualification for an international team was open only to those born in the country, or who had two parents born there. Ireland's first-ever second-generation player was Shay Brennan of Manchester United, who earned nineteen caps between 1965 and 1970. Though Brennan hailed from Manchester, both his parents had emigrated to England from County Carlow. The Granny Rule extended the possibilities further down the genetic line. And for a nation which had spent much of the preceding century exporting its population, to be able to select from the descendants of a diaspora spread across the globe hugely deepened the talent pool.

The last entirely Irish-born football side was the one selected by player-manager Johnny Giles to play Turkey in a European Championship qualifier at Dalymount Park on 29 October 1975. From then on, the net was widened. Giles himself picked Tony Grealish, Mark Lawrenson and Terry Mancini under the new edict a couple of months later. His successor Eoin Hand capped Chris Hughton, Gary Waddock and Michael Robinson, Englishmen all. Robinson's inclusion demonstrated the growing pliability of the Granny Rule: his mother, third-generation Irish herself, became a citizen of the country in order that her son would also qualify for an Irish passport.

But the man who stretched the Granny Rule to the very limit of elasticity was the English World Cup winner Jack Charlton. The first foreigner to manage the Republic team, when he took over in 1986 he was not remotely concerned about his team's wider position as symbols of Irish identity. He just wanted to win. And if they could only do so speaking with an English accent, so be it. As he angrily told an Irish interviewer who wondered if he was forgetting the cultural purpose of international football, victory was all that mattered.

'You want me to compete with the best in the world, I've got to have the fucking best in the world,' Charlton snapped back in characteristically robust terms before continuing:

And it's not here in Ireland that I can find it, I've got to go to England to find it, or Scotland to find the quality that will make you a team that will compete with the best in the world. Now, if you don't want to do that, tell me, and I'll fucking concentrate on the League of Ireland and we'll win nothing. But give me the freedom to produce results and I'll produce results.

> You want me to compete with the best in the world, I've got to have the best in the world.

And Charlton did just that. The closest some of the players had got to Ireland before he selected them may have been downing a pint of Guinness, but he got results. For a decade with him in charge Ireland punched way above their weight. They regularly qualified for international tournaments, where they made a habit of discomfiting the English (they beat the old enemy at the 1988 Euros, drew with them at the 1990 World Cup and, better still, qualified for the 1994 World Cup Finals when the other lot didn't; they made it to the quarter-finals in 1990 and the last sixteen in both 1994 and 2002).

Charlton succeeded by taking a bulldozer to convention. Of the team that beat England in Stuttgart in 1988, only three were born in Ireland (Pat Bonner, Steve Staunton and Kevin Moran). At times the connection between some of the players and the country they represented was flimsy indeed. Charlton's favoured centre-forward Tony Cascarino had the most tenuous of links. He qualified because his grandfather was Irish. But, as the Cockney with the Italian name admitted in his autobiography, that was not really relevant since he was adopted. 'I didn't qualify for Ireland. I was a fraud. A fake Irishman,' he confessed in his best-selling memoir *Full Time: The Secret Life of Tony Cascarino* (2005).

Plastic Paddy he may have been, the epitome of nationality by convenience, but no one could gainsay Cascarino's application in the green shirt. In his eighty-eight internationals he scored seventeen goals and invariably gave his utmost to his adopted country's cause. Though the born-and-bred Cockney never did get round to learning these words from the national anthem: 'See in the east a silv'ry glow / Out yonder waits the Saxon foe / Soldiers are we whose lives are pledged to Ireland.'

While Charlton's team may not have been very Irish, the Irish state tried its best to make Jack Charlton Irish. He was made a Freeman of the City of Dublin, given an honorary doctorate by the University of Limerick and awarded honorary Irish citizenship in 1996. Not forgetting the statue of him in fishing gear and brandishing a salmon which greets anyone arriving at Cork airport.

1988 'The Crazy Gang have beaten the Culture Club.'

John Motson, commentating for the BBC on Wimbledon's victory over Liverpool in the FA Cup final, Wembley Stadium, 14 May 1988.

It was the most extraordinary result in more than a century of the FA Cup. This was not just a simple case of giant-killing, not just another third-round upset. This was a slaying at the altar of English football, at Wembley, a place where the natural order of things is almost invariably maintained. John Motson was describing the humbling of the then most decorated footballing institution in the land. A humbling, moreover, carried out by a club that had only gained entry to the Football League eleven years previously, an outfit that had spent most of its 100-year existence scrabbling around the amateur circuit, a club so unfashionable it had taken as its official nickname the title of a children's story about burrow-dwelling, pointy-nosed creatures who collect and recycle rubbish on Wimbledon Common. For that May afternoon Liverpool, then seventeen-times champions of England, had been beaten by the Wombles. Or, as the sheepskin-coated BBC stalwart Motson put it, in a line you sense he had prepared specially for the occasion, 'The Crazy Gang have beaten the Culture Club.'

The original Crazy Gang were a bunch of comedians in the 1930s who performed at the London Palladium's Crazy Nights, a line-up which included in its number Bud Flanagan and Chesney Allen (no relation to Jon Flanagan and Joe Allen, Liverpool players of 2013–14 vintage). When the Wimbledon team began to emerge in the mid-1980s it seemed an apt description for them. Corralled by their manager Dave Bassett, they were driven by an extraordinary spirit as they made rapid progress up the divisions. They were promoted from the Fourth Division in 1982–3, from the third the next season, and by 1985–6 – just nine years after being elected to the Football League – they were in the top flight.

Theirs was a spirit fostered by an institutionalised tomfoolery, encouraged by the club chairman, the Lebanese businessman Sam Hammam. Pranks were an essential part of life at Plough Lane. In the dressing room clothes were routinely cut up, buckets routinely poured over heads, lavatory seats routinely smeared in superglue. What japes were had, generally to the backdrop of Hammam's infectious cackle.

As the sledgehammer nature of their practical jokes suggested, there was nothing subtle about the Wimbledon way. Their footballing philosophy was route one, hit-and-hope, chuck-it-in-the-mixer stuff. The FA's director of football, Charles Hughes, must have been thrilled to see them exploit so many of his POMOs (see pages 75–6).

Wimbledon embraced a brand of football that most thought had gone out with the dinosaurs. But the Crazy Gang's nakedly confrontational style – instigated by their sharp-elbowed centre-forward John Fashanu, their thuggish midfielder Vinnie Jones and his yapping terrier sidekick Dennis Wise – unquestionably delivered results, even after Bassett departed for Watford, to be replaced by the Bristol Rovers manager Bobby Gould.

Liverpool meanwhile, still recovering from the shame of Heysel (see pages 134–8), had developed a side of rare footballing refinement. The new player-manager Kenny Dalglish had already won one double in 1985–6; now, in 1987–8 – having bought in sublime talent in the form of John Barnes from Watford and Peter Beardsley from

Newcastle – he looked to be heading for another. Crowned league champions a fortnight ahead of the final, his team had arrived at Wembley – in a chilling rehearsal for what was soon to come (see page xv) – by beating Nottingham Forest at Hillsborough in the semi. Wimbledon, meanwhile, had battered their way past Luton at White Hart Lane.

As the two clubs prepared for their final showdown, it seemed certain this was about as far as the Wimbledon story could go. One bookmaker was quoting 5–1 against them winning. But what nobody knew – not the bookies, not Motson, not even the 30,000 Wimbledon fans relishing the high point of their club's existence in the Wembley sunshine – was what was going on in the tunnel as the game was about to get underway. Gould had deliberately altered the clock in the Wimbledon dressing room, putting the hands back a couple of minutes. Thus it was that the Liverpool side arrived in the tunnel well ahead of their rivals. They were lining up for what seemed an age before there was any sign of the opposition, hearing the swirling noise outside, the adrenaline coursing through their veins, the nerves beginning to jangle. And when they finally arrived, Wimbledon's players showed no sign of being intimidated by their opponents' reputation. Far from it, they were right in the Liverpool team's faces, issuing a salvo of snarled threats.

The combative if modestly gifted Vinnie Jones, perhaps rehearsing one of his future movie roles as a violent criminal, loudly informed Dalglish – the finest British footballer of his generation – that he was about to rip off his ear 'and spit in the hole'. As the teams began the walk out to the centre circle, the Wimbledon players kept shouting 'in the hole' to reinforce the threat. The well-brought-up, polite John Barnes looked particularly alarmed by the thuggishness of the opposition. And he subsequently played as if he wished he was anywhere other than sharing a Wembley pitch with this bunch of barbarians.

Direct from the kick-off, Jones behaved as if he were a member of the Seven Samurai – never mind the Crazy Gang – launching into a premeditated assault on Liverpool's midfield enforcer Steve McMahon. Anxious not to appear too fussy too early in the game, the referee Brian Hill let him off with a swift lecture. Hill's response set the tone: Liverpool were nervy and tense; Wimbledon free to be their usual ebullient selves. And by half-time, the Dons were in the lead, Lawrie Sanchez diverting a Wise free-kick into the Liverpool goal.

In the second half Liverpool strained to salvage their reputation. They besieged the Wimbledon area. And when a penalty was awarded (incorrectly as it turned out) for a challenge by the full-back Clive Goodyear on John Aldridge, it seemed as if the proper pecking order was about to be restored. Aldridge stepped up to take the spot kick and fired it firmly to Dave Beasant's left. But the 'keeper dived prodigiously and got his fingers to the ball, becoming in the process the first man to save a penalty in a Wembley Cup final.

His effort seemed to confirm Liverpool's fears that the fates were against them. Their energy largely petered out. And when Beasant recorded a second first by becoming the first 'keeper to lift the FA Cup as captain, the most improbable underdog victory was complete.

The stage was set for Motson to deliver his carefully rehearsed line. Though where the Culture Club reference came from is not entirely clear. Nobody apart from him had ever linked Liverpool FC and Boy George's group of over-dressed New Romantics. By the time Motson made his remark, the band had gone their separate ways, their chart successes and their best days behind them. Perhaps there was an omen in his analogy after all.

1988 'OMA WIJ HEBBEN JE FIETS GEVONDEN' ['Granny We've Found Your Bike']

Banner held up by Dutch fans at the European Championship semi-final against West Germany, Volksparkstadion, Hamburg, 21 June 1988.

Let's just say the Dutch aren't too fond of their eastern neighbours. Which is no real surprise: 206,000 Dutch people were killed during the wartime occupation of the Netherlands by the Germans. And in the Low Countries, memories of the Nazis' 'Rotterdam blitz' of May 1940, in which 900 died and 25,000 homes were destroyed, the drafting of Dutch citizens into forced labour, and the persecution and liquidation of tens of thousands of Dutch Jews took a long time to dissipate. They were certainly still raw in 1974, when Holland and West Germany met in Munich's Olympic Stadium in the final of the World Cup. It was the first competitive fixture

> I don't like Germans. Every time I played against German players I had a problem because of the war.

between the two sides since the war, and it was one freighted with significance. Wim van Hanegem, the Dutch midfielder in that game, had lost his father and siblings during the Nazi occupation and didn't mince his words: 'I don't like Germans. Every time I played against German players I had a problem because of the war.'

The Dutch, espousing the total football developed by Johan Cruyff, anticipated a victory. But the Germans were too strong, too efficient, too muscular for them. When his side lost, van Hanegem left the field in tears. Defeat seemed doubly significant for the Dutch: they needed to win as much for revenge as self-esteem. The West German defender Berti Vogts remembers how even the elegant, cultured Cruyff was not above the bitterness. At the final whistle,

Cruyff refused Vogts's invitation to shake hands.

In 1988, the two countries met again in the latter stages of a major tournament, again on West German soil, this time in the semi-final of the European Championships. If anything, the Dutch were even more convinced of their superiority on this occasion. For this was the team of Ruud Gullit, Frank Rijkaard and Marco van Basten, the gilded threesome whose genius had dismissed England earlier in the competition with the ease of a cat toying with a mouse. This time, however, the Dutch supporters made humorous reference to the past with their banner. During the war, the German invaders had confiscated thousands of bikes across Holland, sending them back to the Ruhr as scrap to be melted down for the war effort. The beery, cheery orange masses, pouring over the border and filling the Rhineland campsites with their loud bonhomie, were conducting a reverse invasion. And they were desperate to see their team return with some booty of their own.

When Lothar Matthäus put the hosts into the lead from the penalty spot, it seemed as if the old order was going to be maintained. But to the accompaniment of a huge, soaring noise from the terracing holding the Dutch fans, Ronald Koeman equalised, also from a penalty. Then, just as the game appeared destined for extra time, the incomparable van Basten found the winner, scoring in the eighty-eighth minute. The Dutch went on to secure their only major trophy to date when they beat the Soviet Union 2–0 in the final in Munich, with Gullit and van Basten on the scoresheet.

But Hamburg was the mythical moment. That was when the Netherlands finally purged some forty years of hurt. As the Dutch coach Rinus Michels put it at the time: 'We all know that the semi-final was the real final.'

1988 'I couldn't settle in Italy – it was like living in a foreign country.'

Ian Rush, Liverpool, August 1988.

It was a comment that came to mark the electric-heeled Welshman as one of football's less rigorous intellects. But he now insists that he never actually said it:

> I was set up. It was someone's idea of fun – probably one of my Liverpool team-mates joked that I'd said it and things went from there. I had just re-joined the club and wanted to get back to playing football, not worry what was being written about me.

Rush is right: there is no evidence that he actually used the words so often ascribed to him. Yet the fact that this apocryphal line gained such widespread currency reveals much about the standing of the footballer in wider society: everyone believed Rush had said it because it sounded exactly the kind of thing a footballer *would* say. After all, these were people with a reputation for talking in clichés about feeling 'over the moon' and 'sick as a parrot'; they were not thought of as being at the front of the queue when the brains were handed out.

One thing, though, that Rush cannot deny is that his season in Turin, playing for Juventus, was not his finest. He had headed there in the summer of 1987 with a glittering return in Liverpool red of 139 goals in 224 appearances. His transfer, smoothed through as part of Liverpool's reparations for the Heysel disaster two seasons previously, set a British record of £3.2 million.

At the time Italian clubs were increasingly looking to England to recruit talent (and England had many more-than-decent players available for hire). The best payers in Europe, they offered significantly better remuneration than their English rivals, the sort of money that attracted Mark Hateley, Trevor Francis and Ray Wilkins. It was a trend that gathered pace after the 1990 World Cup when England's Des Walker, David Platt and Paul Gascoigne joined the English exodus to Italy. As Rush now admits:

> I think if I were to tell the truth, I went there for the financial side of it, but also to learn. Wales were not in the big tournaments – and Liverpool were banned from Europe – and I wanted to go out and play with and against the best players in the world, which were mostly in Italy back then.

And he was treading in august footsteps. Between 1957 and 1962, as he won three Italian championships and topped the Serie A scoring charts, John Charles, a predecessor of Rush's in the Welsh international shirt, had been a Juve legend.

It wasn't to be quite like that for Rush. Challenged by the language, he was surprised to discover that the club did not provide an interpreter. He had to rely on his Danish team-mate Michael Laudrup to translate from Italian into English during team meetings (Rush never saw the irony in a fellow foreigner being so much more verbally acclimatised: he just assumed that was what Danes did). Unable to chat, he found it hard to mix with his colleagues, was isolated in company, and at times felt completely alone. His performances reflected his misery. And the local media were not exactly over-enthusiastic in their welcome, either. One reporter, noting Rush's 1980s moustache, likened him to a cross between Charlie Chaplin and Adolf Hitler (though, surely, a more accurate likeness was Neville Chamberlain).

Not every English footballer abroad was so discombobulated. Gary Lineker became fluent in Spanish during his time in Barcelona (a facility he employs at every opportunity in his role as *Match of the Day* host). The midfielder David Platt played successively for three Italian clubs between 1991 and 1995. During his time at Sampdoria he was asked by an English reporter if he missed the Villa (an allusion to his three-year stint with the Birmingham club). Platt sneered at the very concept of homesickness with his crisp reply that, no, he didn't miss the Villa, he now lived in one.

It was the tactical pattern in which he was obliged to play that most confounded Rush. Used to Liverpool's speedy breakaway style, he became marooned up front, starved of possession by a pragmatic, defensive line-up. Unhappy off the pitch, unhappy on it: it was not a combination likely to produce success. Rush now takes a sanguine view of his ill-fated Italian foray:

> Looking back, Juventus were the right club at the wrong time. We'd just signed seven players and were happy to get 0–0 draws away from home. That negative approach didn't play to my strengths. But I don't regret going. My time at Juventus improved me in every way, both as a person and player. Most importantly, though, it means I can look back on my career and not wonder about what might have been.

When he came back to England, chastened by a return of just seven goals in twenty-nine appearances in his one season in Italy, Rush enjoyed a further seven years in Liverpool red, scoring effortlessly and often, before moving on to Leeds and Newcastle. From the moment he stepped out again at Anfield, he looked like the Ian Rush of old. He looked, in short, as if he had come home.

1989 'It's up for grabs now.'

ITV commentator Brian Moore, Anfield, 26 May 1989.

The plot could not have been better thought through in a Hollywood studio. All season Kenny Dalglish's Liverpool and George Graham's Arsenal had been jockeying for position at the top of the First Division. Their meeting at Anfield in late April had been postponed because of the mid-month tragedy at Hillsborough (see page xv) and was now re-scheduled as the last game of the season, played on a Friday night after Liverpool had already secured the FA Cup.

This was the first season of a new package of rights bought by ITV to provide live coverage of league matches. Until 1983, the only live domestic football on British television was the FA Cup final. Now here, at the very dawn of live football broadcasting, was the most dramatic ending there had ever been to a league campaign; what ITV got for its £44 million outlay was effectively a championship play-off. The mathematics was simple: in order to secure the title Arsenal had to win by two clear goals; any other result and Liverpool would win the double. For the Arsenal striker Alan Smith, the task seemed utterly impossible. 'Blimey, winning a corner up there was usually hard enough,' he recalls of Anfield. 'Never mind comfortably beating a side that had dominated English football for so many years.'

Furthermore, the visitors had to contend with the game's potentially overwhelming emotional undertow. Out of respect for the memory of the ninety-six fans who had died at Hillsborough, the hope that some sort of catharsis might be achieved by a Liverpool victory was shared not only within Anfield, but by many a neutral across the country. Arsenal, though, played the occasion perfectly. Their players trotted out on to the pitch carrying bunches of flowers, which they threw to every corner of the ground, a touching symbol of sporting fraternity. And while the visiting players were utterly focused, Smith remembers the Liverpool team seemed hesitant. 'They didn't know how to approach a match they could lose 1–0 and still end up winning the title,' he says. 'There was a lack of intensity to their play.' So much so, that, midway through the second half, Arsenal took the lead, Smith glancing a header past Bruce Grobbelaar. The Liverpool players were furious with the referee: the goal had come from an indirect free-kick and they were certain Smith had not touched it. 'Oh I headed it all right,' says Smith now. He then breaks into a mischievous smile.

At the time it didn't seem enough, however. As the game drifted towards its conclusion, Moore's co-commentator David Pleat summed up the feeling of the viewing audience when he said maybe poetic justice would be served if the result stayed that way, allowing an Arsenal win, but a Liverpool title. It was a remark that did not endear the former Spurs manager to the North Londoners' fan base.

To the delight of every Gooner in Islington, including Nick Hornby, who memorialised the moment in his book *Fever Pitch* (1992), Pleat was not to prove the most prescient of observers. In the last seconds of the game, Arsenal's 'keeper John Lukic rolled the ball out to the full-back Lee Dixon, who passed it forward to Smith. The centre-forward then flicked it into the path of his colleague Michael Thomas, who advanced into the Liverpool area. 'I was behind him yelling at him to shoot,' remembers Smith, nearly a quarter of a century on. 'But he didn't, he just kept on dribbling.' And as Thomas shimmied past the 'keeper, to roll the ball gleefully into the empty net, Moore came up with his beautifully apposite piece of commentary.

His words entered Arsenal folklore, inscribed on t-shirts by the score. The Gunners' centre-forward remembers hearing it for the first time when he watched a recording the day after the game. 'What made it so special was that it wasn't prepared,' says Smith who, after retiring as a player, forged a broadcasting career for himself at Sky TV. 'The best bits of commentary are always a combination of the heat of the moment and the pictures.' He is right. Out of context, Moore's is not a particularly resonant piece of oratory. When combined with the footage of Thomas's run, however, it still has the capacity to make the hairs on the back of the neck stand up. It was a line that the distinguished commentator would hear repeated back to him by every passing stranger almost every day until his death in 2001, on the day England beat Germany 5–1 in Munich.

But what was so significant about Moore's words was what happened next. From a distance the 1988–9 season – which saw the loss of ninety-six innocent souls in the act of watching football – may have appeared to be the game's lowest point. Yet what this match demonstrated was that the game possessed at its core an unrivalled capacity to enthral a huge television audience. No fictional drama could match the real-life intensity of the Anfield encounter, in which the outcome of nine months of convoluted footballing competition was decided in its very last second. This was the sharpest broadcasting content around.

Such was the popular impact of the match and such was the scale of the viewing figures that many took note. At ITV, the chief executive Greg Dyke – a keen football fan – realised, even as the game struggled to emerge from its darkest hour, that here was the perfect product for the new broadcasting millennium. Others too were watching. Not least the Australian-American media magnate Rupert Murdoch, the man whose influence was soon to transform the English game. Moore was right: it really was all up for grabs now.

1989 'Three years of excuses and it's still crap: Ta-ra Fergie.'

Banner unfurled at the Scoreboard End at Old Trafford, 9 December 1989.

We all make mistakes. Though few have made one as visible as that of a Manchester United fan called Pete Molyneux during his team's home game with Crystal Palace. It was a grim pre-Christmas afternoon as the decade of excess spluttered to a conclusion, and Pete was not exactly suffering from a surfeit of seasonal good cheer. He had had enough. He had followed the Reds since the glory days of Matt Busby. He had done his time on the terraces for nigh on twenty years. And he was not enjoying himself.

Alex Ferguson had been manager at Old Trafford for three years, and Pete couldn't see any progress. Despite spending heavily in the transfer market, Ferguson seemed to have marooned United in mediocrity; they had recently been caned 5–1 by their crosstown rivals and appeared to be heading nowhere. The very idea of their challenging Liverpool for the title was laughable. At the rate United were going they'd be lucky to achieve mid-table security. And, in a pattern that was to repeat itself some twenty-five years later, there appeared to be one overriding explanation for the stuttering and faltering: the manager wasn't up to the job.

Pete had no idea what was going on behind the scenes, had no clue what Ferguson was doing with youth development. All he heard was the manager finding endless excuses for why it was going wrong. He was so fed up he decided to communicate his feelings in the most visible way he could. There was no setting up a Facebook protest group in 1989, no whingeing on Twitter, no calling the radio phone-in to have a 6-0-6-style moan. So what Pete did to register his feelings was purloin a bedsheet from home and some paint from the garden shed and give vent to his anger by making a banner.

After taking it to a couple of previous matches in a carrier bag, his banner of protest was finally unfurled during the wretchedly uninspiring performance against Crystal Palace on 9 December. And there it was for all to see: 'Ta-ra Fergie', an explicit call to the board to sack the manager. At the time there were plenty among the 33,000 disgruntled Reds gathered in the stadium who agreed with Pete. Few criticised the sentiment, nobody accused him of disloyalty, many slapped him on the back for saying what they were thinking.

Amateurish though it may have been, Pete's protest was widely noted. Newspaper photographers homed in on it. There it was in all its glory on that night's *Match of the Day*. Everyone reckoned he was articulating widespread discontent. Besides, it was hard to argue that he did not have a point. United may have won the game 1–0, but no one could deny the football *was* crap. Things had to change.

And change they almost immediately did, though not in the manner Pete advocated. There was to be no dismissal; United's board stuck resolutely to their man. A month after he had flourished his banner, with their manager still badgering from the touchline, United embarked on the FA Cup run that was to deliver the first of thirty-eight trophies of the Ferguson era. History records how right the United board were to stand by a leader whose work they believed would one day blossom into success. What future profits would accrue from the patience they displayed as Fergie found his feet.

> United may have won the game 1–0, but no one could deny the football *was* crap. Things had to change.

Pete's bedsheet protest may look ridiculous in hindsight, but at the time no one could foresee the consistent joys Ferguson would deliver to those of a Red persuasion. Over the next two decades, Fergie would fundamentally alter the mindset of the United fan. Like everyone of his affiliation, Pete came to relish glorious victories in league, FA Cup and on the wider European stage, improbable comebacks and a mountain of unimagined success. And, as Pete quickly came to recognise, that was all thanks to the greatest manager the club has ever known. How many times in those subsequent years did he send up a silent prayer of thanks that no one in the United boardroom had paid any heed to his complaint.

On the day in May 2013 that Ferguson did finally wave farewell from the Old Trafford dug-out, departing of his own volition long, long, long after the banner-flourishing complaints had subsided, Pete was able to illustrate the debt he – and every other diehard Red – owed the retiring manager. He paid homage in the only appropriate way: he found a bedsheet, got out his paint and brushes and made another banner. This time it read: '23 years of silverware and we're still top: ta-ra Fergie'.

PART IV

AFTER THE INTERVAL

1990–99

1990 'Football is a simple game: twenty-two men chase a ball for ninety minutes and, at the end, the Germans win.'

Striker Gary Lineker after his England team lost the World Cup semi-final to West Germany on penalties, Stadio delle Alpi, Turin, 4 July 1990.

It wasn't hard to understand the sense of despair underpinning Gary Lineker's jocular analysis. At the time renowned as a lightning-quick finisher rather than as a television presenter with a penchant for a pun, Lineker articulated precisely the sense of all-consuming inferiority that gripped English football when confronted by anything German. Whatever they did, however well they played, somehow England would always come up short when they met the Germans. Especially when it came to penalties.

As it turned out, Italia 90 was a fleeting feel-good moment for the England national team. Ahead of the tournament there was not much anticipation of anything beyond humiliation. Dismissed as thick-thighed and thick-headed, marooned tactically and technically a long, long way behind the continental sophisticates of France, Germany and Holland, and with their best players barred from competing in European club competition and thus stripped of vital experience, Bobby Robson's squad was reckoned to be there simply to make up the numbers.

Certainly the Italians were not looking forward to welcoming England. Or, to be strictly accurate, their supporters. It was only five years on from Heysel, when thirty-nine mainly Italian fans had died in Brussels before the kick-off of the 1985 European Cup final (see pages 134–8). The hosts, wary and nervy, billeted their Anglo-Saxon visitors on the island of Sardinia for the group stage, where their fans could be contained and controlled. It was dubbed 'Prison Island' by the British press. And a grim, goalless opening encounter with the Republic of Ireland in a stadium in Cagliari, flanked by half the Italian national guard, was an alarming hint of what lay ahead. If this World Cup was to be one giant party, the English were not invited.

Back home, however, the sense of the competition was somewhat different. The BBC made an inspired choice of theme music for the tournament. Luciano Pavarotti belting out 'Nessun Dorma', the tenor aria from the final act of Puccini's opera *Turandot*, gave the footage an epic undertow. But however soaring the soundtrack, Italia 90 was the lowest-scoring World Cup in history (it averaged just 2.21 goals per match), pockmarked with cynicism and on-pitch violence (the body-check by Cameroon's Benjamin Massing on Argentina's Claudio Caniggia, the third of a trio of illegal Cameroonian attempts to end a brilliant jinking run, made the *Observer Sports Monthly's* 'Five Worst Tackles' in their 19 May 2002 issue). Yet the television audience in England was vast. Fronted by the urbane Des Lynam, the live coverage became a must-see appointment with the sofa. Largely because, against type and expectation, it was the English team itself providing the drama.

Challenging assumption with every kick, as they drew with the Irish and Holland, as they beat Egypt, Belgium and Cameroon, what appeared to be emerging was a side of substance. Lineker and the canny Peter Beardsley were a sharp front pair, David Platt and Chris Waddle clever midfielders, Des Walker as good a defender as any in the competition.

But it was Paul Gascoigne who offered hope of real progress. Aged just twenty-three, the Tottenham playmaker approached his trade with an extraordinary insouciance. Unlike so many of those who pull on the shirt decorated with the Three Lions crest, he was not remotely cowed by the responsibility. He played like he was messing about with his mates on the streets of Dunston, back on Tyneside. According to Waddle:

The great thing about Gazza is that he didn't respect who he was playing against. He didn't even know who he was playing against. When I mentioned [Dutch international Frank] Rijkaard to him he thought it was a country.

Off the pitch he was a hyperactive bundle of nervous energy ('daft as a brush' was how his manager referred to him), a presence in the team hotel that was never far short of irritating. On it, he was everywhere, always wanting the ball, always willing to put in the hard yards, always prepared to accept responsibility (though Lineker insisted he 'only ever passed to you when he was too knackered to run himself'). With skill in abundance, he was like an injection of vitality into the moribund body of the English game.

The Italians, initially so sceptical of anything English, loved him: 'A dog of war with the face of a child' was how Gianni Agnelli, the owner of Fiat and Juventus, described him. And his innocent laddishness seemed to percolate into the stands. Taking their lead from their new talisman, the England fans – some of them undoubtedly enjoying a diet of ecstasy, the stimulant of choice in those days, made popular by the 'second summer of love' the previous year – turned out to be nothing like as intimidating as their reputation suggested. Unlike certain of their predecessors, they were in Italy to have a good time, rather than attempt to refight the Second World War.

> The great thing about Gazza is that he didn't respect who he was playing against. He didn't even know who he was playing against.

In the semi-final, the English supporters filled the newly built Stadio delle Alpi in Turin with noise and good cheer. They may have been pitched against the pre-tournament favourites West Germany (playing their last World Cup before reunification would further swell the pool of Teutonic footballing efficiency), but they were determined to enjoy themselves. Back home, a huge television audience hunkered down for an evening with Des and Pav. Everyone was watching. The Rolling Stones were playing a concert at Wembley Stadium that evening, and Mick Jagger kept popping off stage to check the score. He was treated to a wonderful exhibition of what football can offer, a glorious, tense, passionate 120 minutes of skill and enterprise, in which the English, playing the game of their lives, manfully matched their opponents stride for stride, shot for shot, goal for goal. Andreas Brehme had given the Germans the lead when his free-kick was fortuitously deflected off Paul Parker's knee after an hour. Then Lineker's eightieth-minute equaliser gave hope to the watching millions in Blighty.

When Gascoigne was booked, meaning he would be suspended from the final if England were to progress, his legend was sealed. As the lad broke down in disappointment and Lineker was seen pointing out what was happening to the bench, suggesting Robson 'have a word' with the distraught young man, every mother in the country melted. With the media as yet unaware of the mental-health issues that stalked the player, Gazza's tears were analysed to distraction, deemed by many a commentator to be the harbingers of a new, more emotionally expressive masculinity for the millennial age.

But it was what happened after extra time failed to produce a winning goal that really etched this game on the wider national consciousness. For the first time the England team were obliged to participate in a penalty shoot-out. And what television it made. Even if you did not understand the nuances of the game, the format made for unbearable tension. With the penalty-taker trudging slowly from the comfort of their team-mates gathered by the centre spot to the lonely, one-on-one confrontation with the opposition goalkeeper, thus putting his reputation on the line with a single kick of the ball, each penalty was a groan-or-cheer mini-drama. Lineker, Beardsley and Platt scored England's first three spot kicks. But Brehme,

Lothar Matthäus and Karl-Heinz Riedle were remorseless in their efficiency for the Germans. Then Stuart Pearce – as fiercely patriotic an Englishman as ever wore three lions on his chest – missed his effort. After Olaf Thon scored, Waddle had to convert even to compel the Germans to shoot again. His shoulders sagging, his chin down, the Gateshead man approached the ball with all the conviction of a drunk attempting to unlock his car. When he ballooned his shot over the bar, it was all over for England. As Lineker implied: you can do your best, but it won't be enough to beat the Germans.

Gascoigne, meanwhile, was cast as the saviour of English football, the clown prince who was going to lead the nation to football's sunlit uplands, a shoo-in for the BBC's Sports Personality of the Year. When the team returned home to a tumultuous welcome from some 300,000 fans at Luton airport, he sealed his place in popular culture by drunkenly slipping on a pair of false breasts. No doubt he was comforted by the words of his manager, Bobby Robson, on the Turin pitch. 'Don't worry, you've been one of the best players of the tournament. You've been magnificent. You've got your life ahead of you – this is your first.'

> Don't worry, you've been one of the best players of the tournament. You've been magnificent.

Sadly it didn't quite work out like that for the boy from Dunston. His subsequent career never matched the glittering promise of Italia 90. Though, as Lineker implied, it might have done had he been born German.

1992 'It's a whole new ball game.'

Slogan used to advertise television coverage of the fledgling Premier League by BSkyB, July 1992.

It was a grand claim. The newly inaugurated Premier League, ripped from the reluctant donor body of the Football League, was born in the summer of 1992. And it was promoted by its satellite television paymasters with the urgent language of revolution. There was barely a billboard site in the country that did not proclaim that seismic change was in the air. Television and cinema commercials, with a soundtrack by the rock band Simple Minds, endlessly reminded the viewer this was something different, something unmissable, something wholly new. You ain't seen nothing like it. Or so we were told.

But anyone who switched on to watch the first broadcast would have been familiar with what confronted them. Sky's 'whole new ball game' did not seem much different from the old ball game that had been played for the previous 130 years. There were still twenty-two men involved, the grass was still green, the goals still the same width, the running time of matches still ninety minutes. Hoof and hope still remained the preferred tactical ploy. Pretty soon even the razzmatazz grafted onto the presentation in an attempt to make the game seem more glitzy, more American, would disappear. The cheerleaders Sky had tried introducing to the game were made redundant within a year; the fireworks that sparked the gladiatorial entrance of the players were dispensed with even sooner, after a stray rocket escaped Southampton's old stadium at The Dell and landed in a petrol station.

Even so, though we didn't notice it at the time, from the moment Richard Keys began Sky's first live broadcast, on 16 August 1992, by welcoming viewers to the Nottingham Forest v. Liverpool match, things were about to change. Not least because, for the first time, viewers were obliged to pay to watch the action on telly. The thing that was wholly new about Sky's ball game was this: someone had finally found a way of successfully monetising the English obsession with their national sport. And that really did make everything different.

Given its current financial rude health, its relentless twenty-four-hour coverage, its technological gizmos, its multi-camera mega slo-mo, its breaking news breathlessly delivered by silver-haired-uncle-and-blonde-niece presentation double acts, it seems scarcely credible that, back in 1992, Sky was close to financial collapse. Launched by Rupert Murdoch in 1988, Sky had first tried to sell its subscription service on the back of movies. As a sales strategy it didn't work: take-up was sluggish, profits a far distant prospect, the company haemorrhaging money. In 1990 Sky posted losses of £228 million. This on top of loans from its parent company News International of some £450 million, plus a bank overdraft of £33 million. Such were the costs of the start-up and of the remorseless fees for movie rights, Murdoch was looking at borrowings of some £8 billion across his media empire, or roughly half the national debt of Colombia. The figures from Sky offered little hope of resurrection. Frankly they were terrifying: in the early summer of 1992, it cost £6 million a week to run the business, and its income was less than £2 million.

But almost from the moment football was offered as part of its subscription, everything changed. Football could give Sky something that the movies could not: fans in the grip of obsession. Unlike movie watchers, football supporters brought commitment. Picked up with the birth certificate and surrendered at the grave, this was a lifelong dedication to the cause that would compel the sufferer to do whatever was necessary to maintain their fix. For decades, the only live football the fan had experienced on television was the FA Cup final and an international

> I think it is wrong that only dish owners get access to such major sporting events.

tournament every two years. Now, after ITV had shown the way with its coverage of the last day of the 1989 season, here was an offer they simply could not refuse: an endless diet of the game's weekly league dramas, beamed live into their own home. Whole channels dedicated to their sport: for football fans it was as if they had died and gone to heaven. Sure, it came at a cost. But the kids could do without supper once a week.

Murdoch, moreover, was able to use his newspapers to talk up the new competition. This was the perfect demonstration of the benefits of vertical business integration, a cartel in operation. In the Murdoch-owned tabloid *The Sun*, extra pages were immediately allocated to trumpeting the game. Market forces compelled his media rivals to match the coverage. Every day, as the papers insisted the Premier League was the sexiest, most compelling offering in the civilised world, so more subscribers were brought into the fold. Soon, no fan could be without their weekly top-up of live football, viewed from their sofa. Either that, or they watched down the pub, where the landlord paid a sizeable fee to show games.

Some people didn't like the idea, raising philosophical objections to the manner in which the national game had gained a sudden exclusivity. The Olympic hero Sebastian Coe, by now a Conservative MP – and a Chelsea supporter – was not alone in expressing reservations when he said: 'I think it is wrong that only dish owners get access to such major sporting events.'

But there was little anyone could do to stop the juggernaut, certainly not a free-market-oriented government perpetually cowed when it came to challenging Murdoch's expansionism. The mogul had in his grasp the perfect business circle. It meant that within months Sky was able to post whole new figures. And its profits have been on an upward trajectory ever since.

Sky's – or rather its subscribers' – money has subsequently transformed the game in this country. The endless gushing torrent of cash has buffed up stadia, recruited the best international talent and turned ordinary players into multi-millionaires, keeping Ferrari dealerships across the land in business. Richard Scudamore, the Premier League's canny chief executive, has been tireless in his efforts to ensure that the broadcaster pays ever more colossal rates for the right to show his product.

And football in turn has been very good for Sky. At the time of writing, in the summer of 2014, the company is the most successful broadcast business in the world. No one makes profits like Sky. And not even the most forensic accountant poring over the books could deny that its success is due to one thing and one thing only: the fact that it bought the rights in 1992 to charge fans to watch Premier League football from their armchairs. For Rupert Murdoch it was a whole new ball game indeed.

▲ They really didn't like each other: Johan Cruyff leads the Dutch protests against the loathed Germans in the World Cup final, 1974. Franz Beckenbauer, meanwhile, is modelling what appear to be the shortest shorts ever worn in international football.

▲ Summit of the Macs: 'What will you do if you win the World Cup?' asks a young Trevor McDonald of Ally MacLeod as the Scotland team prepare to head out to the 1978 World Cup in Argentina. The team manager's response is short and indicative: 'retain it', he said.

▲ Big Ron Atkinson in happier times, taking on Brendan Batson in training at West Bromwich Albion, 1980, long before he was let anywhere near a commentator's microphone.

▲ Glasgow constabulary on one of their regular mass mobilisations known locally as The Old Firm match, 1980.

▼ The Hand of God: he may have been eight inches shorter than the 'keeper, but Diego Maradona rises high above a leaden-footed Peter Shilton to unleash the most famous mitt in football, Mexico City, 22 June 1986.

▲ Football's 1980s diplomatic corps in action: England fans brawling on the terraces in Basle, 1984.

▲ Vinnie Jones, self-styled
Wimbledon hard man,
attempts an onfield
vasectomy on Paul
Gascoigne, 1987.

◀ Tears of a clown: Paul
Gascoigne, Stadio delle Alpi,
Turin, 4 July 1990.

THE Sun

**WHO'S THIS?
FIND OUT IN
SUN WOMAN**

20P

Wednesday, November 24, 1993   **20p**   Audited daily sale for October 3,778,312

Jackson . . . 'guards brought him boys'

THAT'S YER ALLOTMENT

At last turnip Taylor turns up his toes

Jackson ordered guard to 'tear up photo of nude boy'

From CAROLINE GRAHAM
in Los Angeles

SUPERSTAR Michael Jackson ordered a bodyguard to destroy a photograph of a naked boy hidden in his bathroom, it was claimed last night.

The snap showed the side view of a boy aged between 10 and 14 and revealed everything.

Minder Leroy Thomas destroyed the Polaroid after Jackson phoned him with instructions.

Thomas was one of five bodyguards sacked by the singer after years working for him at his parent's mansion and his Neverland ranch in California.

Jackson regularly instructed the guards to bring young boys to spend the night with him, they allege in a 22-page document filed to Los Angeles Superior Court.

The boys were taken to Jackson's parents' home after the star had first checked that the couple were either away or asleep, says the document.

The minders claim unfair dismissal and are suing for damages. They say they all got the boot because the star could not remember who had destroyed the picture and who had escorted boys to his rooms.

Full amazing story – Page 5

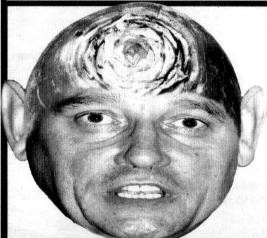

By PETER SEABROOK,
our Gardening Correspondent

ENGLAND soccer manager Graham "The Turnip" Taylor hurled himself on to the compost heap yesterday.

Taylor — England boss for three years — finally admitted he had lost the vegetable plot and resigned.

The 49-year-old Turnip quit just six days after England failed to reach next year's World Cup finals.

He said: "No one can grasp the depths of my personal disappointment at not qualifying.

"I do, however, naturally wish my successor the best of good fortune in England's endeavours to win the 1996 European Championship."

The Sun awarded Taylor his nickname after even the Swedes gave us a 2-1 bashing in last year's European championships.

NOURISHING

Last night we were so concerned at The Turnip's future we called in our gardening expert Peter Seabrook.

Peter said: "A good idea would be to cut the top off The Turnip and put it in a saucer of water on a window sill.

"It will produce green shoots and the leaves can make a nourishing soup. Makes sense, as Taylor has dropped English soccer well and truly in the soup."

Don Howe — an ex-England No 2 manager and now part-time coach at non-league Newbury Town — is stepping in as caretaker boss.

Sun Says: Page 6; Turnip II: Back Page

THE OFFICIAL A-LEVEL REPORT See pages 23, 24, 25 / **£26,000 SUN BINGO** See page 22

▲ *The Sun* gets its man, 25 November 1993: Britain's biggest-selling paper enjoys the demise of Graham Taylor, football's most renowned root vegetable.

▲ Eric Cantona arrives, barely noticed, at Croydon Magistrates Court, to be tried for affray, March 1995.

▼ This one's for you, Alan: Manchester United's youthful team demonstrate precisely what it is you can win with kids, May 1996.

▲ A young Ryan Giggs, a player who always enjoyed scoring.

▲ Refuelling issues: Paul Gascoigne and team-mates replay the dentist's chair to celebrate his goal against Scotland, Wembley Stadium, 15 June 1996.

◄ Why didn't you just belt it? Gareth Southgate adds to the ever-growing list of English penalty flops, Wembley, 26 June 1996.

▶ The Alsatian Professor: Arsène Wenger's arrival at Highbury in August 1996 triggered a revolution in coaching in the English game.

▼ *Liberté, égalité, Coupe du Monde*: France's multi-racial winning side in the 1998 World Cup was a timely slap in the face for the country's election-seeking xenophobes.

▲ Alex Ferguson demonstrates why an invitation from *Strictly Come Dancing* was never forthcoming, as he celebrates Manchester United's last-gasp victory in the Camp Nou, Barcelona, 26 May 1999.

▶ The Beckhams in their floppy-fringed pomp: backstage after a Whitney Houston concert at London's Wembley Arena, 1999.

1993 'Mr Clough likes a bung.'

Entrepreneur Alan Sugar at the High Court, London, 10 June 1993.

Back in 1993, Alan Sugar was just plain Mr Sugar. Not yet Surrallan, certainly not Lord Sugar, he was still a commoner, albeit a commoner who was chief shareholder in Tottenham Hotspur. And as such he was not exactly thrilled with the way in which Terry Venables, the player-turned-manager-turned-would-be-club-owner, was going about the business of being Tottenham's chief executive. Four years earlier, Venables – who had long nurtured an ambition to sit at the head of the directors' table – had needed Sugar's money to negotiate a takeover of the outfit he had played for in the 1960s. The pair had gone into partnership, Sugar encouraged to do so by his business associate Rupert Murdoch, who was anxious to stymie the plans of his newspaper rival Robert Maxwell, who was circling Tottenham at the time (and who wanted a business ally on the inside of the game's ownership structure).

Venables was looking for someone who was happy just to invest without taking any further interest in the day-to-day running of the club. Sugar, though, was not one to surrender his cash without close scrutiny, and he turned out to be the most alert of sleeping partners. Astonished at some of the practices he had uncovered when examining the books, the entrepreneur had quickly moved to oust Venables, a man regarded as a saviour by the club's fans. But in those pre-*Apprentice* days, nobody paid much heed when Sugar pointed his finger and told them they were fired. Certainly not Venables, who sued him, seeking substantial compensation.

And their feisty spat in the High Court – observed from the public gallery by several dozen Venables-supporting Tottenham fans who hissed at Sugar like he was a pantomime villain every time he took to the witness stand – was to have repercussions in the game. Not least in the manner in which it brought a new term into wider circulation. Until Sugar gave evidence that day a 'bung' was generally thought of as a little rubber widget that you shoved in barrel to keep the beer from spilling out. After he had spoken, it became the favoured slang word for a cash inducement.

Though it came out like that, Sugar's target in his witness statement wasn't actually Clough. The pair had never met, certainly not to exchange brown envelopes. Sugar's purpose in his allegation was to expose the wider corruption in football and try to expose his former colleague Venables in the process. But it was Clough who was most obviously compromised. And it was Clough who was characteristically vocal in his own defence.

The Nottingham Forest boss insisted that his managerial record was unimpeachable. He had a point. After all, he had steered unfashionable, unconsidered Forest from thirteenth place in the Second Division in January 1975 to promotion to the old First Division in 1977, to the League Championship in 1978 and thereafter to consecutive European Cup victories in 1979 and 1980. This was a staggering – surely never-to-be-matched – sequence of achievements. It was true that the club had just been relegated that May from the newly inaugurated Premier League, a decline that had precipitated Clough's retirement. It was also true that, with his powers visibly in decline, undermined by an ultimately fatal drinking habit, Cloughie had appeared in his last season to be a man struggling against the modern world, raging against the dying of his own light. But this was still Brian Clough whom Sugar was bad-mouthing. Not some two-bit upstart. This was the man still widely regarded as the finest manager the England team never had.

Sugar, however, gave a much less benevolent view of the man known as 'Old Big 'Ed'. His evidence suggested that Venables had authorised a cash payment of more than £50,000 to Clough in the autumn of 1992, in order to smooth the transfer of Teddy Sheringham. It was, Sugar claimed Venables had told him, standard practice when dealing with Cloughie. Unethical, illegal, it also struck Sugar as profoundly unbusinesslike. He had reacted with horror to the notion; it was not the way he was used to doing things. Yet he insisted that Venables had brushed off his reservations, assuring him that was the way football operated.

Clough did not attempt to duck the allegations. He charged at them like an enraged, if somewhat tipsy, bull. The following week, on the television show *Sport in Question*, after liberally indulging in the green room hospitality, he accused Sugar of being 'a spiv' who was 'in need of a shave'. To much raucous amusement from the studio audience, he challenged the satellite dish manufacturer to say again what he had said in court, this time away from the libel-free protection of the witness box, adding that were he to do so, he would 'sue the arse off' him.

After he won his case against Venables, Sugar was never inclined to repeat the claim. The MP Kate Hoey, however, was less reticent. She used parliamentary privilege to name Clough as one of the managers who had 'siphoned off millions from the game in back-handers, bungs and fixes'. Another of those she named was George Graham, the Arsenal boss who was to be fired by his club in 1995, after it emerged that he had taken a hefty cash bribe from a Norwegian agent.

Faced with a growing suggestion of institutionalised corruption, the FA set up an inquiry into illicit payments. It was led by the first chief executive of the Premier League, Rick Parry. After taking four years to compile a 10,000-page report, Parry's investigations uncovered substantial evidence to support the suggestion that illegal hand-outs had indeed lubricated the Sheringham transfer. A sum of £58,750 had been paid in cash by Spurs to the agent Frank McLintock. The former Arsenal double-winning captain had then passed the money on to Ronnie Fenton, Clough's assistant. The revelation that the money had changed hands in the Alan Partridge-esque surroundings of the Posthouse Hotel, Luton, gave the episode a bleakly comic edge. But the implication was clear and Parry recommended that charges be brought. He thought the book should be thrown at Clough. By the time the report was published, however, the great managerial maverick's health had deteriorated to the point that the FA decided it would be impolitic to pursue him.

So it was that, when he died in 2004, Clough's reputation had suffered only minor abrasions from the heavy shells fired at it by the future star of *The Apprentice*. And the fact was that even if Mr Clough did like a bung, as Sugar insisted, the lifelong socialist at least went to the grave with his reputation as one of the game's sharpest managerial brains and quickest wits intact. As he himself once said: 'I wouldn't say I was the best manager in the business. But I was in the top one.'

> I wouldn't say I was the best manager in the business. But I was in the top one.

1993 'THAT'S YER ALLOTMENT'

Headline in *The Sun* the day after Graham Taylor resigned as England manager, 25 November 1993.

Few managers in the history of football have suffered the personal abuse Graham Taylor did when he was in charge of England. Certainly none were as routinely likened to a root vegetable. So associated with rutabagas did he become that, when he left the job, a gardening pun could be employed by the country's biggest-selling newspaper in the certain knowledge that everyone would get the joke.

Poor Taylor; how he had wanted to do the right thing when he was appointed to succeed Bobby Robson as manager of the national team in the autumn of 1990. He was determined to be open and honest, to have nothing to hide. An ebullient character, he was bullish and upbeat. When asked on his appointment to reveal his ambitions he said they were simple: to qualify for the Euro 92 tournament and win it, then to qualify for the World Cup 94 and win that.

When he took on the job there was much to be optimistic about. He was inheriting an England team on the rise. Semi-finalists at Italia 90 (see pages 162–6), they were blessed with a healthy balance of experience – John Barnes, Chris Waddle, Des Walker and David Seaman – and potential, in the shape of Alan Shearer and Matthew Le Tissier. Plus he had at his disposal Europe's most effervescent talent in Paul Gascoigne.

Taylor began with a clear view on how he would set about making the team gel. 'I'd like to be the most tracksuited manager England has ever had,' he said. This was his plan: he would roll his sleeves up and work, work and work again to bring success to the national side he loved.

A career coach, Graham Taylor had been the youngest manager

in Football League history when he took over at Lincoln City as a twenty-eight-year-old in December 1972, his own playing career at Grimsby and Lincoln curtailed by injury. His hands-on approach had been part of the success he had subsequently brought to Watford – a club he had elevated from the Fourth to the First Division in just five seasons in charge – and then Aston Villa – whom he had steered to promotion to the top division, then on to become runners-up in 1990. After Brian Clough and Jim

> I'd like to be the most tracksuited manager England has ever had.

Smith, he was only the third English manager to have managed over 1000 league games. Taylor was an honest toiler. With a PE teacher's demeanour rather than a metropolitan sophisticate's, his favoured tactical methodology was characteristically unpretentious. There was nothing subtle in his game. A graduate of the Charles Hughes school of coaching (see pages 75–6), he believed in a system in which the aim was to get the ball forward as quickly as possible, without paying much attention to what he considered irrelevancies like control or possession. As he took control of the national side, his style was not without its critics. As Ken Bates, then chairman of Chelsea, put it: 'Hump it, bump it, whack it. That might be a recipe for a good sex life, but it won't win England the World Cup.'

It soon became clear that Bates had a point. While such a rugged tactical system might have served Taylor well in the hectic environs of the Football League, it was to prove utterly inadequate in international competition. England were embarrassed at the 1992 European Championship. After two 0–0 draws with Denmark and France, England needed to defeat the hosts Sweden to advance to the knock-out stage. In the event, they succumbed 2–1, Taylor drawing opprobrium for substituting Gary Lineker in his final international and thereby depriving the striker of the chance to draw level with – or even surpass – Sir Bobby Charlton as England's leading goalscorer.

Perhaps because of Lineker's unwavering popularity, the manager and his antediluvian tactics were singled out for blame. A man incapable or organising victory against a bunch of Swedes, he became, to *The Sun*, Turnip Taylor. Few footballing nicknames have stuck quite so obstinately. And the paper brought all its verbal and visual dexterity to bear in rubbishing the man: a picture of Taylor, his head transmogrified into a turnip, became a standard visual reference point, the template for future tabloid hammerings of England managers.

Looking back, Taylor is certain that *The Sun* had a purpose behind their endless sniping. Their football correspondent – the late Brian Woolnough – was a keen advocate of Terry Venables for the England position. Almost from the moment he was appointed, Taylor believed, *The Sun* wanted him out and Venables in his place. And to that end they agitated against him from day one, convinced they had the power to see any incumbent removed.

While there may have been something in that, results were Taylor's best way to silence criticism. But results never went his way. Taylor's problem was that little he achieved in office proved his legitimacy to hold it. Besides, it was hard not to identify the source of Graham Taylor's failings as Graham Taylor himself. When Gascoigne sustained a career-jeopardising cruciate ligament injury in a reckless challenge on

> Hump it, bump it, whack it. That might be a recipe for a good sex life, but it won't win England the World Cup.

Gary Charles of Nottingham Forest in the 1991 FA Cup final, Taylor was deprived of his talismanic playmaker for the entire forthcoming season. In Gazza's absence, he promoted the plodding Sheffield Wednesday midfielder Carlton Palmer to the England squad for Euro 1992. Taylor still robustly defends his decision today:

I get this all the time: 'why did you pick Carlton Palmer?' I say to people who ask me that, right, well, before I answer tell me this: who would you have picked? They say, so and so and I say, good, so would I. But he was injured and he was and he was. You picked who was available.

Taylor may not have been well served by fortune, it is true. But he hardly made his position any easier when he invited the documentary maker Ken McGill to follow England's 1994 World Cup qualification campaign for a Channel 4 film. To Taylor the idea seemed reasonable enough: he wanted to be open, to give insight into the complexities of his job. Instead, McGill, enjoying access which would never again be afforded to a man in Taylor's position, came away with a portrait of a hapless inadequate, not waving but drowning on the touchline. Footage of the manager, squeezed into an under-sized tracksuit, ranting as England succumbed to Holland was excruciating to watch. His tactical shortcomings ('can we not knock it?') his strangled syntax ('do I not like that?') his wounded self-pity ('tell your mate he's cost me my job') combined to deliver a portrait of a manager impotent in the face of circumstance. Many of his contemporaries in such a position would doubtless have been similarly exposed. It was Taylor's misfortune that, by inviting in the documentary-maker, he exposed the stark truth of a managerial inadequacy that the world had long suspected.

'When you're committed and fail, the pain doesn't go away. Twenty years on and we're still talking about it,' he reflects ruefully. 'People say I'm silly, but the truth is I'll take this to the grave with me: I am the England manager who failed to qualify for the World Cup.'

The fallout from that dire campaign, which ended in the ignominy of England failing to beat San Marino by the required seven clear goals while hoping that Poland won at home to Holland (they didn't) was brutal. A profoundly decent man, Taylor's first instinct was to accept his culpability and resign. No clinging on, no holding out for compensation, he went immediately. Even so, such an honourable move did not stem the tide of vilification. Nor did it prevent his elderly parents being door-stepped by aggressive

> I'll take this to the grave with me: I am the England manager who failed to qualify for the World Cup.

reporters, his children being humiliated at school, his wife being abused in the street. As for Taylor himself – who, as *The Sun* had long hoped, was succeeded in the England dug-out by Terry Venables – the reputational damage was lingering. Driven by that press caricature, he has never been allowed to forget it.

I remember I met Kelvin MacKenzie, who was the editor of *The Sun* at the time, and he told me I was being over-sensitive to complain about his paper calling me a turnip. He said it was a bit of fun. Well, I'll say this. I was at a match in Brentford maybe as long as ten years on from it, making my way to my car when I saw out of corner of my eye two yobbish-looking people coming out of the pub with a pint in each hand. They were shouting 'there's the fucking turnip' and they chucked the pints over me. If it wasn't for the swift action of the Brentford security people, I reckon it would have been worse. Was that just a bit of fun, Kelvin? Was it?

1994 'FIFA cut my legs off, just as I was proving to my daughters that I could play with twenty-year-olds.'

Diego Maradona after being expelled from the World Cup in the USA, 4 July 1994.

The five banned substances found in Diego Maradona's urine following a routine test conducted after his team's game against Nigeria in the group stages of the 1994 World Cup Finals were listed as ephedrine, phenylpropanolamine, pseudo-ephedrine, non-pseudo-ephedrine and methylephedrine. As Michel d'Hooghe, one of Fifa's medical panel suggested, that sort of agglomeration of proscribed stimulants does not arrive in the bloodstream by chance. Nor, indeed, by supping on a sports drink, as Maradona claimed. The thirty-three-year-old Argentine was, it appeared, doped up to his drooping eyelids.

Mind you, it didn't take the results of a urine test to spot that the world's most celebrated player had counteracted the effects of ageing by seeking the assistance of a chemist. After Maradona scored in his country's victory over Greece in the game before his failed drug test, the Argentine captain had raced to the pitchside camera and embraced it with a goggle-eyed derangement which suggested that this was a man floating through the tournament on the contents of his medicine cabinet. Gurning and cackling, and apparently trying to tongue the lens, the player fêted as the greatest since Pelé looked certifiably insane.

For Maradona, the USA World Cup was the final chance to prove to an increasingly sceptical world that he was still a potent footballing force. The man who had single-handedly propelled his country to victory in the 1986 World Cup (see pages 138–41) and to second place four years later, had subsequently sunk into a trough of decadence. Playing for Napoli in the Italian league from 1984, he took the unfashionable southerners to their first Serie A title in 1986–7 and a second three years later, in the process becoming idolised by the Neapolitan supporters. But his lifestyle became a parody of blinged-up excess. He was pursued by paternity suits, with acknowledged children born to a variety of partners, and by allegations of friendship with members of the Camorra, and was banned from all football for fifteen months in 1991 after admitting to taking cocaine ahead of a Serie A match. He left Napoli in disgrace in 1992 and played for Sevilla in Spain until he first retired in 1993.

By 1994, as he attempted to make a comeback, it was apparent that Maradona had not exactly retired to live in a monastery. In February of that year, he fired a pellet gun at reporters camped outside his home in Buenos Aires, then, five days later, he and six members of his bloated entourage assaulted a photographer. He was holed up in Argentina after fleeing Europe as the Italians were seeking to prosecute him on drug charges. Despite this, following a disastrous 5–0 home defeat to Colombia, public demand in his homeland insisted that coach Alfio Basile bring him back into the team for Argentina's qualifying play-off. When Basile hesitated, he received a call from President Carlos Menem suggesting it might be a smart idea to select Diego. So it was that Maradona returned to the side as they beat Australia in the play-off; after securing qualification, he handed the Cuban president Fidel Castro his blue striped jersey.

Given the player's almost god-like status, Basile had little choice but to include him in the squad for the finals in the USA. His weight ballooning, his chest ever more resembling a barrel, his eyes swivelling, Maradona did not exactly look a man ready to undertake demanding physical toil. But the hope was that his inclusion in the squad alone might be the only stimulant the player required. Some hope. In the event, he became only the third player in World Cup history to be sent home from the competition for failing a drugs test. 'They have retired me from soccer,' he said on his return from the USA. 'I don't think I want another revenge, my soul is broken.'

His soul recovered sufficiently for him later to display a level of paranoia unusual in those clean of drugs. Maradona cast himself as the victim of a Byzantine conspiracy. In his subsequent autobiography he claimed that FIFA had reneged on an agreement to allow him to use medication for weight loss before the competition in order to be able to play. They needed him there for publicity reasons and then turned on him once he arrived, he complained.

> They have retired me from soccer. I don't think I want another revenge, my soul is broken.

Well, that was one way of looking at it. His failed drugs test signalled the end of his international career, which had lasted seventeen years and yielded thirty-four goals from ninety-one games. His game was over. And his twenty-year addiction to cocaine was to have serious effects on his health, which deteriorated after his retirement, with a major heart attack in 2004. Still, at least FIFA had failed in the bid to cut off his legs.

1994 'Gazza said that scoring was better than an orgasm. Lee Chapman reckoned it wasn't as good. I'll go with Pelé – he thought it was about the same.'

Ryan Giggs in his first autobiography *My Story*, published in September 1994.

It was just a throwaway line, a bit of a filler to pad out a life story published before he was even twenty-one. But unwittingly Ryan Giggs – who would go on to become the most decorated footballer in British history – may have been on to something. In 2002, after measuring the responses of dozens of football fans, researchers at the Institute of Neurological Sciences in Glasgow discovered that seeing your team score a goal triggers a reaction in the same part of the brain that responds to sexual stimulus. When the ball crosses the line, the anterior cingulate cortex lights up as it might if its host had just been invited into the shower by Scarlett Johansson. 'Back of the net!' is how Alan Partridge might have summarised the report's findings.

And if that is the effect produced by just watching, imagine how the brain must respond if it is you doing the actual scoring. No wonder players sometimes lose all contact with reality when they make the net bulge. No wonder they dash about the pitch, faces contorted with the it's-so-pleasurable-it's-painful gurn of a pornstar at the moment of climax, before flinging themselves to the turf to writhe in ecstasy with their team-mates. No wonder the modern Premier League kit man keeps several spare pairs of shorts in the changing room. A goalscorer's brain must be jiggling about like Elvis's trousers.

Giggs was just twenty years old at the time he put his name to the book, near the start of a career that was to set new records for longevity and trophy-gathering. But the young Welshman's remark told us rather more about his own interests in life than the player perhaps intended.

Giggs's arrival in the Manchester United first team in the early nineties coincided with a sudden and dramatic upturn in the capacity of football's commercial engine. Driven by clubs' new marketing departments, footballers were beginning to be sold like boy bands. And for United, there was no one better to drive the sales of duvet covers – and instant picture-book autobiographies – than the floppy-fringed Welshman. United promoted Giggs as the sharpest, sexiest superstar around. They pushed him as the new George Best; they even released a video of Best and Giggsy out on the town together. After being more than impressed watching the young man training, the forty-something George Best made the marketeers' day when he said: 'One day they might even say that I was another Ryan Giggs.'

> One day they might even say that I was another Ryan Giggs.

Giggs may have reluctantly played along in those early days, but he wasn't remotely interested in that sort of fame. All he wanted to do was to become a very, very good footballer. Driven by a determination not to squander his talent on frippery and excess in the same way his rugby-playing father had, relentless in his urge to commit himself to the dull stuff like training and fitness, he did his best to avoid living his life in public. How thrilled he was when his club-mate David Beckham came on the Old Trafford scene in July 1991, eager to soak up all the available attention. It gave him the space to do his thing unhindered.

And if the rest of us thought Giggs was rather dull, rather one-dimensional, that was fine by him. Eating his greens, doing his yoga, keeping himself fit, he quietly set about the process of accumulating more silverware than anyone else in English football history. By the time Giggs retired in the spring of 2014, he had unostentatiously stuffed in a drawer, somewhere in his house, the small matter of medals for thirteen Premier League titles, four FA Cups, four League Cups and two Champions Leagues. In the two decades and more that he graced the United first team, there was no going off the rails, no dispute with authority, nothing to frighten the horses. So widely admired was Giggs that even those who found United to be the epitome of all that was wrong with the modern game quietly appreciated him.

Those in the know, however, hinted at a secret life. 'Innocent Giggsy is not,' wrote Roy Keane in his autobiography, published in 2002. 'He's got away with murder over the years and he laughs about it.' Regulars on the Manchester social scene spoke of the way his eyes would sparkle when approached by an attractive woman. Mostly, though, we had no idea what he did in his spare time. His careful dead-bat deflection of attention ensured that little came his way.

But then, not long after he had been voted BBC Sports Personality of the Year in 2009, the rumours began to circulate that he was taking a little more direct action to stifle interest in his personal life. This was the time of the super-injunction, when massively well-paid Premier League players were among those using the law to maintain tabloid silence on stories about what they got up to off the pitch. John Terry had tried it. Others, too. Manchester City's Garry Flitcroft had taken out an injunction to stop *The People* publishing details of an extramarital affair as early as 2001. Ultimately, for all of them, it proved a waste of money and time. The internet burst through the old-style legal apparatus, and soon the web-based stories about Giggs became commonplace. It was well known on social media that he had taken out an injunction to prevent publication of a kiss-and-tell story sold by the pneumatic Welsh model Imogen Thomas. To the extent that on 22 May 2011 the Scottish newspaper *The Sunday Herald* printed a picture of him with the deliberately threadbare disguise of a photoshopped blindfold with the word 'CENSORED' printed over the player's eyes. A day later, Giggs was identified in the House of Commons as the footballer who had indeed taken one out.

That December, the High Court decided the legal curb had been breached so often on the web that it was no longer valid. At which point, Giggs suddenly found himself exposed. And it turned out he had somewhat changed his view on the relative merits of sex and goalscoring. Here was a man whose vice was not booze or drugs or gambling, but scoring of a more fundamental kind. In addition to the dalliance with Thomas, Giggs had engaged in an eight-year affair with his younger brother's wife.

Even as the tabloids printed allegation after allegation across their front pages of what he had got up to, Giggs never suffered the sort of public humiliation he must have feared when he took out the injunction in the first place. His wife stood by him, his team-mates laughed it all off, his club maintained his contract (indeed, in the spring of 2014 he would briefly serve as Manchester United's interim player-manager, before being appointed assistant to Louis van Gaal).

And yet, though Giggs is on the very shortest of shortlists when it comes to enumerating British footballers of outstanding quality (up there with Matthews, Finney, Best, Charlton and Moore), the reputational damage had been done. Any idea of giving him the knighthood that his achievements might be thought to have justified was probably shelved the moment the details of his private life were made public. While most football fans will have envied Giggs his general sexual success, there was a widespread distaste for what was revealed. Even in the amoral world of modern football, a line is drawn by many a fan at the idea of screwing your brother's missus.

1995 'When seagulls follow the trawler it is because they think sardines will be thrown into the sea.'

Eric Cantona, Jury's Inn Hotel, Croydon, 31 March 1995.

In February 2014 Shia LaBeouf confused the Hollywood journalists attending a press conference to promote his new movie *Nymphomaniac*, the latest offering of the boundary-crossing Danish director Lars von Trier. The actor had just been asked about shooting the sex scenes – of which, as the title implies, there were plenty – when he said: 'When seagulls follow the trawler it is because they think sardines will be thrown into the sea.' He then stormed out of the room.

When news of LaBeouf's comment reached France, how Eric Cantona must have smiled. Twenty years on and his infamously gnomic utterance had been pilfered wholesale by a young American star seeking to cast himself as a character. That the plagiarist in question was an actor would have made the Frenchman's grin all the wider.

It was first heard, the fishing metaphor, in the less than gilded surroundings of a Croydon hotel on 31 March 1995. Cantona, then a Manchester United player, had been arrested a couple of months earlier when the mother of all footballing fracas erupted at Crystal Palace's Selhurst Park ground during a Premier League game on 25 January. Having been sent off for kicking a Palace defender, the Frenchman, *en route* for the tunnel and an early bath, found himself the target of a gobby home fan who seized the opportunity – as the miscreant player passed the family stand – to give him some advice (to paraphrase, it was something about hurrying home to France where he might commune with his mum). Cantona's reaction was to launch a kung fu kick at the fan in question, followed by a volley of punches. After the match, Cantona was charged with affray, for which, the Croydon magistrate Mrs Jean Pearch insisted, the appropriate judicial response was a fortnight's prison sentence.

Following an appeal, his punishment was commuted to 100 hours of community service. And Maurice Watkins, the Manchester United director and solicitor who had been advising the Frenchman throughout the case, thought it might be appropriate to make some sort of statement to the waiting media representatives, who had turned up at the Croydon courtroom in their hundreds. So a room in a nearby hotel was hastily requisitioned for a press conference.

The gathered reporters didn't know what to expect of Cantona. If this was any normal footballer, they would anticipate maybe a touch of contrition, maybe an apology, perhaps a thank-you to his lawyers for quickly heading off the prospect of a night or two in Wormwood Scrubs. Or maybe, as the Arsenal player Paul Merson was to demonstrate a couple of years later, a few blubbed tears of self-pity. If nothing else, some evidence of relief.

But Eric Cantona didn't do normal. Elusive, aloof, from the moment he had arrived in the country, he had cunningly exploited the latent English inferiority complex about all things Gallic. Back in his homeland he was widely regarded as little more than a thug and had been driven into footballing exile after his temper had frayed once too often. Once in England, however, he was shamelessly cast by his sponsors Nike as the coolest of continental sophisticates. He read philosophy, we were told; he quoted poetry; he played backgammon; his hero was not Rambo (the Sylvester Stallone vigilante) but Rimbaud (the Symbolist poet). Here was someone different all right.

Behind the scenes on the day of his sentencing, as the press waited, Watkins asked the player what he was going to say to them. Cantona said he had an idea. Watkins, who these days is chairman of Barnsley FC, takes up the story:

We started to draft a speech on a piece of paper and he asked what the boat was that catches fish. So I told him. Then he asked what the birds were that fly over the sea. So I told him that. Eric went on writing, then showed me what he wanted to say.

Watkins and Cantona then entered the room, which was full to bursting with newspapermen, television cameras and radio reporters. The lawyer welcomed the media and said that his client had a statement he wished to make, but would not be answering any questions. At which point Cantona – who had committed the lines to memory – said what he had to say. And the moment he finished, he got up and left the room with a mumbled 'thank you'.

Driven by the rapacious Murdoch news operation, which recognised in Cantona the perfect soap-opera villain to drive sales of Sky satellite subscriptions, The Frenchman's words became the most written about in the history of the game. Whole pages were dedicated to their deconstruction. Editorials pondered its import. Linguistics experts were commissioned to unpick them. Though all sorts of significance was attached to the words, they seemed a pretty straightforward allusion to the parasitical nature of reporting. The press were the seagulls, he was the trawler and we all fed off the titbits that might be chucked from its deck: it was no deeper than that.

And as it turned out, Cantona was perfectly right in his analysis. His press conference may have been brief, but his musings featured sufficient sardines to keep the media occupied for an age. The satirist Willie Donaldson – the jocular pen behind *The Henry Root Letters* – wrote a whole book inspired by it called *The Meaning of Cantona*. That was how big the player had become in the spring of 1995: there was even money to be made being by sarky about him.

But watching the YouTube footage of him making his statement at some twenty years' distance, what is most apparent is that he is loving every moment of it. Midway through delivering his line, he has to take a sip of water. He does so not to lubricate his throat but to stop himself laughing. As he admitted when I once had the opportunity to ask him about what happened at Selhurst, the whole thing was just a game to him. 'Yeah, I played that moment,' he said of the press conference. 'It was a drama and I was an actor.'

> Yeah, I played that moment... It was a drama and I was an actor.

Even as a player, he knew precisely how to give a performance. The upturned collar, the statuesque goal celebrations, the refusal to conform: it was all part of the act. And no one before or since could pull off one like it. What was revealed in Croydon that day was that he could do it off the pitch too. It gave a hint of the second career on stage and screen he would undertake after he retired from football.

Given that it has become one of the game's most famous quotations, known wherever the game is played and even borrowed by Hollywood A-listers, Maurice Watkins, Cantona's collaborator on the day it was coined, often wishes that he had been a touch more forward-looking. Had he pocketed the notes the player made when they were discussing what he might say, he would have in his possession a document of real value. Unfortunately for his pension, he was left with only memories of his participation. 'Everyone thinks because of the expression on my face that I didn't know what he was going to say, but I did,' he recalls. 'And I so often wonder whatever happened to that piece of paper.'

1995 'And you? You're in fucking Latvia.'

Neil Warnock delivers a half-time address to his Huddersfield Town team, who were losing 2–0, Gay Meadow, Shrewsbury, 22 April 1995.

The half-time team talk is one of football's most mystique-fuelled rituals. The fifteen minutes when oratory can be employed to make a difference has become routinely mythologised. In the subsequent retelling, words spoken in the intensity of the dressing room gain a significance way beyond their meaning. Losing positions are turned around by a word or two, inspiration derived from a verbal gee-up.

Sometimes, words don't even have to be exchanged. There is a story about Brian Clough, the master natural psychologist, when he was manager at Nottingham Forest. Two–nil down at half-time, the Forest players trudged back into the dressing room alarmed at the verbal pelting they were about to receive from a boss whose tongue, they knew all too well, could lacerate at twenty feet. But when they got there, there was no sign of the manager. They waited for him to arrive, but when he failed to show, they started to make tactical switches of their own to ensure improvement in the second half. The captain did the team talk. It was not until the referee had knocked on the dressing-room door to tell them time was up that Clough finally appeared. It was the briefest of interventions. Sticking his head around the door, all he said was: 'Sorry, lads. My fault: picked the wrong team.'

Every football reporter – every football fan – yearns for the opportunity to be a fly on the dressing-room wall, to be a witness to the processes of the half-time talk. Every Sunday morning on park pitches up and down the land, the managers of mini-league teams unleash their inner Ferguson, hair-drying their young charges in imitation of what they imagine goes on in the inner sanctums of the professional game.

And in the mid-1990s, for the first time, we began to get glimpses of what did indeed go on. As the Premier League elevated and enhanced football's cultural profile, television started to take an interest in the phenomenon. At the top of the game, the rituals were too hallowed to be compromised by wider exposure, so despite numerous requests, what happened at Manchester United, Liverpool and Arsenal at half-time remained a matter of mystery. But lower down, in the game's middle reaches, every club had its price. Thus it was that the Channel 4 cameras were there at Gay Meadow on a very wet Shropshire spring afternoon when a young Neil Warnock had the briefest of opportunities to have a positive influence on his team's performance.

On a pitch that redefined the phrase 'a bit slippy', Huddersfield had found their promotion charge out of Division Two compromised by a determined Shrewsbury Town side. Some 2000 Trotters fans, soaked to the skin by not so much an April shower as an early monsoon, had seen their favourites leak two goals without reply. Warnock was not happy. Having composed himself with a cup of tea and carefully removed his sweatshirt before confronting his players, he reveals himself to be a man on the very point of spontaneous combustion. 'Any injuries, lads?' he asks, opening in an apparently calm and rational manner. When no one replies, he proceeds to answer his own question: 'Stupid fucking question that. Of course there's not any fucking injuries, none of you have been anywhere near the fucking ball.'

> Of course there's not any fucking injuries, none of you have been anywhere near the fucking ball.

And so it continues, a meltdown of volcanic proportions, which at one point becomes so heated that the lens steams up and the cameraman is obliged to apply a cloth so the television viewer can continue to observe the rant in all its unhinged glory. It makes deeply uncomfortable viewing: in the course of an epic tour de force,

Warnock accuses his players of all manner of failings, from sloppy defending to a lack of commitment to the cause, culminating to this frankly bizarre geographical observation about his full-back's positioning for the first Shrewsbury goal: 'And you? You're in fucking Latvia.'

It sounded nonsensical. But that is the way of the half-time talk. What's more, those who have been inside dressing rooms when the emotional charge is at its most electric insist that television gives a misleading view of coaches by capturing them in their most unguarded moments.

'I can't think of any manager who has let the cameras in and come out with any dignity,' reckons Ian Hendon, who was a player when Channel 4 turned up in the dressing room for the documentary *Leyton Orient: Yours for a Fiver* (1995) which aired around the same time as the Warnock piece. That film made an anti-hero out of manager John Sitton, immortalising a half-time rage that added little to the history of oratory. This was no tracksuited Aneurin Bevan we saw fuming in the dressing room. The cameras recorded a lengthy and bizarre offer to fight his own players. It made no sense, followed no known patterns of English grammar. But it was riveting viewing:

> You, you little c***, when I tell you to do something, and you, you fucking big c***, when I tell you to do something, do it. And if you come back at me, we'll have a fucking right sort-out in here. All right? And you can pair up if you like, and you can fucking pick someone else to help you, and you can bring your fucking dinner. Cos by the time I've finished with you, you'll fucking need it.

Despite being on the receiving end of this foul-mouthed diatribe, Hendon has nothing but sympathy for Sitton: 'The programme portrayed him as an absolute madman, when actually he was one of best coaches I've worked with. It pretty much ended his career in professional football.'

Soon after his verbal explosion was shown (and you can still see it in all its unhinged glory on YouTube), Sitton was sacked, drifting out of management to become a cab driver. The downward trajectory of his career serves as a warning of what can happen to a manager who lets outsiders in: nobody would have known what went on behind closed doors had he kept them firmly shut.

Warnock was luckier. He survived his brief moment of national scrutiny, going on to enjoy nigh-on twenty more years in charge at seven clubs, including QPR and Leeds United, before turning poacher and becoming a television pundit on BT Sport. Not that his career stopped in the studio. In the summer of 2014, he defied both chronology and expectation by being appointed Crystal Palace manager at the age of sixty-five, a dinosaur resurrected in the age of the sleek, sophisticated, scientific manager.

But perhaps Warnock owed his managerial survival at Huddersfield less to good fortune than to the simple fact that in the very same year as his televised meltdown he led the club to promotion. Despite losing the game at Shrewsbury 2–1, they went up to the First Division (now the Championship) via the play-offs. He achieved what he set out to do. There was method in his madness. Maybe it is time for the Harvard Business School's management class to conduct some research to assess exactly what impact utterly incongruous geographical observations can have on sporting motivation.

1995 'You can't win anything with kids.'

Alan Hansen, BBC *Match of the Day* studio, Shepherd's Bush, 19 August 1995.

Over the years since he uttered these singularly ill-chosen words, Alan Hansen's bold dismissal of Manchester United's young team on the opening day of the 1995–6 season has been a source of rich ridicule. It sits high and proud in the shortlist of sporting predictions that history has most undermined, alongside Ally MacLeod's promise of Scottish World Cup glory in 1978 and England cricket captain Tony Greig's vow to make the brilliant West Indian cricketers 'grovel' in 1976. After United's brilliant youngsters went on to win the double that season, and to dominate English football for the next decade, it grew to look ever more ridiculous, the opposite of prescient, as if Hansen was consulting the foggiest of crystal balls. T-shirts were issued with his words printed across the front, banners were flourished at Cup finals. Blimey, some smartarse even used it as the title of a book about youth football.*

And a day barely passes when the man himself isn't reminded of it by wise-cracking taxi drivers or passing white-van drivers, a ribbing he takes with unfailing good humour. But the truth is, at the time it looked as though he was on to something. When he said it, no one was laughing. In fact, in Manchester, there were many who were nodding sagely in agreement with the ex-Liverpool defender.

The previous season, 1994–5, United had been frustrated at every turn. They had seen their best player suspended for nine months after assaulting a spectator (see pages 187–90), they had blown a league and cup double at the last hurdle; in short, they had looked like an institution fraying at the edges. And then, over the summer, their

---

*The present author's *You'll Win Nothing with Kids: Fathers, Sons and Football* was published in 2007.

manager had taken drastic action. Alex Ferguson had demolished a side which had won two titles in the previous three seasons. He sold Mark Hughes, Paul Ince and Andrei Kanchelskis, respectively to Chelsea, Internazionale and Everton, a ruthless purge of the old guard that prompted one observer to suggest that the Scot had become intoxicated with his own legend and it was really time he stood down and allowed a manager with a broader vision to step in. That observer wasn't Alan Hansen, incidentally. Nor was it someone who worked for the mainstream media. It was a writer for the United fanzine *Red Issue*.

What worried the doubters was that Ferguson had not replaced his championship-winning stars with better imports. He had not bought anybody of renown over the summer. Instead, he had promoted the recent graduates of his youth system to his first team, lads who had no experience of how to pursue a championship challenge. It seemed to many to be the most reckless of gambles, threatening to sink United in an excess of callowness. So when United, stripped of established stars and with six players under the age of twenty in their line-up, lost their opening match of the season 3–1 to Aston Villa, the BBC's man was by no means alone in shaking his head in puzzlement.

The list of young players written off by Hansen now reads like a roll-call of recent United greats: Gary Neville, Paul Scholes, Nicky Butt, Phil Neville and David Beckham (Ryan Giggs was injured) were to be the mainstay of Ferguson's trophy-gathering behemoth over the next decade, their names indelibly inscribed in the annals of Manchester United. But in those days they were household names only in their own households. Indeed, a couple of seasons previously, when the manager had blooded them in a League Cup tie against Port Vale, he had caused such consternation that Joan Walley, Labour MP for Stoke-on-Trent North and a staunch Port Vale supporter, saw fit to demand in the House of Commons that football clubs be obliged to give value to ticket holders by playing their established stars.

But Ferguson knew something those watching from outside did not: that the cohort of home-reared young players he had at his disposal was simply too good to hold back, that for the good of them and his club, he needed to clear the path ahead of all obstacles. As he was about to demonstrate, Giggs, Scholes, Butt, Beckham and the Nevilles were the legitimate heirs to the tradition established by the Busby Babes.

And how he was proved right. Hindsight has never worked as quickly as it did that season to smack Hansen in the face. Ferguson's youthful charges may have looked naïve and exposed in that opening game against Villa, but once the captain Eric Cantona returned to the team in October, the manager's investment and faith in youth would begin to pay triumphant dividends.

Just nine months after he made it, Hansen's point looked ridiculous: the kids had won quite a lot. But that is the peril of television punditry: events hold the speaker at their mercy. And, unlike so many recently retired players who hold on to the omertà of the dressing room even when being paid to analyse, Hansen at least voiced an objective view. He did not duck the issue. He did not sit on the fence, the smell of creosote lingering in his every opinion. Indeed, looking back, he now feels the comment sealed his reputation as a pundit. Not because of what he said. But because he was prepared to say it.

> That is the peril of television punditry: events hold the speaker at their mercy.

1995 'The Old Firm match is the only one in the world where the managers have to calm the interviewers down.'

Celtic manager Tommy Burns, 29 November 1995.

As a summary of the hysteria surrounding the Glasgow derby, Tommy Burns' observation is hard to beat. On days when Celtic meet Rangers, Scotland's largest city grinds to a halt. A freedom of information request in 2011 revealed that it costs Strathclyde Constabulary more than £300,000 to police a single encounter between Celtic and Rangers. Violent crime increases substantially as prejudices held in check during the week erupt on the Old Firm match day, and the 'ninety-minute bigots' – as the Rangers and Celtic diehards were neatly characterised by the former Rangers chairman David Murray – act out the long-familiar sectarian script. If there is not a rival fan to berate, then male supporters take it out on the wife: domestic abuse call-outs rise significantly on days when the fixture is played.

> At the end of the day, let's not kid ourselves. These supporters hate each other.

'This is like a scene out of Apocalypse Now... We've got the equivalent of Passchendaele and that says nothing for Scottish football. At the end of the day, let's not kid ourselves. These supporters hate each other,' was how the commentator Archie Macpherson reported rioting on the pitch after the 1980 Scottish Cup final between the two sides.

The root causes run deep; in the Old Firm can be found most of the fault lines that cut through Glasgow society. The clubs represent two halves of a long-divided city. Roughly, Rangers stand for the Scottish and Northern Irish Protestant Unionist tradition, while Celtic is the favoured club of the descendants of Irish Catholic immigrants. These are not two groups inclined to integration. Or tolerance. Or mutual understanding. The division is of long standing and assumed by many to be permanent.

And that divide is an essential strand in the DNA of both clubs: Rangers came into being as long ago as 1873, founded by a group of rowing enthusiasts from the west of Scotland, and the club soon became a focus for Presbyterian Unionist identity, faced by an Irish Catholic community that was coalescing around Celtic, founded in 1888. There are other rivalries based on sectarian tradition in Scotland. But Hibernian and Heart of Midlothian in Edinburgh cannot match the Glaswegian clubs' visceral and combustible hatred of one another.

Maybe that is because the two have dominated Scottish football, constantly battling each other for ultimate supremacy. Outside Glasgow, the term 'Old Firm' has derogatory connotations of carve-up and institutionalised success. And no wonder: Rangers FC, based at Ibrox in the southwest of the city, have won the Scottish League championship no fewer than fifty-four times; their Parkhead-based, East-end rivals, Celtic, have lifted the trophy on forty-five occasions. But if success has been omnipresent for both clubs, so has bitter, sometimes violent, sectarian rivalry between their supporters. As the journalist Sandy Strang once remarked: 'A Glaswegian atheist is a bloke who goes to a Rangers–Celtic match to watch the football.'

When he was managing Celtic, Jock Stein – himself a Protestant; Celtic have always been marginally more ecumenical than their rivals – was once asked which player he would sign first, a Catholic or a Protestant. To which he replied, the Protestant. His interviewer seemed rather annoyed by that. Why would he go against the traditions of his club so wilfully? 'Because I know Rangers would never sign the Catholic, so I'd get him as well,' was the reply. It was a line that neatly flagged up the absurdity of historic Old Firm prejudices.

Though it gave precious little suggestion of how they might be countered. As Mo Johnston discovered in 1989 when he became the first significant Catholic player to sign for Rangers; even as he led his new team to the Scottish title, many a supporter in Ibrox refused to acknowledge his presence, publicly claiming the manager Graeme Souness was fielding only ten men in matches.

Yet however absurd and poisonous the history of Old Firm enmity may appear to outsiders, many in Glasgow enjoy the fizzing sense of excitement that attends the fixture. The noisy atmosphere at these encounters is unmatched anywhere in Britain. When it matters as much as this derby does, the intensity is infectious. The Glasgow press – derided by their English colleagues as 'fans with typewriters' – have long invested the matches with a seriousness which belies the fact that this is merely a game. Knowing how much it means to their readers – how much it means to them, for that matter – the pressmen ascribe huge significance to every nuance.

> A Glaswegian atheist is a bloke who goes to a Rangers–Celtic match to watch the football.

It is because of the high level of sectarian sensitivity that Celtic and Rangers have long shared the same shirt sponsor: any company associated with one of them alone would be putting their product beyond the reach of half of the consumers in the city. So it is with the media. Fans of either side pore over match reports sniffing out bias for the other lot. Which is why so many media folk in Glasgow claim publicly to support Partick Thistle – a small club that prides itself on offering a non-sectarian alternative to the blue and green of the Old Firm – in the attempt to maintain a veneer of impartiality.

But Tommy Burns knew they could not hide their true affinity. In the emotional hurly-burly of Old Firm week newsmen betray their allegiances with their every over-excited response. Although he played for the club on more than 300 occasions, the Celtic boss regarded Scotland's sectarian divide as a hopeless anachronism in a modern society, and spoke out against it at every opportunity:

> Educate the kids to integrate with one another and not pay any attention to who's a Catholic and who's a Protestant or any of that rubbish. Just go out there, support your team, make good friends and get on with your lives.

When Burns died of skin cancer in 2008, Ally McCoist, then the assistant, now the Rangers manager, paid tribute to his rival boss's inclusive instincts. 'If you didn't like Tam Burns then there was something wrong with you. He was one that crossed the divide,' McCoist said. 'Not having an enemy in the world is a great legacy to leave behind.'

Whether that legacy has had any effect on cross-community behaviour is yet to be determined. Since Rangers were liquidated following the discovery of serial fiscal chicanery in 2012, and a new club begun in their stead was elected to the very bottom tier of the Scottish League, the football calendar has lacked one of its most anticipated and colourful events. In Glasgow, everyone is waiting for Rangers to make their way back to the top division, so that Old Firm hostilities can resume. Sadly, you suspect their eager anticipation is not driven by an anxiety to shake hands with their neighbours and engage in a fraternal hug.

Not having an enemy in the world is a great legacy to leave behind.

1996 'And I'll tell you, honestly, I will love it if we beat them. Love it.'

Kevin Keegan, speaking after his Newcastle team had just beaten Leeds United, Elland Road, 27 April 1996.

It was not so much what he said as the way he said it that made the then Newcastle manager's unhinged tirade stick so resolutely in the mind. Kevin Keegan was talking to Sky television after one of the concluding games in a tight race to the title and his agitation was evident. Sporting a pair of headphones atop his bouncing badger quiff, with his finger jabbing and his eyes blazing, he appeared to be at war with the world, besieged by his enemies. He looked like a man on the verge of a nervous breakdown.

The 'them' he would have loved to beat were Manchester United, Newcastle's principal rivals in the gallop for the finishing line. Newcastle had been out in front in the Premier League race for so long – at one point in February 1996 they led their Mancunian rivals by twelve points – that a bunch of optimistic Geordies had commissioned a banner to hang from Tyne Bridge announcing their title victory. But the young team from Manchester had gradually reeled them in, winning a critical match at St James' Park and breathing so heavily on the back of his collar that Keegan's fragile self-control began to fray.

What had sparked his immediate ire were comments by the United manager Alex Ferguson about the motivation of the Leeds players ahead of their game with Newcastle. The Scot had questioned whether they would be as keen to beat Newcastle as they had been recently to beat his own Manchester United side. Fergie's remarks were typically jaundiced, and characteristically calculating:

I can't understand Leeds United. Their manager doesn't deserve to have his players playing like that only when they come to Manchester United. No wonder managers get the sack. He has done a great job for that club, it's pathetic the way his team have been playing. If they had played every week like they did tonight it would be a different story. I think we can accept any club coming here and trying their hardest – so long as they do it every week.

It was a classic Ferguson intervention, designed to goad the Leeds players into thwarting Newcastle's ambition. But it achieved a lot more than that. It exposed a fundamental flaw in his rival's psychological make-up. Suddenly Keegan looked a man ill-equipped to cope with the pressures of a title challenge. His players were said to have taken one glance at their boss foaming at the mouth beneath those headphones and seen him in a new and distinctly less flattering light. They could no longer believe that the enthusiast whose bubbly creativity had taken them to the brink of success was a man with the necessary heft to carry them over the line. This was the moment that Keegan torpedoed his own reputation live on air.

Right from the off in the interview, it was clear something was amiss. The words with which Keegan prefaced his famous rant may have sounded familiar, but, in the order that the overwrought Newcastle manager spoke them, they made no sense at all:

I've kept really quiet but I'll tell you something, he went down in my estimations when he said that. We have not resorted to that. But it really has got to me. I've voiced it live, not in front of the press or anywhere. I'm not even going to the press conference.

Keegan's very public meltdown was the first recognised triumph of the newly manufactured discipline of managerial mind games. It may have been collateral damage – after all, the intended targets of Ferguson's verbal mischief-making were the Leeds players – but Keegan's implosion was subsequently credited to the United manager's Machiavellian wiles. He had out-thought his rival to the point where Keegan could no longer cope. Look at the footage again on YouTube and you can almost hear Ferguson's evil cackle in the background.

Poor Keegan. He has never been allowed to forget the moment he exposed himself so badly to the nation. When the competition reached its twentieth birthday in 2012, his was voted the most memorable quote in Premier League history, beating such gems as Alan Hansen's 'you can't win anything with kids' (see pages 195–7), Eric Cantona's 'when the seagulls follow the trawler' (see pages 187–90) and José Mourinho's 'I am a Special One' (see pages 271–5). And this from a man who has provided a rich seam of memorably fatuous sayings over the years.

> Our current financial situation means that if we want to buy, we have to spend.

'I don't think there is anyone bigger or smaller than Diego Maradona,' was one of his, for example. As was: 'Our current financial situation means that if we want to buy, we have to spend.' And not forgetting: 'The Premier League is in danger of becoming one of the most boring, but great, leagues in the world.'

But it was his 'Love It' rant that sealed his legend. Not least because the scenario that Keegan so craved did not come to pass. As Manchester United eased past Keegan's Newcastle to pip the Geordies for the 1995–6 Premier League title, Kevin never did get to feel the love.

1996 'If he farts in front of the queen we get blemished.'

Paul McGaughey, Adidas spokesman, on the risks of a sponsorship deal with Paul Gascoigne, May 1996.

By the mid-1990s, there was money in football. Real money. Big money. The injection of cash from satellite television had pushed up Premier League players' salaries to a level undreamt of in the past. At the same time, as the game found a new place in the culture, there was an upsurge in commercial sponsorship by organisations keen to ride on its coat tails. Premier League footballers began to be presented as the hottest thing around, as Britain's answer to Hollywood's A-listers. Sportswear companies, fashion houses, grooming-product manufacturers, even vegetarian-snack-food providers were anxious to use these freshly discovered young celebrities to promote their product. And they were happy to pay top dollar to attach their brand to a footballer's renown. In financial terms, things had come a long way since Billy Wright slicked on some Brylcreem or George Best sizzled a sausage. There were millions on offer to the new footballing product endorsers.

But, as with all exciting new fashions, there was a risk involved. The never-once-booked-in-his-career Gary Lineker was unlikely to imperil the corporate integrity of Walker's Crisps and the fresh-faced determination of Ryan Giggs (in the days before he besmirched his own brand with an off-piste dalliance with his sister-in-law) seemed the ideal vehicle to promote Quorn. But with some players things could at any moment go pear-shaped; a carefully constructed commercial image could be compromised with a single red card. As Adidas's marketing man suggested (and indeed as the same organisation came to appreciate some eighteen years later when their client Luis Suárez turned cannibal at the Brazil World Cup), a company choosing to associate itself with a sportsman might end up with egg on its face. Especially if the footballing superstar whose endorsement they were anxious to secure was Paul Gascoigne.

Actually, with Gazza it wasn't a risk. It was a certainty. He wasn't violent, or aggressive or unpleasant. Or at least not too often. He didn't mean to embarrass his backers; he was not deliberately subversive or destructive. It was just that with Gazza there was no 'off' switch. He was the living definition of juvenile. If you took the plunge and sponsored Gazza, at some point you were going to be compromised. As Jimmy Greaves put it at the time, he was the only footballer 'capable of breaking leg and wind at the same time'.

We know now that Gascoigne's ceaseless attention-seeking was the product of a sadly fractured psyche. But at the height of Gazzamania following his brilliant and mercurial performance in Italia 90 (see pages 162–6), we just thought he was a buzzing, over-excitable eccentric. Those obliged to share dressing rooms with him, however, quickly tired of his ceaseless tomfoolery and of the wrecking-ball that was his scatter-gun energy. Already damaged by childhood trauma (he witnessed at close quarters the death of his best friend in a road accident when he was just ten), he was riven with insecurities. And one of his biggest fears was that people might not like him. Because, after all, he could not stand himself.

Paul Stewart, who was asked to keep an eye on him when he was laid off injured at Tottenham Hotspur in the 1991–2 season, recalls a kind of manic self-loathing which manifested itself in an endless determination to change his appearance. Every day Stewart came home from training he found Gazza had dyed his hair, or shaved off his eyebrows, or bought a new outfit. And every day he heard the same question: 'do you think I look good?'

Looking back, the clues about how damaged he was were evident from the start. A mild form of Tourette's long informed his public utterances. When asked by a Norwegian television reporter if he had a message for the people of Norway ahead of England's opening World Cup qualifying game against their country in October 1992, he couldn't help himself. His response, 'Yeah, fuck off Norway,' was broadcast live and was the headline in the newspaper *Dagbladet*. For Gazza, microphones were always an open invitation to belch. Just as a glass was an open invitation to be emptied.

Any message for the people of Norway, Mr Gascoigne?

So it was that, now playing for big bucks at Glasgow Rangers after a brief, injury-ravaged sojourn at Lazio in Rome (1992–5), he was promoted as England's talisman at the commercially enormous Euro 96, the first major international football tournament to be staged in Britain since 1966. He was the biggest name in the biggest sporting event to hit the country in thirty years. There was every chance that if things went well he would be introduced to the queen. The thought of which induced sweaty palms among his backers.

But before that, before the competition even started, England went on a bonding trip to Hong Kong. There, the newly installed manager Terry Venables, appreciating that there were still a couple of weeks to go ahead of kick-off, allowed his players to enjoy a night on the tiles, to let off steam. Incapable of discreetly shrinking into the background, Gazza became the focus of the shenanigans, at one point being strapped into a 'dentist's chair' in the middle of a bar while liquor was poured down his throat by cackling team-mates.

It was something that might have passed without comment, a 'what-goes-on-on-tour-stays-on-tour' bit of horseplay, had Gazza not been involved. But the player was now a magnet for headline writers, and there was money to be made from him. And snaps taken by others present in the bar found their way onto the front pages of the tabloids back home.

The pictures prompted outrage. Players who were supposed to be representing their nation in the most significant tournament in three decades were dismissed as behaving like revellers at a drunken stag party. The sexy young brand ambassadors were now chastised by the popular press as booze-swilling losers. 'Disgracefool' was the headline in *The Sun*. 'Look at Gazza,' read the copy below pictures of him in a drunken stupor, strapped to the chair. 'A drunken oaf with no pride.'

Such condemnation was not to last. After the same drunken oaf scored a wonderful solo goal in the group game against Scotland – which he celebrated by lying on the turf and getting his team-mates satirically to squirt liquid down his throat (this time water from a sports drink bottle) – the *Daily Mirror* ran a memorable editorial. Headlined 'Mr Paul Gascoigne: An Apology', it continued 'Gazza: is no longer a fat, drunken imbecile. He is, in fact, a football genius.'

> Gazza is no longer a fat, drunken imbecile. He is, in fact, a football genius.

Well, for now he was.

1996 'Why didn't you just belt it?'

Barbara Southgate, after being asked by a reporter if she had a message for her son, Gareth, after his penalty miss in the Euro 96 semi-final, Wembley Stadium, 26 June 1996.

Euro 96 was billed as the tournament when football came home. To the infectious accompaniment of 'Three Lions', Frank Skinner and David Baddiel's amiable homage to the great moments of English football history (with a little musical help from Britpop band The Lightning Seeds), and barely more than a decade on from the disgrace of Heysel, it repositioned the English game internationally as a bulwark of good-humoured self-deprecation, providing the first hint of the mood of benevolent patriotism that would reach its apogee at the London Olympics sixteen years later.

The feel-good cheer was driven in part by the performance of the England team. Every tournament needs its hosts to do well, to sustain local enthusiasm. Under the stewardship of Terry Venables, available after his shortlived move into the boardroom at Spurs, the England side flourished. Playing with a sophistication and awareness seen all too infrequently in England sides (and fired by a 'we'll-show-em' reaction to the tabloid vilification they had suffered after their drunken carousing in Hong Kong), they had reached the semi-finals, dispatching such distinguished opponents as Holland and Spain along the way.

Unlike his immediate predecessor Graham Taylor, Venables had been blessed in having most of his leading performers fit for the tournament. Alan Shearer, the muscular Blackburn forward, was available to him in a way he rarely was for Taylor. And, crucially, England's talisman, the fizzing box of tricks that was Paul Gascoigne, was close to his best, full of invention and sparkle, the wellspring of so much of England's creative potential.

To this promising mix Venables added a gloss of tactical fluency that had not been evident under Taylor. When analysed, the 4–1 group stage victory over the Netherlands was a masterclass in managerial manipulation. The coach adapted his plan perfectly to exploit the technical strengths of Teddy Sheringham, Darren Anderton, David Platt and Steve McManaman, as well as Shearer and Gascoigne. Compared to his England, the Dutch look sluggish and one-paced. For perhaps the first and only time in the post-Cruyff era, England made the Dutch look old-fashioned.

And England had even managed to win a penalty shoot-out. After a goalless 120 minutes against Spain in the quarter-final, they had delivered a perfect set of kicks, beating the Spaniards 4–2 with not a shot missed. When Stuart Pearce, who had seen his effort saved six years earlier in the Stadio delle Alpi (see pages 162–6), hammered his shot into the Spanish net and roared out his relief in the most visceral of celebrations, it seemed as if England had finally conquered their nervy inferiority when faced with the twelve-yard showdown.

Indeed, Gareth Southgate, the centre-back who had not been called upon in the shoot-out against Spain, was remarkably upbeat about the possibilities of involvement when interviewed ahead of the semi-final. 'I've only taken one penalty before, for Crystal Palace at Ipswich,' he revealed. 'I hit the post and we went down that year. But I think I'd be far more comfortable now than I was then.' His tone suggested that English football was finally reaching psychological accommodation with the penalty. Which, given that the shoot-out had been a fact of footballing life since the first one was played out in a Watney Cup tie between Manchester United and Hull City in 1970 (United won, even though Denis Law missed his effort) was about time.

Yet everyone watching the ensuing semi-final against the Germans still feared what lay ahead if the scores were tied. And, after Shearer had scored within three minutes of the kick-off, and the aptly named Stefan Kuntz equalised for the Germans, followed by a tense, fraught extra time in which Gascoigne missed connecting with a cross by the length of a stud to score the golden goal that would have put England in the final, the pant-wetting finale duly arrived. England's hopes in an international competition once again depended on spot-kicks. Just six years after the semi-final of Italia 90 it seemed as if fate was mocking the English game.

When the shoot-out started, however, England approached it apparently in the best of cheer. After all, their goalkeeper was David Seaman, a man who had made a habit of saving spot-kicks for his club Arsenal. And for once England had a group of more experienced penalty takers than Germany, as was evident when Shearer, Platt, Pearce, Gascoigne and Sheringham all scored. So good were their efforts, the German keeper Andreas Köpke dived the wrong way for four of them. Gascoigne's shot hit the inner side netting before bouncing into the back of the goal.

Unfortunately, the Germans had converted their five penalties with similar efficiency, Seaman getting close to only one of them. So it was down to sudden death. The England players available to take the first of the kicks included McManaman, Anderton, Paul Ince and the skipper Tony Adams, who had scored from the spot in Arsenal's European Cup Winners' Cup victory shoot-out two seasons before. All of them seemed better bets than Southgate, the centre-back with the professional spot-kick record of one taken, one missed. But Venables, recognising that the most important quality for a player in a shoot-out is nerve, was impressed by Southgate's willingness to volunteer. He gave the player the responsibility, and told Anderton he would take the seventh shot if required.

Southgate approached the task with his head held high, apparently immune to the fact that 25 million of his countrymen were watching him on television. He took half a dozen confident steps up to the ball and then − to the watching nation's disbelief − underhit it feebly. Köpke, who had been seen to move illegally well before Sheringham took his shot, didn't have to bother again with such subterfuge. Time seemed to stand still as the ball dribbled tamely towards him. He simply waited until it was nearly upon him, dived and saved it.

For the Germans the outlook was suddenly sunny. All that was required now was for their sixth man to score and they were through to the final. Up stepped Andreas Möller, whose effort was almost as unconvincing as Southgate's. He shot straight down the middle. But Seaman, his morale apparently punctured by his colleague's miss, had already tumbled to his left. The ball barely had sufficient power to hit the back of the net. But it did, and England were out.

> No matter how much the other players try to console me, I'm still left with the feeling that I let everybody down.

Southgate was mortified by his momentous miss. 'No matter how much the other players try to console me, I'm still left with the feeling that I let everybody down,' he said at the time. Though later that year the Villa man would enjoy the lucrative consolation of appearing in an advertisement for Pizza Hut, making light of his Euro heartache alongside his fellow penalty-shoot-out bunglers – of 1990 World Cup vintage – Chris Waddle and Stuart Pearce.

Nor was that the end of England's penalty-shoot-out misery. Two years later, at the World Cup finals in France in 1998, Venables's successor Glenn Hoddle convinced himself that the only way to win a shoot-out was through incessant practice, and had his players take penalty after penalty in training. But his approach turned out to be no more effective. Hoddle's England failed to make it out of the last sixteen, being beaten on spot-kicks by their other World Cup nemesis, Argentina, in a second-round match otherwise distinguished by the wondrous finishing of the teenaged Michael Owen and by the petulance – and resulting sending-off – of David Beckham.

Everyone's an instant armchair expert when it comes to dissecting

England's footballing flops. In the aftermath of their exit from Euro 96, even Southgate's mum got in on the act, asking the question that was on the lips of the entire watching population. Why hadn't he belted it? Experts and psychologists have long insisted that is the best method, eradicating as it does such distractions as doubt and fear. Though when England were – yet again – dismissed on penalties in the quarter-final of Euro 2012, Italy's Andrea Pirlo confounded Mrs Southgate's theory by deftly, gently, dinking the winning strike over Joe Hart's prone body. Nobody, least of all his mama, was required to ask him why he hadn't just belted it.

1996 'ARSENE WHO?'

Headline in the *London Evening Standard* above an article about Arsenal's new manager, 18 September 1996.

So unknown was Arsène Wenger when he first arrived in England that nobody was certain even how to pronounce his name, let alone be aware that there was an accent on that first E. When the reporter from *The Standard* contacted Arsenal, the club which had just appointed him, a spokesman admitted nobody there knew if you pronounced his surname in the German manner, with a V, or the English way with a W. Or maybe there was a French compromise somewhere in between. The truth was, as he arrived in the marbled halls of Highbury that autumn, the man from Alsace was not a manager who had built much of a name for himself.

Hard as it might be to imagine in this era of José, Manuel and Roberto, back in 1996 foreign coaches were a rarity in English football. There had been a handful in charge of clubs in the top flight – Ossie Ardiles at Newcastle (1991–2) and Spurs (1993–4), Jozef Vengloš at

Aston Villa (1990–91) – but none had troubled the trophy engravers. More to the point, none had challenged the conventional assumption in British football that a manager was a growly bloke who did a lot of shouting from the touchline, generally in a Scottish accent. Wenger did not even look the part. Tall, angular and bespectacled, he had the appearance of someone who should be peering down a microscope in a laboratory, not issuing instructions to professional footballers on the training pitch. The tone of the *Standard*'s article suggested that Arsenal had made a very odd appointment. One which, the writer was convinced, was unlikely to be a long-term one.

Wenger did not feel diminished by such reporting; he happily admitted his background was not something to generate much excitement – particularly in a footballing culture as inward-looking as England's. He had won the French League with Monaco in 1988 and the Japanese Cup with Nagoya Grampus Eight in 1994, but he accepted his approach had not been tested at the highest level. Nor was he too surprised when his new charges quickly reached for a cultural stereotype when weighing him up. He was a bit awkward physically and he was French, so the Arsenal players called him 'Inspector Clouseau'.

> One of the biggest bets was how long I would last.

'One of the biggest bets was how long I would last,' Wenger recalled when he reached his one thousandth game in charge of Arsenal in the spring of 2014. 'Everybody was betting I would be gone by January 1st.'

Seventeen years later, Wenger was still in place, the one fixed point in a footballing culture that has become increasingly short-term in its employment practices. In the spring of 2014 he signed a contract that should see him into his third decade of employment in North London. He had presided over an era of unprecedented growth at his club, transforming Arsenal into one of the most financially secure footballing institutions in Europe, playing their home games in the most lavishly appointed stadium in Britain. More fundamentally, Wenger has changed the way in which the football manager is regarded. It is because of him that men of the calibre of Brendan Rodgers, Mauricio Pochettino and Roberto Martínez are employed by the country's leading sides. If we had never discovered who Wenger was, the chances are English football would have continued ploughing its traditional narrow furrow. He was the unknown who sparked a revolution.

Wenger was the Premiership's first student of methodology, its first football professor. Just as the influx of foreign players attracted by the Premier League's money were bringing new attitudes, new focus, new professionalism to English football, so he now brought new systems, new approaches to preparation, a new appreciation of sports science. Not to mention an encyclopaedic knowledge of dietary supplements.

Inheriting a stalwart though ageing defence of Tony Adams, Steve Bould, Lee Dixon, Martin Keown, Nigel Winterburn and David Seaman, Wenger immediately won them over with the promise that his approach would lengthen their careers (and thus, as football's wages suddenly began to spiral, bolster their pensions). Pre-match stretching, the regular use of osteopaths and massage, an energy-rich, vegetable-heavy, fat-free diet: such procedures may now be routine, but they were largely alien to the English game when he introduced them. Also, despite being the son of a bar owner, he made clear his suspicion of alcohol to a group that hitherto had been in thrall to booze.

The main thing, though, was the change of attitude he brought. His predecessor at Highbury, the Scot George Graham, had been old-school, a verbal bully. The atmosphere around the club reflected his aggression. Things often got heated in the dressing room: words were slung around, the sparring was hostile. It could be a harsh place. Wenger was very different. He worked by encouragement, by collaboration, by treating his players as grown-ups. As Martin Keown recalls, Wenger was unusual among football managers at the time:

> He was just incredibly calm, respectful, the best word is nice. That was what was so great about him. In a sense he is proof that nice guys can win in this game. You wanted to play for him because you liked him. He made the club a happy place to be.

So much so that just twenty months after he arrived, in spring of 1998, Wenger's gently holistic methodology had borne fruit. His Arsenal side – the stalwart English back five skilfully attached to a front six illuminated by the continental flair of Patrick Vieira, Emmanuel Petit, Marc Overmars, Nicolas Anelka and the incomparable Dennis Bergkamp, with Romford's Ray Parlour making up the numbers – had made up an eleven-point deficit opened up by Manchester United and won the Carling Premiership. They also won the FA Cup. No one was referring to Wenger as 'Arsène Who' on 16 May 1998, when Tony Adams raised the famous old trophy to make Arsenal the only side to equal Manchester United's record of two league and cup 'doubles'. By now, everyone knew his name.

1998 'Short back and sides while you're there, Eileen love.'

Ray Parlour to England manager Glenn Hoddle's spiritualist assistant Eileen Drewery, before the 1998 World Cup.

The 1997–8 season was Ray Parlour's best. The Arsenal midfielder – known around Highbury as 'the Romford Pelé' – had been so instrumental in his team winning the double he was anticipating a call-up to the England team. When it came and he was invited to a pre-World Cup training camp, he was delighted. So when he succumbed to a calf injury, his frustration was evident. As he waited in the medical room at Bisham Abbey for a scan, the manager Glenn Hoddle came into the room and told Parlour he could help. He suggested that, before he underwent diagnosis, the player should go to see Eileen Drewery, the spiritual healer who at the time was attached to the England set-up. A jaunty sceptic, Parlour only went because he was told to do so by the boss and the boss had the power to realise his World Cup ambitions. But when she laid her hands on his head and started intoning something, his response was that of the typical footballer. He made a gag about it. She laughed too. Though that might have been out of politeness, he acknowledges.

But when he told the other England players what he'd said – and one of them leaked the quip to *The Sun* – Hoddle was not amused. There was no tittering from the boss; the terms 'Hoddle' and 'sense of humour' rarely co-exist in the same sentence. Parlour found himself excluded from the eventual World Cup line-up (which one newspaper, in reference to the manager's psychic predilections, called 'The Hod Squad'). And the player remains convinced his humorous undermining of Eileen was the reason he was not picked.

Hoddle's flirtation with spiritualism was an odd episode in the history of the game, one which eventually cost him his position as England manager. He was a teenager, and dating her daughter, when he first met Mrs Drewery in 1976. At the time he was the most promising young player in the country, but his progress was being compromised by a persistent groin injury. He mentioned this to his girlfriend, who said her mum might be able to help. And help she did: so convinced was Hoddle that it was Eileen rather than conventional medical attention that had resolved his groin problem, that he became ever more attached to her, long after his relationship with her daughter had cooled.

Throughout his playing career he sought her intervention when his body was ailing. He was not the only footballer who tried to speed up recovery from injury by recourse to alternative treatment methods. Manchester United's captain Bryan Robson had a faith healer in Blackpool he insisted was more use than the entire medical team at Old Trafford put together. But Hoddle took things one stage further: when he became manager of the national team in September 1996, after three years at Chelsea, he integrated Eileen Drewery into the England set-up.

Most of the players were dubious about such stuff. Gary Neville mocked Hoddle's superstitious insistence that the staff walk round the pitch ahead of the World Cup second-round tie against Argentina in an anti-clockwise direction ('sadly it didn't do us much good'). Paul Gascoigne – another to be overlooked for France 98 – joked about Eileen's name ('I thought Hoddle was telling me to go visit a brewery,' he said). Dennis Wise said she reminded him of his mum. Hoddle, meanwhile, was obliged to defend his employment of Drewery when it was revealed that the two of them were partners in a pricey spiritualist healing venture that was benefitting enormously from the publicity he had drummed up for his ex-girlfriend's mother.

It wasn't his promotion of Drewery, however, but an interview he gave on 30 January 1999 to Matt Dickinson of *The Times* – in which he attempted to defend himself from criticism arising from the Drewery affair – that sealed his fate as England coach. In that interview Hoddle expressed some distinctly odd views on reincarnation and disability:

> My beliefs have evolved in the last eight or nine years, that the spirit has to come back again, that is nothing new, that has been around for thousands of years. You have to come back to learn and face some of the things you have done, good and bad. There are too many injustices around. You and I have been physically given two hands and two legs and half-decent brains. Some people have not been born like that for a reason. The karma is working from another lifetime. I have nothing to hide about that. It is not only people with disabilities. What you sow, you have to reap.

In the past, a remark in the middle of an interview that appeared in the sports pages of a broadsheet newspaper would not have ramifications. But at a time when football had become a barometer for national opinion, it was unlikely to slip by unnoticed. When no less a figure than the prime minister appeared on daytime television to condemn Hoddle for his comments, he was in deep trouble. Tony Blair, on a breakfast-TV sofa, opining about the England manager's attitude to the disabled: as a snapshot of the interface between politics, football and the media in the late 1990s, it said it all.

Initially Hoddle tried to bluster his way out of resigning by claiming he had been misrepresented by his interviewer. 'I never said them words,' he insisted. But Dickinson, a trusted and trustworthy reporter, would have required some imagination to make up such bizarre beliefs.

And when it became clear that Hoddle had used almost exactly them same words in a previous radio interview, he had nowhere to go. Despite boasting a win rate of 60 per cent during his spell as manager, a tally bettered only by Sir Alf Ramsey and Fabio Capello, on 2 February 1999 – to a backdrop of approving noises from representatives of disabled groups – he was removed from his post by an embarrassed Football Association. His job was given to the hapless Kevin Keegan, a man who, for all his tactical shortcomings, had never knowingly picked a squad according to whether they believed in spiritual healing.

As for Drewery, without her principal sponsor, she faded into the background, her five minutes basking in the limelight as the country's most renowned exponent of mumbo-jumbo were over. At the time of writing, copies of her autobiography are available on Amazon for the princely sum of 1p. Even at that price, it is unlikely Ray Parlour has a copy on his shelves.

1998 'Winning the World Cup is the most beautiful thing to have happened to France since the Revolution.'

Emmanuel Petit, Stade de France, Paris, 12 July 1998.

The pony-tailed Arsenal midfielder Emmanuel Petit was not alone in his extravagant response to his country winning the World Cup on home soil. The entire centre of Paris ground to a halt on the night the captain Didier Deschamps lifted the trophy after his side's comprehensive 3–0 victory over Brazil. More than one million people filled the Champs-Élysées in a glorious, spontaneous outpouring of national pride. All down the historic boulevard, the sound of 'La Marseillaise' filled the air, as victory was toasted in a flood of champagne. It was a magnificently inclusive, good-humoured, joyous occasion. To paraphrase the poet William Wordsworth's observation on witnessing the revolutionary events of 1789, for many a French-man bliss it was in that evening to be alive.

This was a victory, moreover, that made a profound statement about the condition of modern France. The beauty of it went beyond mere triumphalism. The nature of the team that had delivered the golden trophy in its home tournament was as significant a pointer to the social and racial make-up of the country at the dawn of the millennium as it was possible to imagine. This was a side constructed of black, white and mixed-race players, of Muslims, Christians and those not

> African, Arab and Caucasian passing and moving together, united in the French cause.

entirely sure. There were Patrick Vieira, Marcel Desailly and Zinedine Zidane playing alongside Deschamps, Petit and Fabien Barthez in a glorious testament to cooperation and integration. African, Arab and Caucasian passing and moving together, united in the French cause.

And the importance of the symbolism was not lost on one observer. Just after Petit himself had scored the third goal in injury time to seal the win, in the VIP area of the newly built Stade de France, President Jacques Chirac was to be seen heading for the nearest television camera. He was desperate for his face to be the first on the national news after victory was confirmed. And there he was, broadcast across the country, beaming out his congratulations even as Petit and his colleagues hugged each other on the pitch below.

What Chirac wanted more than anything was to associate himself with triumph. Not just because it is always good for politicians to bask in national success, not just because he was addicted to self-promotion. But because the multi-racial team that had just secured the win tallied perfectly with the political message he wanted to convey. At stake here was the future direction of France itself.

Chirac was at the time contesting mid-term elections against the growing threat of the National Front led by the crypto-fascist Jean-

Marie Le Pen (father of the party's present leader, Marine Le Pen). The unabashed representatives of the far right were picking up a significant section of an electorate who felt the French way of life was being threatened by immigration. Offering a manifesto that pledged immediate forced repatriation for legal immigrants, the National Front and its ethnic-cleansing agenda were gaining real momentum, particularly in the south of the country. Le Pen had already distanced himself from Petit and his colleagues, publicly sneering earlier in the tournament about the fact that a couple of the black players had not joined in the national anthem before matches (conveniently ignoring the fact that a couple of the white players hadn't exactly belted it out either).

What better way was there for Chirac to demonstrate the values of a multi-ethnic society – and thus undermine the fundamental premise of Le Pen – than to celebrate the victory of this rainbow French team? This was a side that reflected a very modern, united France that embraced difference and gave opportunity to all. The kind of France that Le Pen wanted to see destroyed and Chirac was happy to encourage. What the president was doing as he grinned in the camera arc light was insisting that if the French public wanted to win the World Cup then the only way they might do so in future was to consign the National Front to electoral oblivion. Vote Chirac and win the World Cup: seizing his moment, this canniest of political operators was sending out the most persuasive of electoral messages.

1999 'Two Andy Gorams, there's only two Andy Gorams.'

Celtic fans respond to the news that the Rangers goalkeeper had been diagnosed with a mild form of schizophrenia, Ibrox Park, Glasgow, 7 November 1999.

In the main, terrace wit does not repay the retelling. You really need to be there to appreciate the repartee of the crowd. But just occasionally speed and spontaneity are not the only things worth celebrating about a collective chant. Here are ten examples of magnificently quick-witted – not to mention devastatingly pointed – group humour from the years that followed the Andy Goram song.

Oh Teddy Teddy, you might have won the Treble but you're still a c***.
Arsenal fans rephrase their chant about the former Tottenham forward Teddy Sheringham, who, they insisted, moved to Man United but won fuck all, the season after he won the Treble in 1999. Sung to the tune of pop group Chicory Tip's 1972 hit 'Son of My Father'.

There's only one Carlton Palmer and he smokes marijuana / He's six feet tall, his head's too small / Walking in a Palmer wonderland.
Stockport County fans serenade their new player-manager, 2002.

His name is Rio and he watches from the stand.
West Ham fans adapt a Duran Duran hit to mock their former player Rio Ferdinand while he was undertaking a lengthy ban for missing a drugs test while with Manchester United, 2004.

He's red, he's sound, he's banned from every ground, Carra's dad, Carra's dad.
Liverpool fans after Jamie Carragher's father was arrested and subsequently given a banning order for being drunk and disorderly at a game, 2005.

Don't blame it on the Biscan / Don't blame it on the Hamman / Don't blame it on the Finnan / Blame on Traoré / He just can't, he just can't, he just can't control his feet.

Liverpool fans respond with one of the finest spontaneous chants of all time, reworking the Jackson Five's 'Blame It on the Boogie' after Djimi Traoré scores a painful own goal in an FA Cup third-round tie against Burnley, 18 January 2005. Four months later the hapless full-back was a Champions League winner.

U-N-I-T-E-D that spells fucking debt to me / With a knick-knack paddywack give a dog a bone / Ocean Finance on the phone.

Manchester City fans rework their rivals' old song about them to mark the arrival of Malcolm Glazer and his leveraged buy-out, 2005.

Deep-fry your pizzas, we're gonna deep-fry your pizzas.

To the strains of the song 'Guantanamera', Scots fans threaten the ultimate culinary sanction on their Italian opponents during a World Cup qualifier, 2007.

Monday, Tuesday Habib Beye / Wednesday, Thursday Habib Beye.

Newcastle fans turn all Fonz-like in their enthusiasm for their new French full-back, 2007.

When you're sat in Row Z and the ball hits your head / That's Zamora.

Fulham fans bring out their inner Dean Martin in homage to the wayward shooting of their striker Bobby Zamora, 2013.

You're shish and you know you are.

Chelsea supporters welcome followers of the Turkish side Galatasaray to Stamford Bridge for a Champions League tie, 2014.

1999 'I find it difficult to understand how someone in Stan's position, with the talent and money he has, is stressed. I wonder how a twenty-nine-year-old at Rochdale, in the last three months of his contract, with a wife and three kids, copes with stress.'

Aston Villa manager John Gregory on Stan Collymore's battle with depression, January 1999.

Looking back, this was not John Gregory's finest moment. The more we learn about depression and about the reality of Stan Collymore's battle with this most debilitating of conditions, the more the dismissive tone taken by the former Aston Villa manager looks like an act of casual bullying.

Collymore may not have been an easy person to love. Arrogant, aloof, self-obsessed, he could suck the oxygen from a dressing room. And Ulrika Jonsson is unlikely to endorse his candidacy for the world's cuddliest life partner.* But the fact was in the winter of 1999 he was in the grip of a disorder he did not yet even know the name of, let alone understand. Confused, hurt, alone and evidently suffering, crippled by his inability to make the most of his unquestioned talent, what he needed was coherent, clear-headed, practical advice. And what he got from the man supposed to be drawing the best from him was mockery and derision, seasoned with an assumption that only the financially bereft have reason to feel depressed. It was not exactly enlightened man-management.

In football, as in all professional sport, mental strength has long

---

* Collymore's relationship with the Swedish weathergirl and television presenter Ulrika Jonsson ended after he punched her in a Paris bar in 1998.

been regarded as a primary asset, one of qualities that set the excellent above the merely talented. Being able to cope with the ups and downs of the game, being capable of making the best of any given situation, these have long been regarded as essential prerequisites of a good player. So admitting to having problems, to being down or confused, feels to the vulnerable sportsman akin to admitting weakness. Your head isn't up to it. You can't hack it. You're second-rate.

In an environment as competitive as the professional football dressing room (where the biggest competition comes from those seeking your first-team place), to confess that you are suffering is not a step that many are willing to take. Those in the grip of depression (and statistics suggest that it afflicts up to 10 per cent of the population, which means at least one player in every team in the country) have been faced with a workplace in which there can easily appear to be no assistance. This was not a subject that was talked about. Sufferers had to learn strategies to hide their problems. As the former Wimbledon hard man Vinnie Jones, a long-term depressive, puts it: 'If you told anyone you were suffering from depression in my day in the Wimbledon dressing room you'd have got a clip round the ear.'

> If you told anyone you were suffering from depression... you'd have got a clip round the ear.

We now know that the athlete's brain is a complex mechanism. But when Gregory was in charge of a top football team a manager was regarded as a cutting-edge psychologist if he recognised that some players 'need an arm round the shoulder and others a kick up the backside'. Gregory tried both approaches with his most talented forward and ended up, he said at the time, 'tearing my hair out'.

What Collymore needed, however, was proper psychological intervention, professional diagnosis and assistance in finding coping strategies. What he got instead was a transfer. And he went on to play only twenty-four more league games. After the forward had moved to Fulham, Gregory announced: 'It is in the best interests of everyone that he has left Villa. Now I can get on with more important matters than talk about him, and that is all I seem to have done since I became manager.'

Collymore's travails, however harshly they were dismissed by so many at the time, were to prove a significant milestone in the recognition of depression as an issue among sportspeople. After his revelations of mental problems, the England Test cricketers Marcus Trescothick and Andrew Flintoff both admitted to succumbing to bouts of crippling self-doubt, the former quitting England's 2006–7 tour of Australia owing to a stress-related illness (a fate that would befall Jonathan Trott on the Ashes tour seven years later). Neil Lennon, the former Celtic manager, revealed in his autobiography that there were times in his career when depression affected his ability to function. Former Hull City striker Dean Windass was another footballer who spoke eloquently of his struggles. And when they did so, these sportsmen were treated with far more understanding by the wider world than Collymore had been. Certainly none of their workmates told them to think of the money they were earning, pull themselves together and stop behaving like a self-indulgent moaner.

But it was the suicide of the former Leeds and Newcastle United midfielder Gary Speed on 27 January 2012 that did most to change attitudes. This tragic event followed the death in November 2009 of the German national goalkeeper Robert Enke, who had thrown himself in front of a train despite apparently being in possession of all of life's trump cards. The remarkable thing is that there is no evidence that Speed, at the time the Wales manager, was suffering from depression when he took his own life. Indeed at the inquest, his former doctor at Sheffield United suggested that Speed was among the most mentally robust characters he had ever worked with. So uncertain was he as to Speed's motivation, the coroner recorded a narrative verdict.*

Nobody, though, kills themselves without reason. Especially not someone as outwardly successful as the former Leeds, Newcastle and Bolton midfielder, a man who appeared blessed with every physical and material advantage life could offer. Indeed, less than twenty-four hours before his wife found her husband hanging in their garage, Speed had appeared, relaxed and smiling, on BBC TV's *Football Focus* and then watched his old club Newcastle play Manchester United at Old Trafford with his former team-mate Alan Shearer. The most plausible explanation for his desperation was that he was suffering from clinical depression but had spent his career finding strategies to disguise his affliction. Instead of seeking proper help, instead of finding a way through the problem, he hid it to the point of despair.

> Instead of seeking proper help he hid it to the point of despair.

After Speed's suicide, the Professional Footballers' Association circulated a flier to all members giving advice, informing players that depression is not a weakness and that trying to hide its symptoms only exacerbates a person's problems. It gave a list of numbers of those who can help. For the first time, here was official recognition of the issue. As Dean Windass says, talking about it is the best way to confront depression. Even if talking about it is the last thing you want to do.

Collymore – now a successful broadcaster – long ago buried the hatchet with Gregory. He continues to suffer occasional recurrences of the condition. But mental-health professionals have acknowledged that the very fact he came out into the open about his depression back in the late 1990s has been of huge significance in the treatment

---

*A verdict available to coroners in which the circumstances of a death are recorded without attributing the cause to a named individual.

of the disease, not just in football but across society. It gave it far greater prominence, opened up media discussion and generally increased public awareness. And for many a sufferer, to see someone as apparently blessed as Collymore publicly admitting to being afflicted was a huge boost. Knowing that you are not alone, that you are not cast adrift, and most importantly that you are not to blame, is of enormous assistance in tackling the condition.

Gregory was not to know, but the ironic consequence of his sneering at Collymore is that a major mental-health issue is now much more widely understood. And football managers are now far more attuned to their players' psychological state.

PART V

THE SECOND HALF UNFOLDS

1999–2012

1999 'Football: bloody hell.'

Alex Ferguson, Camp Nou, Barcelona, 26 May 1999.

In his time as the finest accumulator of silverware the English game has ever known, Alex Ferguson was renowned for many things: his temper, his ferocious competitiveness, his unscrupulous manipulation, his elephantine memory for perceived slights, his enthusiasm for financial reward. But what was revealed in the aftermath of his side's astonishing victory against Bayern Munich in the 1999 Champions League final was the characteristic that went to the very core of his make-up. As he stood, glassy-eyed, grinning, hugging those around him, uttering over and again the phrase that came to be associated the most glorious season of his most glorious career, one thing became abundantly clear: this was a football romantic.

When he arrived at Old Trafford from Aberdeen to replace Ron Atkinson as manager in November 1986, the first thing Ferguson did was study the history of Manchester United. He absorbed everything that had been written about the club, hoovering up the tales of its historic commitment to youth, of the desire for glory in European competition, of the innate requirement for the team to entertain its followers with the free-flowing football played by local boys.

It took him a while to get there (see page 157), but once Ferguson started winning he ensured he did so in a manner that conformed to Old Trafford's most cherished traditions. By 1999, the finest team that he assembled in his time as United boss was at its glorious, swashbuckling best. Fergie's team of all the talents boasted the exotic, the quixotic and the very expensive. He had happily broken the British transfer record to bring in Roy Keane (£3.75 million from Nottingham Forest), Andy Cole (£7 million from Nottingham Forest) and Dwight

Yorke (£12.6 million from Villa). Only Alan Shearer – Tyneside-bound for £15 million – eluded the ambitious Scotsman's purchasing power. He had balanced them with bargain-basement buys: the Danish 'keeper Peter Schmeichel (from Brøndby), Denis Irwin (from Oldham) and Ole Gunnar Solskjaer (from Molde in Norway). But at the heart of the squad were the six home-grown lads he had promoted from the youth team, the half-dozen Alan Hansen had once disparaged (see page 195), the boys who characterised what his club was about.

Ryan Giggs, Paul Scholes, Nicky Butt, David Beckham and the Neville brothers had been instrumental in clinching Ferguson's third 'double' as United manager. With the 1998–9 Premiership title and 1999 FA Cup already won – despite the attentions of Arsène Wenger's brilliant first Arsenal team (the previous season's double winners; see pages 213–16) – they had arrived in Barcelona for the Champions League final with a unique achievement still on the cards: to become the first English team ever to win the treble.

And they were not alone in their journey from Manchester. Officially, United were allocated 38,000 spaces in Barcelona's giant arena. But at least 55,000 supporters turned up, many paying up to £600 a ticket from the Manc touts patrolling Las Ramblas. The sense of belonging that day was tangible. In every bar and every restaurant, there were people bound by affection for the Reds and their young core. They came from all backgrounds and income groups, people who in normal circumstances would never have breathed the same air. There were monied Sloanes and working-class blokes, the posh and the poor, Mancunians and Southerners. People of all races, several sexes and a huge variety of sizes. Of the tens of thousands of Red fans gathered in the Catalan capital, maybe as many as half a dozen approached the Camp Nou sober.

The mood among these beery, cheery fans was very different from the one that had characterised European nights in the 1970s and 1980s. This footballing occasion brought nothing like the violent

> Don't you dare come back here unless you have given everything to make sure you don't lose.

excesses in Turin described in Bill Buford's *Among the Thugs* (see pages 127–30). Regular European travellers, the United fans were drunk but not disorderly, loud but not disrespectful, boisterous but not confrontational.

These were the people Ferguson hoped to uplift. Although for ninety minutes, it did not look as though he would. Bayern – a side bristling with seasoned German internationals including Lothar Matthäus, Oliver Kahn and Markus Babbel – led at half-time thanks to a goal by Mario Basler. Ferguson needed all his motivational skills to rouse his team – with several of its finer talents played out of position – from what was a distinctly uninspired, un-United display. Unlike the time in 1994 when he had shouted at Butt for giving away possession in this very same stadium ('You've fucking lost me the European Cup, Butt. Are you happy?') he was measured in the dressing room, calm and to the point. Repeating an observation he had heard the former player Steve Archibald once make about his own experience of failure in the competition with Barcelona in 1986, he told his players:

> If you lose, you'll go up to collect loser's medals and you'll be six feet away from the European Cup. But you won't be able to touch it. I want you to think about the fact you'll have been so close to it and for many of you that will be the closest you'll ever get. And you will hate the thought for the rest of your lives. Don't you dare come back here unless you have given everything to make sure you don't lose.

Initially, his words appeared to have had little effect. As the second half progressed rapidly towards its conclusion, Bayern remained in control; United's chance looked to be slipping away.

Like many of the reporters covering the game, with eighty-five minutes gone and United still behind, I had all but completed a piece for the first edition of my paper which lamented that the treble had been an impossible dream. In it, I dwelt on the players' exhaustion and blamed Ferguson for the defeat because of his poor team selection. It was never printed. Other media Mystic Megs were not so fortunate, and Ferguson is said to have kept a selection of the negative first editions as a handy *aide-mémoire* of those who slighted him. It was not just the media, however, who assumed it was over. As the ninety minutes drew to a conclusion, as the fourth official held up a board saying only three more would be added, George Best had left the stadium looking for a bar, unable to face watching his team lose. We should have known better. As Clive Tyldesley put it on the ITV commentary: 'United have to score. They always score.'

With time seemingly gone, United won a corner from which Teddy Sheringham, on as substitute for Yorke, scrambled the ball home from close range. The strike was timed at 90:36 minutes. From the kick-off, on the bench Ferguson's assistant Steve McClaren was yelling at the manager to re-arrange the team, get them back into shape for extra time. But Ferguson wasn't listening. He was watching Denis Irwin hump the ball forward, where it spun off a Bayern player for another corner. Beckham took it. Sheringham flicked it on. And Solskjaer, reacting faster than his dumbfounded, traumatised, statuesque Bayern markers, stuck out his right leg to prod the ball into the roof of the net. The match clock read 92:17. Peter Schmeichel cartwheeled in delight in his penalty area; the Bayern players, slumped and shattered, could not bestir themselves for the game's dying seconds. 'Name on the trophy,' yelled Tyldesley.

Down on the pitch Sammy Kuffour, Bayern's Ghanaian centre-back, pounded the turf with his fists. Other Bayern players lay flat on the ground, utterly spent, overwhelmed by the

United have to score. They always score.

suddenness of what had befallen them. They had led for eighty-four minutes, then seen their chance for immortality snatched from them in less than three minutes of added time.

When the whistle went seconds after Solskjaer's winner, on the touchline, Ferguson did his trademark arrhythmic dad-dance in celebration. And he didn't stop dancing for the rest of the night, dancing with anyone he saw, dancing with newsmen, UEFA officials, club directors; a woman whom he passed in the corridor of the hotel where the celebratory party was to be held was whisked off her feet for an impromptu victory waltz. The manager was delirious. And to everyone he met he repeated his assessment: 'Football, bloody hell.' What he realised that evening was that the game had unique properties, capable of delivering torment or euphoria within a heartbeat. That night in Barcelona was the pinnacle, the very apex of what the game could produce. As it lived up to its romantic potential and beyond, football had given him a moment of unsurpassable joy. Even as he said those words, Ferguson knew he was unlikely to match that feeling ever again.

2000 'SUPER CALEY GO BALLISTIC CELTIC ARE ATROCIOUS'

Headline in *The Scottish Sun* the day after Inverness Caledonian Thistle's 3–1 win in the Scottish Cup at Parkhead, 8 February 2000.

Britain's tabloid newspapers have long relished their power to hasten a football manager's dismissal. Graham Taylor was finished as England manager the moment he was likened to a root vegetable (see pages 175–9), Don Revie before him was browbeaten into seeking alternative employment by a ferociously antagonistic popular press. In the history of the game, however, John Barnes is probably the only boss to have been hurried on his way by a piece of Mary Poppins-inspired word play. When it came to Barnes's career at Celtic, it was the pun wot done him.

Barnes, the silky-smooth Liverpool and England winger, had taken over at Parkhead in the summer of 1999. He arrived promising to turn Celtic into a paradigm of passing football. He said he would bring a continental swagger to the place. He certainly brought continental quantities of backing staff; one reporter viewing the dug-out for Barnes's first game in charge, crammed as it was with physios, fitness coaches and dieticians, said it was so full it resembled a bus stop during a drivers' strike.

Indeed, the Glasgow press were largely sceptical. It was not just that Barnes was a management newcomer, it was not simply that as a player he was remembered more as an individual than a team man, it was not just that he was young. There was something more in the instant dismissal of his chances; there was undoubtedly a touch of racism. Not so much concerning the colour of his skin. But rather the fact that John Barnes had been an England international.

In the fiercely parochial and protective environs of Scottish football – which means principally Glasgow football – anyone whose worldview does not revolve around the poisonous rivalry of Rangers and Celtic (see pages 198–201) is reckoned to be without the required qualifications to take such a prominent part in the proceedings. Barnes may have been a very fine footballer, but what did he know of Old Firm lore? What would he – an outsider – understand of the fierce sectarian divide? How would he ever be capable of appreciating the fixture's deep cultural significance?

And no matter how much the Celtic directors insisted that this was the point, that by his very distance from Glaswegian footballing tradition he might be able to bring a sense of perspective to the club and thus lead it in a new direction, Barnes was regarded by many within the Glasgow media – and among the Celtic support too – as an interloper.

It didn't help his cause that the performances he elicited from his team were a long way short of the ambition he set himself of restoring the European competitiveness the club once enjoyed. Never mind competing with Barcelona and Bayern Munich, they were struggling to keep pace with Hearts and Aberdeen. As for Rangers, the old enemy was a mile off. Having won the 1999 Scottish Premier Division under Dutch manager Dick Advocaat, Rangers were comfortably on target to bag their eleventh Scottish championship in twelve seasons.

So it was that when his side stuttered and stumbled out of the Scottish Cup to lowly Inverness, Barnes was subject to the press's nuclear option: ridicule by pun. And what a cracker it was too. Not one of the wearisome word-play headlines that accompany virtually every goal by Wayne Rooney ('Roo Beauty' or 'What a Heroo!'). But rather a superb flourish of a one-liner which not only told the reader what had happened but encapsulated the pitiful situation in which Barnes's Celtic now found themselves. Every aspect of the homage to the Shermans (the two brothers behind the *Mary Poppins* score) supported the thrust of the argument. There was praise for the underdog ('Super Caley'); wide-eyed rejoicing at their performance ('go ballistic'), together with – and this was the significant bit – a hefty swipe at Celtic's horribly misfiring team of under-achievers ('Celtic are atrocious').

The headline fizzed round the world, commented on the next morning by breakfast news outlets across Britain and beyond. People with no interest in football chortled and guffawed. For Celtic it doubled the humiliation of defeat, reckoned the worst in thirty years. It made the club look foolish. And it meant Barnes was effectively finished, hammered by a headline. Having enjoyed a mere eight months in charge, he was removed from office two days after the paper was published. He was replaced by Kenny Dalglish, a man of unimpeachable Celtic heritage.

Sub-editors at *The Scottish Sun* were so pleased with their work that they repeated the line years later. In December 2007, when Don Cowie scored the winner for Inverness, this time against a Celtic side managed by Gordon Strachan, it was the scorer of the injury-time victory goal who was name-checked: 'Super Cowie Goes Ballistic, Celtic Are Atrocious'. If it seemed a familiar gag, the headline writers could at least claim they were only plagiarising themselves.

Except they weren't. In the aftermath of the paper's first widely noticed use of the quip, someone on Merseyside pointed to a dog-eared cutting from the *Liverpool Echo,* dating back to the mid-1970s. Reporting on the midfielder Ian Callaghan's majestic contribution to a Liverpool victory against a struggling Queen's Park Rangers, the *Echo's* sub-editors had reached for a line familiar to anyone who had seen Walt Disney's classic: 'Super Cally Goes Ballistic, QPR Atrocious'.

Small comfort to John Barnes, perhaps. But the verbal jugglers in his old Liverpool stamping ground had beaten the Scottish punsters to the gag by nearly three decades.

2000 'I've still got my old school report. It says I was dyslexic, backward, mentally deficient and illiterate – all the qualifications you need to be a football club chairman.'

George Reynolds, chairman of Darlington FC, May 2000.

There have been many crooks in football's directors' box over the years. With all that cash clacking through the turnstiles every week, the boardroom has long been a handy place for anyone looking to launder the proceeds of nefarious activity, a place where assets can be stripped, profits pocketed and corners cut. Take Thaksin Shinawatra at Manchester City, or Carson Yeung at Birmingham City or Ken Richardson, the man who burned down his own club Doncaster Rovers in 1995. None of them are what you might term straight.

But no one has been quite so brazenly bent as George Reynolds, chairman of Darlington FC for five years from 1999. Before he took up the role, Reynolds made no secret of the fact he had convictions for burglary, theft and safe-cracking. He had done two lengthy stints inside in the 1960s and 1970s. On being released from prison the second time, he had built up a fortune in a home-improvements business. By 1999 the Sunderland-supporting businessman featured on the *Sunday Times* rich list, though he reckoned his position of 112th was an insult. He should have been, he said, much higher. After all, Sporty Spice was his neighbour in Hampstead; he had to be somebody if he lived next door to a Spice Girl. This was not a man prone to self-doubt. At the time his business card read: 'George Reynolds, gentleman, entrepreneur, adventurer, maker of money, and utter genius.'

In 1999 he was invited to take over Darlington FC. Where he showed his utter genius by installing 60,000 earthworms on the pitch at Feethams, the club's tumbledown home, in an attempt to improve drainage. So pleased was he with his initiative, he invited Sky Television along to report on the invasion by worms. 'By the time I faced the cameras every seagull from Hartlepool to North Shields had flown in to partake of George Reynolds' barbecue,' he recalls. 'There were so many seagulls on the pitch it looked as though it was covered by snow.' He attempted to divert attention from the birds by telling the Sky reporter he recognised him from prison. Was he a fellow inmate? The interview was abruptly terminated.

George Reynolds, gentleman, entrepreneur, adventurer, maker of money, and utter genius.

Reynolds' appointment may have gone down well with the local birdlife, but it was not hugely popular among the fans, who were immediately suspicious of the motives of the crook who had got his hands on their club. On one occasion, as he and his wife left Feethams after a game, they were obliged to make their way through a hostile gathering of home supporters complaining about his stewardship. He heard a commotion behind him and looked round to see that someone had upended a wheelie bin on his wife's head. All that was visible were her legs sticking out of the bottom.

Reynolds popularity among the playing staff was hardly enhanced when he admitted – in advance of the annual round of salary negotiations – that he had bugged the dressing room to discover his players' intentions. 'First guy comes in and I knew he was going to ask me for £35 grand,' he explains. 'Before he could say a word I said "if you think I'm going to pay you 35 grand you've got another thing coming. Best you'll get is 25." And he walked out of the room convinced I was psychic.'

Despite their misgivings, he vowed to win the supporters round.

Reckoning it was Feethams, worms notwithstanding, that was holding the club back, as part of his stated aim to steer Darlo into the Premier League he announced he would build a new 27,000-seater stadium on the edge of the town. Given that the average crowd Darlington attracted in the fourth tier of English football was under 4,000 it was an ambitious project. But he claimed the place would transform the club's fortunes, and vowed to create a team to play there that would bring in the crowds. He offered Paul Gascoigne £1000 a week to turn out for them, to which Gazza replied that sort of money wouldn't keep him in Mars bars. He reached an agreement with the former Newcastle striker Faustino Asprilla to play for a more substantial return. But, after arriving in a helicopter on the pitch ahead of a match, the Colombian took one look at the contractual small print and headed straight back to Bogotá.

Still, the stadium was built. Christened, with characteristic modesty, the Reynolds Arena, it opened at the start of the 2003–4 season, attracting a crowd of 11,600 to the first game against Kidderminster Harriers. Unfortunately for the chairman, he was only able to enjoy the run of the place's lavish hospitality areas for nine months before he was arrested in June 2004 on money-laundering charges. He had been stopped by police and found to be carrying £500,000 in cash in the boot of his Mercedes. Subsequent inquiries into his business arrangements suggested he may not have been entirely scrupulous in his tax affairs.

> He wouldn't even know what a tax return was.

Removing the wheelie bin from her head, his wife leapt to his defence. 'He is illiterate and needs people around him to look out for him,' Susan Reynolds insisted. 'He wouldn't even know what a tax return was.' The judge at Newcastle Crown Court was less inclined to regard him as blameless. Summing up the case Judge Whitburn said: 'Your investment in the stadium project cost you your fortune, but it was not quite as altruistic as you make out.' The arena had been built, the judge decided, as an elaborate front for tax evasion and, taking into account his illegal use of company funds to subsidise a lifestyle of pricey cars, choppers and champagne, he sentenced Reynolds to three years' imprisonment.

Still, at least the by-then-former chairman was released in time to see Darlington finally escape the fourth tier of English football: they were relegated to the Conference in 2010. Saddled with debt brought on by the ludicrous white elephant that was the Reynolds Arena, they went into administration and were demoted a further four divisions for financial irregularity. In 2012 they went out of business entirely, reforming as Darlington 1883, owned by the fans and playing their football in Northern Football League Division One. The phoenix club don't, incidentally, use the Reynolds Arena. Ownerless and tenant-free, that sits on the outskirts of town, locked up and mildewed, a sad memorial to one man's *folie de grandeur*.

As for Reynolds himself, in June 2013, by now touting himself as an after-dinner speaker telling yarns about his time in football's boardrooms, he was in court once again. This time he was accused of breaching minimum-wage legislation in his chain of sandwich bars, in which it was alleged some full-time workers were being paid no more than £100 a week. Sometimes it appears that reputation does not lie.

2000 'They have a few drinks and probably the prawn sandwiches, and they don't realise what's going on out on the pitch. I don't think some of the people who come to Old Trafford can spell football, never mind understand it.'

Roy Keane talking to BBC Radio after Manchester United's Champions League tie with Dynamo Kiev, 8 November 2000.

Roy Keane was at his dismissive best after his team had negotiated their way through a tricky group stage tie to qualify for the Champions League knock-out. The combative, opinionated Manchester United captain's observation about the sound of silence emanating from the Old Trafford stands, however, was not an original one; his manager Sir Alex Ferguson had complained about the lack of support from the crowd during home matches the previous season. Keano was in a long line of those who lamented the way that what had once been the most fearsome of atmospheres, one which had shaken the building to its foundations on European nights in the past, had rapidly diminished over the previous decade. This was not mere wistful nostalgia. This was fact: at Old Trafford, they weren't singing any more.

And it wasn't a problem confined to Manchester, either. At Arsenal the home support was frequently derided as 'The Highbury Library'. At Stamford Bridge the once-fearsome Shed had gone quiet. Across the Premier League, frequently the only noise to be heard at games came from the gaggle of away fans. 'Shall we sing a song for you?' was chanted by visiting supporters, as they relished making disparaging remarks about a thin, desultory atmosphere they recognised only too well from their own home grounds.

In the past English football was renowned for the noise its fans made. Teams turning up at Anfield in the 1970s would quake at the roar emanating from the Kop. Now even that stand had gone quiet, the singing of the Liverpool anthem 'You'll Never Walk Alone' before games stage-managed via the public address system. And the players had noticed it, too: Keane was voicing a growing concern. At times he and his colleagues needed the adrenaline gee-up provided by the supporters. Yet frequently in the Premier League era, they played in a silence so complete the only noise came from their manager, yelling intemperate instructions from the touchline.

For many fans the reason for the aural decline was simple: the Taylor Report (see page xv) was to blame. While no one would argue against the need for stadiums to be updated and upgraded and for the supporters' safety no longer to be compromised, the legislative insistence on the removal of terraces had utterly changed the watching experience. Now that everyone was obliged to sit where their season ticket was allocated, no longer could groups of like-minded fans gather to chant. And sit was the operative word. Anyone who stood up to engage in encouragement was immediately told to sit down by dozens of those behind whose view was being blocked.

Envious glances were cast by English supporters at Germany, where safe-standing areas, with crash barriers on every row, had been introduced into newly built grounds. In the Bundesliga the fan culture remained sacrosanct. At Dortmund's Westfalenstadion, the South Terrace – the so-called Yellow Wall – provides an astonishing backdrop to any game Borussia Dortmund play, with 25,000 fans belting out their support for the team. 'Every time you walk out onto the pitch it's like being born again, except with a lot more applause,' the Dortmund manager Jürgen Klopp once said of the

> Every time you walk out onto the pitch it's like being born again, except with a lot more applause.

atmosphere there. 'You come out, and it just explodes.'

But it is not solely a matter of accommodation. What has happened in English football since the arrival of the Premier League and the implementation of the Taylor Report has been a systematic social cleansing of the game. It may not have been deliberate, it may have been the result of no more than financial opportunism on the part of club directors, but the prodigious increase in the price of attending games has led to an entirely different demographic sitting in the stands. If nothing else, the regulars are much older: a season ticket is beyond the pocket of most teenagers. In 1967, when the Stretford End swayed and sang at the sight of Best, Law and Charlton, the average age of those watching from that part of Old Trafford was seventeen. By the time Keane made his observation, it was forty-one.

Keane, though, sensed something else. In his reductive phrase 'have a few drinks and probably the prawn sandwiches' he was referring to the rise in corporate entertaining. A huge number of those attending games were now doing so as part of packages, bought by business associates to entertain clients. They didn't just sit in the ring of glass-fronted boxes around the stadium's upper tier, either. The best seats in the Stretford End had been given over to those who liked a nibble and a glass of something interesting with their football. Keane's point was that these match-goers were consumers, not contributors. They enjoyed the atmosphere, as long as someone else provided it. These were not the hard-core obsessives who once dominated the Old Trafford crowd, they were passing trade, treating the football as they might a night at a pop concert or an afternoon at the racing, sitting back and waiting to be entertained.

Such was the accuracy of Roy Keane's remark, 'prawn-sandwich brigade' quickly established itself as the term of choice for disparaging the well-heeled supporter. Everyone used it. It appeared as a line in the 2009 film version of David Peace's *The Damned United*, even though that was set some twenty-five years before the phrase was coined.

Pithy as his observation was, though, there were ironies in what Keane said. Not least that the principal beneficiaries in the enormous rise in gate receipts generated by the arrival of the prawn-sandwich brigade were players like him, who by 2000 were enjoying salaries matched only by the highest fliers in the City of London. There was something else too. The moment Keane said it, curious reporters made inquiries as to the menu on offer in the corporate sections of Old Trafford. What they found was that no one in the expensive seats was offered anything as derisory as a prawn sandwich. The food being served was way posher than that.

As a fellow diner once said to me during a pre-game meal at the Etihad Stadium, in which we were treated to what the menu described as a 'Deconstructed Sunday lunch of pulled pork and fondant potato towers': 'It's not a football match, this. It's the final of bloody *Masterchef.*'

> It's not a football match, this.
> It's the final of bloody *Masterchef.*

2001 'At 6.45 a group of Millwall supporters were taken under escort towards the stadium. As they passed a public house, a group of some thirty to forty males came out and bottles were thrown and pub windows smashed. After a while it became apparent that both groups were from Millwall and each thought the other were Bristol City supporters.'

Extract from the National Criminal Intelligence Service (NCIS) report on Bristol City's Division Two match with Millwall, Ashton Gate, Bristol, 17 March 2001.

Back in the 1970s, when football hooliganism first became a subject of interest to the media, a film crew from *Panorama* spent some time following a bunch of Millwall supporters. The young lads called themselves 'F-Troop' and on the terraces they wore operating gowns and masks liberated from St Thomas's Hospital, where one of them worked as a porter. On one occasion the cameras tracked them to an away match at Bristol Rovers. The most vocal member of the crew, a chap called Harry the Dog, explained somewhat disingenuously that while his cohort didn't look for trouble they were ready for it whenever it occurred. Perhaps unaware of geographical specifics, as his minibus headed westward down the M4, Harry explained that he and his mates were not going to take any insult that day from the home team supporters: 'If any of them Northern bastards...'

It seems from that NCIS report that twenty-five years on Bristol was still a source of confusion to followers of the southeast London club; so befuddled were they by West Country ways (or perhaps the local cider), they were fighting amongst themselves.

Just as football had evolved over the years, so had football hooliganism. As it became ever more difficult to stage a scrap at football matches, as grounds were revamped into grand all-seater stadiums with every corner covered by CCTV, as police surveillance became ever more sophisticated, so fighting around the game became a more isolated pursuit. Although largely invisible by the turn of the century, rowdyism didn't disappear entirely. It just narrowed its range.

Intriguingly, as it became a minority preoccupation, so the average age of those involved seemed to rise. It appeared that those still addicted to fighting in the street were the same bunch who had kicked off back in the 1970s and 1980s, when every game, it seemed, took place against a backdrop of breaking glass. When a group of West Ham fans were arrested in 2012 for organising an off-piste meet with some Millwall followers, the ages of those picked up were forty-one, forty-three, forty-six and fifty-six. These were not teenaged hotheads who were issuing threats by text. These were Hell's Granddads. For such superannuated yobs, dressed in their Stone Island anoraks and peaked caps pulled down to cover their bald patches, a rumble at the game was a chance to relive the adrenaline-charged escapades of their youth. This was the opportunity for instant nostalgia, to engage in football as it used to be, before money arrived to spoil the fun.

> These were not teenaged hotheads who were issuing threats by text. These were Hell's Granddads.

Although they may have got it wrong outside that Bristol pub in 2001, the Millwall old boys were still more than capable of causing a stir. Even as the game rapidly gentrified they maintained their fearsome tradition of fomenting unrest: no one liked them and they didn't care. In May 2002, after their team lost a Championship play-off game to Birmingham City, the mayhem around the New Den was described by the BBC as one of the worst cases of civil disorder seen in Britain in recent times. A police spokeswoman said that forty-seven officers and twenty-four horses were injured. So significant was the damage to its resources, the Metropolitan Police considered suing the club.

A League Cup tie at West Ham in 2009, too, saw the kind of large-scale violence that took many observers back to 1985, when Millwall fans – augmented by cohorts from other London clubs – had rioted at Luton Town. At Upton Park, twenty fans were injured, one of them brutally stabbed. Then in 2013, during the FA Cup semi-final at Wembley against Wigan Athletic, trouble at the Millwall end flared up throughout the second half. This time, rather like the Bristol pub incident, the Lions fans appeared to be fighting amongst themselves. The arrival of the police created a new focus for violence, which went on for at least half an hour. The live television audience was witness to pictures of a man in his thirties with his face covered in blood. Another man who would not see thirty-five again was tracked by the camera as he gleefully ran away from the action with a purloined policeman's cap hidden under his jacket. In the middle of it all, a young girl, there at Wembley to enjoy her first semi-final, stood sobbing in the ugly confusion as the older generation turned back the clock. At the football, she was discovering, no one could pretend adults know best.

▶ A permanently riled Roy Keane prepares to issue unlikely anatomical instructions to his international manager, June 2002.

▼ Not a man for a crisis: a passion-free Sven-Göran Eriksson looks on as England's players respond tearfully to defeat in the World Cup, 2002.

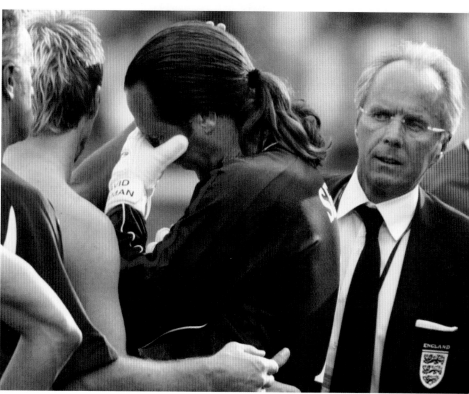

▲ José and his merino coat, on the touchline
with Chelsea, first time around, 2005.

▲ No way to bow out: Zinedine Zidane, in his last ever game, engages in some banter with Italy's Marco Materazzi, World Cup final, Berlin, 8 July 2006.

▶ Abbey Clancy makes a heroic effort to talk on the same level as her husband Peter Crouch, 2012.

▲ Sian Massey points
the way to the exit for
Richard Keys and
Andy Gray, January 2011.

▶ I am Zlatan: the ever
modest Ibrahimović
auditioning for the role as
the next Bond villain, 2012.

Fly
Emirates

▲ Djbril Cissé leaves no inch un-inked in his race to be recognised as football's most decorated body.

◄ Lost for words: Fernando Torres's late goal for Chelsea in the Champions League semi-final against Barcelona, Camp Nou, 25 April 2012.

▼ Sergio Agüero's late, late show for Manchester City, Etihad Stadium, 13 May 2012.

▲ David Moyes is welcomed to Old Trafford, August 2013. Within eight months, the banner and the man it celebrated were gone.

▼ Nicolas Anelka engages in gesture politics, Upton Park, 28 December 2013.

▲ Washed down with a nice Chianti: Luis Suárez dines out on an Italian, Natal, 24 June 2014.

▼ Mario Götze celebrates becoming the first substitute to score in a World Cup final, Rio de Janeiro, 13 July 2014. Behind him Thomas Müller appears to be channelling his inner Luis Suárez.

2002

'The face of an angel and the bum of a Greek god. Rumour has it that his tackle is enough to not only take your breath away but possibly do you serious damage.'

Editorial in the magazine *Attitude* when David Beckham appeared on its cover, June 2002.

Just ahead of the 2002 World Cup in Japan and South Korea, Beckham-mania was at its height. Four years on from France 98, when his sending-off in a game against Argentina was widely depicted as an act of treason and a dummy of him was ritually hanged outside a pub in Kent, he had been transformed into the nation's hero. After scoring a wonderful long-range free-kick against Greece to secure qualification, Beckham had enjoyed the best season of his career, his energy, skill and selfless determination marking him out as a singular talent. When he had broken a metatarsal three months before the finals were due to take place, *The Sun* newspaper – one of those which had berated him four years before – printed a picture of his foot on its front page and invited readers to unite in prayer for its speedy recovery. On Beckham did so much depend.

Attitude magazine, meanwhile, photographed a lot more than his foot. The gay-lifestyle publication ran a series of artfully posed semi-naked shots accompanied by breathless prose suggesting unseen glories. On its cover, Beckham beamed beatifically. He took, the world knew well, a very nice picture.

For a footballer, especially the England captain, it was a bold departure. At that point, contrary to every known statistical probability, only one English player had ever revealed themselves to be gay, the tragic Justin Fashanu, who had taken his own life after being accused of sexual assault by a young footballer he was coaching.

But Beckham had an uncanny natural ability to surf controversy and steer it to his advantage. As he said later about the photoshoot:

> To be honest, I wasn't thinking about politics, or how it might affect attitudes, or how it would be perceived in the future. I was just doing what felt right. I have always had a very open attitude to other people and try to be inclusive. Isn't that what life is about?

That was the thing about Beckham: everybody loved him. He was the most widely renowned sportsman of his generation, his apparent malleability allowing him to be championed by advocates of every lifestyle. In the newspapers, columnists waxed lyrical about his metrosexual qualities, women's magazines trembled at his new-man credentials, gay men went weak at the knee at the thought of what went on inside his sarong. His photogenic smile (there has never been a bad picture taken of him) made him the most commercially sought-after man of his age. Just a month before the pictures appeared in *Attitude*, the film *Bend It Like Beckham* was released, sealing his position as the country's most recognisable popular-cultural figure.

It didn't matter that he had shown absolutely no suggestion of being gay. This, after all, was the country's most celebrated married man. When he got hitched to Victoria theirs was a ceremony that was beyond posh. It was regal. Costing a rumoured half a million pounds, staged in an Irish castle, swathed in episcopal purple, it featured a golden throne for Goldenballs (as his Spice Girl wife referred to him). Now with a growing stable of offspring, not to mention the gorgeous, pouting young women making unproven allegations that they had been participants in affairs with him, he was as hetero as they came. Not, as the editors of *Attitude* cannily appreciated when they used his image to secure their biggest-ever monthly sale, that such reality ever put a stop to fantasising.

'The thing about David Beckham is he can do no wrong,' commented the American cultural blog *Juice with Junior*. 'He has no problem that he has many gay fans, but has never pandered to gay people. We all know he's straight but we love him, the kids and Victoria. He's a Teflon gay icon.'

It was a facility which had substantial financial implications; every brand wanted to be associated with a man of such wide-ranging appeal. With his commercial career cannily guided by Simon Fuller, the man behind the Spice Girls, the rewards for Beckham were substantial. For more than a decade he has generated huge income, far more than any of his English contemporaries. In June 2013, eleven years after his *Attitude* moment and in his final season as a player, *Forbes* magazine listed him as the highest-earning footballer in the world, with an annual income – thanks to his commercial endorsements – in excess of $46 million (£29.3 million). And with his broad smile, impeccable manners and beautifully tailored suits, Beckham appeared to be loving every minute of his celebrity.

> The thing about David Beckham is he can do no wrong.

There was one person, however, who baulked at all the attention the footballer was getting. In 2002, his manager at Manchester United believed the ballyhoo surrounding him was distracting him from his principal purpose: playing for United. Alex Ferguson was convinced the player's association with Victoria had blurred his focus. Never mind that the couple remained devoted to each other to a degree rarely seen in either football or showbusiness, Ferguson marked her down as an unequivocally bad influence.

'He was never a problem until he got married. He used to go into work with the academy coaches at night time, he was a fantastic young lad,' Ferguson said in 2007. 'Getting married into that entertainment scene was a difficult thing – from that moment, his life was never going to be the same. He is such a big celebrity, football is only a small part.' Ferguson could never understand that. For him, football had to be everything.

The pair were to have a spectacular and brutal falling-out, when, in mid-rant in February 2003, Ferguson kicked a boot in the United dressing room, which flew up and cut his star player above the eye.With much fanfare, including a royal tour of the United States wearing outfits tailored exclusively in white, Beckham moved that summer to Real Madrid.

In his suspicion of the player's celebrity, however, Ferguson was in a dwindling minority. Everyone else appeared to adore him. In Japan, the venue (with South Korea) for the 2002 World Cup, adoration of Beckham was no less intense than in his homeland. One Tokyo website reported on the obsessive devotion of a pair of female Japanese Beckham fans who had spent the tournament camped outside the England team hotel in the hope of catching sight of him. After England had returned home following their quarter-final defeat to Brazil, the twosome discovered which room the object of their desire had been staying in. They checked into it and then photographed each other lovingly licking the lavatory seat. Oddly, those pictures have never appeared on the cover of a magazine.

2002 'Mick, you're a liar... you're a fucking wanker. I didn't rate you as a player, I don't rate you as a manager, and I don't rate you as a person. You're a fucking wanker and you can stick your World Cup up your arse. The only reason I have any dealings with you is that somehow you are the manager of my country. You can stick it up your bollocks.'

Roy Keane addresses the Ireland manager Mick McCarthy during a team meeting at a pre-World Cup training camp, Saipan, 23 May 2002.

It was by a quirk of footballing fate that Roy Keane was in Saipan at all that day. Had Manchester United won their Champions League semi-final against Bayer Leverkusen, he would have played in the final against Real Madrid that very evening and would not have joined up with the Irish until they had arrived in Japan.

But United hadn't won, so Keane, the Irish captain, fetched up in the tiny American protectorate of Saipan seemingly itching for a fight, his mood soured by his club's inability to overcome entirely beatable opposition and provide him the chance to play in a European final after being denied by suspension in 1999. He was stroppy and niggly from the moment he arrived at the camp, a short acclimatisation stop-off before the squad headed to Tokyo for the 2002 World Cup. He immediately found fault with the accommodation, the training pitch, the travel arrangements. He had a go at the goalkeeping coach for apparently letting the 'keepers off lightly in a training session. He told an Irish pressman this would be his last outing in Irish colours, he would retire once the competition was over. He had had enough, he added, of the relentless amateurism of the Irish set-up.

And the man he chose as the target to unleash his ire was his international manager, Mick McCarthy. McCarthy had soon got wind of his captain's volcanic displeasure. The bluff Yorkshireman, who had enjoyed a lengthy international career as one of Jack Charlton's 'Granny Rule' Anglos (see pages 142–5), thought it best not to let the discontent grow. He announced there was to be a clear-the-air team meeting at which grievances could be expressed, without recrimination. It did not take long for the grievances to surface. At the meeting, Keane's opening remarks were brisk, targeted and devastating. Never mind no confidence in his manager, he made clear his contempt in the most contorted of physiological instructions: 'You can stick it up your bollocks.' These, it turned out, were his last words as an international footballer. As last words go, no one could deny they were memorable.

After he had stormed from the meeting room, Keane rang his club manager. Alex Ferguson warned him of the consequences of walking out on his country, warned him of the traumatic effect the inevitable bad publicity might have on his children and urged him to talk the issue through with McCarthy immediately. 'As bad as the conditions were, Roy shouldn't have pushed his anger to such levels. But that was Roy. He was a man of extremes,' Ferguson wrote in his autobiography. There was to be no chance of a meeting of minds. McCarthy, perhaps not surprisingly believing his position to have been fundamentally undermined, called a press conference at which he announced that his captain was to be sent home with immediate effect for breaching squad discipline. Cue pandemonium.

> That was Roy. He was a man of extremes.

As Keane made his way to the airport, where a private jet chartered by his club had been arranged to bring him back to Manchester, in

Ireland the country went collectively berserk. No issue – not the Catholic Church, not divorce, abortion or the IRA, not even Sinéad O'Connor – has so divided the population as this, the nation's most gifted footballer walking out on his team.

For roughly half the country it was an act of unforgivable treachery, jeopardising hopes in the tournament on some prima donna pretext, whining about a bumpy training pitch and the dirty condition of the bibs when he should be have been subsuming his ego into the wider cause of ensuring the Irish team had a good World Cup. For the other half it was an act of selfless principle, a man prepared to sacrifice his own ambition for the betterment of others.

Geography played a part in the reaction. In Cork, Keane's hometown, his walk-out was perceived as a regionalist act of defiance against an autocratic Dublin-centric system; he was reckoned a revolutionary hero, a Michael Collins for the twenty-first century. In Dublin, meanwhile, he was dismissed by many as no more than a thuggish hick. 'What do Roy Keane and Michael Collins have in common?' ran the Dublin joke furring up the nation's in-boxes. 'They are both traitors from Cork.'*

In Saipan, the Irish football press corps, expecting to do little more than report on the occasional thigh strain, worked as they never had before to feed an insatiable news media. Over the next few days there were countless rumours that a rapprochement might be reached. McCarthy, it was reported, was prepared to accept the player back, provided he apologised. Outside his house in Cheshire, Keane was photographed on a daily basis taking his dog out for a walk. To the pack of reporters who followed his every speedy step, he said nothing. Though his steely glare suggested he was not a man ready to admit culpability.

---

*After successfully withstanding British attempts to crush the Irish nationalist insurgency of 1919–21, Collins notoriously went to war with his former IRA colleagues when they rejected the terms of the independence treaty that he negotiated with Britain in 1921.

For ten days this was the biggest story of the World Cup, an episode that came close to sparking verbal civil war in Ireland. Even Keane's dog Triggs became a star. A Labrador cross seen lolloping out in front of him every morning on every news channel, Triggs was given his own column in a newspaper, ghosted by the satirist Paul Howard. The columns were eventually collected in a single volume which topped the Irish book sales charts: Triggs ended up with a best-seller.

But then, just as McCarthy and Keane appeared to be reaching compromise, the rest of the Irish players made it clear they would rather he wasn't recalled. A vote was taken and most – reckoning him a black cloud at the best of times – thought it best if Keane stayed away. He might have been a good player, probably the best they had, but they would enjoy the competition a lot more without him glowering at them.

McCarthy, after disentangling his inner organs, tried to maintain a philosophical air as his team prepared for the competition in Japan (in a training facility, incidentally, reckoned the second-most luxurious at the tournament, after the one the French had taken). Though even then he seemed aware that the incident would come back to haunt him. As he put it at a press conference ahead of his team's tie with Nigeria. 'I'll probably be walking down the street with my dog and flat cap and ferret in my pocket in Barnsley at eighty, and someone shouts "oh there's that bloke who sent him home from the World Cup." '

As for Keane, it was not long before he discovered what it was like to patrol the other side of football's cultural divide. After falling out with Ferguson, he retired from the game and became a manager. Following spells in charge of Sunderland (2006–8) and Ipswich (2009–11) – and a turn on television as ITV's curmudgeon-in-chief – he was appointed assistant to Martin O'Neill as manager of the Irish national side in October 2013. Keane had clearly been forgiven by the authorities he had so vigorously bad-mouthed eleven years earlier.

Quite what McCarthy, then managing Ipswich, felt about Keane's elevation we were never to find out. Asked six times at a pre-match press conference for his view on the appointment, he refused to comment. But we can guess what he thought. And it probably involved bollocks.

2002 'We needed Winston Churchill and we got Iain Duncan Smith.'

Gareth Southgate on Sven-Göran Eriksson's half-time team talk during England's World Cup quarter-final loss to Brazil, Shizuoka, Japan, 21 June 2002.

Tactics win football matches. Speedy analysis wins matches. Strategy wins matches. Forget the Henry V tradition, or the stirring battlefield oration of William Wallace or General George S. Patton, what can best make a difference in a dressing room at half-time is cogent, clear-headed, panic-free instruction. Though nobody ever remembers that. In English football, what everyone remembers are words.

And whatever words Sven-Göran Eriksson, the Swede in charge of England, may have issued on a baking hot evening in Shizuoka were immediately lost in the collective memory. Eriksson's side were playing Brazil in the quarter-final of the 2002 World Cup. They had gone into the lead through Michael Owen's sharp opener, but the Brazilians had equalised just as the half-time whistle was about to sound. Psychologically it was a bad time to concede. When they arrived in the dressing room the England players looked as if they had had the air removed from their lungs, as if their bubble had been burst.

These were young men brought up in a tradition that values

rhetoric, a tradition in which words carry a message and a value beyond their literal meaning. What these English footballers needed as they slumped onto their benches was something to clear the head of negative thoughts, something to help them refocus, something to restore their flagging morale.

According to Southgate, such a something did not come. Instead of a speech to rival the wartime eloquence of Churchill, there were little more than a few mumbles from the softly spoken Swede known in his homeland as 'Svennis'. They were all looking to Eriksson to appeal to the bulldog spirit of never-say-die English resolve, but Southgate reckoned that what they heard was about as inspiring as a speech by Iain Duncan Smith, the uncharismatic leader of the Conservative Party from 2001 to 2003 – a man apparently permanently afflicted by a frog in his throat, and a politician capable of curing an epidemic of insomnia with every vocal intervention.

Sven simply failed to rise to the occasion. Which was no surprise to some. After all, this was the man who, after once stirring the emotions of the fiery Nancy Dell'Olio, was given a resounding thumbs-down by another of his conquests, his fellow Swede and sometime television presenter Ulrika Jonsson: a night with Sven, claimed the former weathergirl, was 'as dull as putting together Ikea flat-pack furniture'.

However, when Eriksson first took charge of England following the resignation of Kevin Keegan in 2001, his hands-off, light-touch, treat-the-lads-as-grown-ups approach was seen as a necessary corrective to the fearsome sergeant-major tradition of English management. Compared to Keegan, who admitted when it came to tactical analysis he occupied the shallow end of the gene pool, Sven – with his background of managing major club sides in Portugal and Italy – seemed sophisticated. His approach was to let the players get on with it. And for a while it seemed to work.

But occasionally, just occasionally – and especially on this occasion – continental sophistication was not appropriate. What was required was a return to the old school. The expectation from the players was that the manager would, in a match as vital as this, in a game carrying the hopes of an entire nation, try to revive their performance with his words. That was what Alf Ramsey had done in 1966 with

> Occasionally, just occasionally – continental sophistication was not appropriate.

his speech before extra time: 'you've won it once now go out and win it again'. That was what Alex Ferguson had done in 1999 at the Camp Nou (see page 234). That is what Cloughie and Don Revie – even Neil Warnock – had done.

What Southgate – these days no doubt getting all verbal in his role in charge of England's Under-21s – was hoping for was a touch of the American football coach played by Al Pacino in the movie *Every Given Sunday*. He wanted a bit of Pacino's 'inch by inch'. He wanted some 'we're in hell right now, we can stay here, or we can fight our way back'. He yearned to be sent out for the second half with 'in any fight it's the guy who's willing to die who'll take that inch' echoing in his ears. But such words were not forthcoming.

José Mourinho, a manager who is second to none in his technical and tactical preparation, would never gainsay the value of saying the right thing at the right time. Even if it is not him doing the saying. After a Chelsea victory against eventual title-winners Manchester City at the Etihad in February 2014, he revealed that the stirring half-time oration which had inspired his players to victory had been given by Billy McCulloch, the team masseur:

> I didn't speak. It was Billy who spoke to the team. He was screaming so much in Scottish – grrr, grrr, grrr – that I didn't understand him. I am serious. But the players were clapping. It was Billy's team-talk and he was fantastic. I didn't understand but it looks like the players understood.

Never mind that McCulloch is from Swindon, the point still stands: at certain times in a dressing room what players need and want is the right words. But instead of delivering the right words, Sven remained his usual self: enigmatic, aloof and disengaged, mumbling gently in his accent that sounded ever more reminiscent of the Muppets' Swedish chef. And England, without a 'Band of Brothers' moment to inspire them to glory, faded in the second half, losing to a ten-man Brazil, missing their clearest opportunity in a generation to reach the summit of the game.

But if Eriksson was to blame, he was not prepared to take responsibility. In a newspaper interview ten years later, he was asked his reaction to Southgate's comment. 'I gave a normal team-talk,' he said to *The Times*. 'When we defeated Germany 5–1 [in 2001] I was not Winston Churchill then, either. It's stupid of Southgate and that's it. I know what I've done in football and I have my style. If it's not good enough for Southgate, I can live with that.'

> If it's not good enough for Southgate, I can live with that.

So there you have it, it was a normal team talk: maybe that was Southgate's point. This was an occasion which demanded not the ordinary but the extraordinary.

2002

'**Michael Owen has already** given me a nickname. It happened quite naturally in training. It's Dioufy.'

El Hadji Diouf, Liverpool's newest signing, reveals how he is adapting to life in the Premier League, August 2002.

It is possible that England's diminutive striker was making a subtle cultural reference. Sensing his new Senegalese colleague's artistic temperament, maybe the nickname Owen handed the newcomer to the Liverpool dressing room was a cunning allusion to the French Fauvist painter Raoul Dufy. But probably not. More likely Owen was reaching for the footballer's standard nickname mechanism: if in doubt, add a 'y'.

In English football, the rules of the nickname are clear: long names are shortened (Jamie Carragher becomes Carra) while short names are lengthened, generally by the addition of a 'y' (thus Ryan Giggs is invariably Giggsy). For Owen there was no question – when the young striker arrived from the French club Lens – but that he should be welcomed in the traditional manner: Dioufy he was to be.

A pity that Owen had not done a modicum of research on his new colleague. If he had, he would have learned that Diouf already had an impressive nickname. In France he had acquired the memorable soubriquet of 'Serial Killer'. This was not a suggestion that in his spare time he had a habit of stalking the streets with a large hunting knife, persuading passengers waiting for the night bus that he might give them a lift home. Nor was it a nod to the fact that, as a youth team player, he had crashed a team-mate's car into a wall. Rather, it was

The former Derby defender Christian Dailly was known as Parish Newsletter.

a reference to an alleged killer instinct in front of goal. Which was somewhat misleading, given that in four seasons in French football his combined goals tally was fewer than twenty. Maybe, after all, Dioufy *was* more appropriate.

If Dioufy's Liverpool dressing-room sobriquet seems less than inspired, not every footballing nickname is so impoverished. There have been some magnificent monikers bestowed on British footballers. Here are five of the best:

- The former Derby, Blackburn and West Ham defender Christian Dailly was known as *Parish Newsletter*.

- The erstwhile Crystal Palace, QPR and Watford defender Fitz Hall was universally called *One Size*.

- The moment he signed for Everton from Rangers in 1994, where he had developed a sizeable reputation for drink-fuelled excess, Duncan Ferguson was dubbed *Duncan Disorderly* (though probably not to his face).

- When he was on loan at Manchester City from his parent club Atlético Madrid, Kiki Musampa was dubbed by team-mates, with a nod to the seasonal, *Chris Musampa*.

- Neil Pointon, the Everton, Oldham and Manchester City defender, laboured throughout his career with the not altogether complimentary nickname of *'Dissa' Pointon*.

2003 'To put it in gentleman's terms if you've been out for a night and you're looking for a young lady and you pull one, some weeks they're good-looking and some weeks they're not the best. Our performance today would have been not the best-looking bird but at least we got her in the taxi. She wasn't the best-looking lady we ended up taking home but she was very pleasant and very nice, so thanks very much, let's have a coffee.'

Ian Holloway, manager of Queens Park Rangers, Saltergate Stadium, Chesterfield,
11 February 2003.

The former manager of Bristol Rovers, QPR, Plymouth, Leicester, Blackpool, Crystal Palace – and at the time of writing boss of Millwall – has a way with a metaphor. A Hollo-way you might say. Delivered in his characteristic Bristolian drawl, pockmarked with the most unlikely verbal imagery, Ian Holloway's after-match press comments are rarely dull. Some managers tell it like it is. He tells it as it might be in an acid-fuelled dream.

Sometimes – as in the case of Holloway's comments following his side's 4–2 win at Chesterfield in a Second Division encounter in 2003 – analysis does not add much. Besides, analysis is not always possible. So, in homage to the man and his metaphors, here is a bald, straightforward and unadorned list of some of his finer verbal moments:

- *I couldn't be more chuffed if I were a badger at the start of the mating season.*
  After QPR beat Cardiff, 2003.

- *Every dog has its day – and today is woof day. Today I just want to bark.*
  After QPR's promotion-clinching win at Sheffield Wednesday, 2004.

- *He's six-foot something, fit as a flea, good-looking – he's got to have something wrong with him. Hopefully he's hung like a hamster. That would make us all feel better.*
  On Cristiano Ronaldo, 2008.

- *Having said that, my missus has got a hamster and his cock's massive.*
  When later reminded of his previous observation.

- *I love Blackpool. We're very similar. We both look better in the dark.*
  Marking his appointment as boss of the Seasiders, 2009.

- *If you're a burglar, it's no good poncing about outside somebody's house, looking good with your swag bag ready. Just get in there, burgle them and come out. I don't advocate that obviously, it's just an analogy.*
  Holloway extends some advice to his Blackpool players after the 4–1 defeat by his future employers Crystal Palace, 2009.

- *I am more than happy and I am afraid the chairman will need a hell of a tub of cream to get rid of me – I'm like a bad rash and not easily curable.*
  Denying reports that he was seeking alternative employment while still at Blackpool, 2010.

- *In the first half we were like the Dog and Duck, in the second half we were like Real Madrid. We can't go on like that. At full-time I was at them like an irritated Jack Russell.*
  After his Blackpool side fought back to draw 2–2 against Crystal Palace, 2010.

- *Right now, everything is going wrong for me – knowing my luck, if I fell in a barrel of boobs, I'd come out sucking my thumb.*
  Bemoaning a run of ill-fortune at Blackpool, 2010.

- *My arms withered and my body was covered with pus-like sores, but no matter how bad it got I consoled myself by remembering that I wasn't a Chelsea fan.*
  His response to queries about his health, following his resignation as Crystal Palace boss, 2013.

2004 'What I said was racist, but I'm not a racist. I am an idiot.'

Ron Atkinson in an interview with *The Guardian*, 23 April 2004.

Actually, what Big Ron Atkinson said on the night of 20 April 2004 when he was commentating on the Champions League semi-final in Monte Carlo was both racist *and* idiotic. After the live feedback to England had ended, Atkinson, then ITV's leading pundit, was wittering away about the less-than-stellar performance of Chelsea's French defender Marcel Desailly in the club's 3–1 defeat to Monaco: 'He is what is known in some schools as a fucking lazy nigger,' he chuntered.

Unbeknownst to Atkinson, the line was still open and his comments were broadcast to several television stations in the Middle

East. In the few days after it had become clear what he had said, the immediate repercussions were extensive. He resigned from his job at ITV, he had to give up his column in *The Guardian* and he lost a fortune when other commercial projects were ditched by the companies with which he was associated.

But perhaps more significant than the financial implications, his racist remark totally undermined the standing of a man who had done more to promote black players in the English game than any of his contemporaries. This was not so much a foot-in-mouth moment as an act of reputational suicide.

Before sitting behind a microphone, Ron Atkinson had enjoyed a gilded career as a football manager. He won trophies at Manchester United, Sheffield Wednesday and Aston Villa. It was, however, his innovations at West Bromwich Albion in the late 1970s which marked the most distinguished chapter of his working life. His Albion were a superb team: swift, imaginative, clever. It was their scintillating 5–3 victory at Old Trafford in 1979, driven by a young, frizzy-permed Bryan Robson, that served as a most compelling audition for Atkinson's appointment as United boss.

But what was most pioneering about that side was the inclusion within it of three black players: the full-back Brendan Batson, the centre-forward Cyrille Regis and the winger Laurie Cunningham. It seems almost ridiculous these days, when half the England team is black or mixed race and every squad in the country is a polyglot mix of nationalities, creeds and skin tones, to suggest that the inclusion of three black players was somehow revolutionary. But in the 1970s – the decade, let us not forget, that gave us the appalling sitcom *Love Thy Neighbour*, which featured liberal use of the term 'nig-nog' – Atkinson was a real agent of change, a man who made a significant difference. 'Hey, we did all right, didn't we?' he says now of his time with the Baggies.

Looking back, the level of racism in football the 1970s, as elsewhere, was astonishing. Recalling what used to be chanted from the terraces at the very sight of a black player is enough to induce shame in every spectator. It was vicious, nasty and by no means restricted to isolated cases; it was universal. But it wasn't just the monkey chants, Nazi salutes and projectile bananas that pockmarked progress back then. It was the institutionalised dismissiveness that pervaded the game. Coaches routinely made crass generalisations based on race: black players couldn't defend, they couldn't be trusted to carry out instruction, they were reckoned to go missing on a wet Wednesday night away at Rotherham. A scandalous amount of talent was left untapped through widespread ignorance. The attitude wasn't merely inhumane, it was utterly self-destructive. Atkinson had no truck with that sort of prehistoric prejudice. What he wanted were the best players around, regardless of their background or colour. 'Any manager who doesn't select the best he can get is a fool,' he says. 'And let me tell you there were a lot of fools around in the Seventies and Eighties.'

Batson, Regis and Cunningham were certainly good. Atkinson was happy, too, to promote them as something new, something exotic, something to be admired. He called them 'The Three Degrees' after the all-female African-American disco outfit of the time, and the threesome were inevitably photographed with the group when they were on a British tour, Cunningham in particular looking as though he was rather enjoying being wrapped up in a fur coat with a curvaceous soul singer.

> Any manager who doesn't select the best he can get is a fool.

The reputation Atkinson earned for such novel thinking followed him through his managerial career into retirement, when he became one of the country's most respected television pundits. His popularity was largely based on his verbal inventiveness, the strangulated syntax that became known as Ronglish. 'Giving it eyebrows', 'the lollipop', 'early doors': he created a whole new footballing lexicon. It was his way with words that allowed him to develop a lucrative second career, a succession of commercial partners cheerfully exploiting his strange yet memorable phraseology.

Which is what made his outburst against Desailly all the more surprising. This was a man who had not only championed black players, but understood the power of words. And yet he blithely used a word that, in the mouth of a white man, is the most profoundly offensive of all racist terms. It may not have been intended for broadcast, but what Atkinson said was utterly unacceptable in a game that had moved on from the 1970s, making huge strides to become inclusive, open and free of such rancorous terminology. As his shamed response recognised, there was no excuse for it.

Initially, after his verbal slip-up, he was supported by many within football. Carlton Palmer, whom Atkinson had managed at Sheffield Wednesday in the early 1990s, said of him: 'I'm black and I'm going to stand up for Big Ron because I know what he's like as a bloke. If we're going to deal with racism then let's deal with the bigger picture of racism not about a throwaway comment that wasn't meant in that manner.' The man himself still maintains a vigorous defence of his reputation. 'I'm not a racist, a racist is someone who won't give a black man a chance. My actions over the years prove that I have no problem with that,' he says.

But his reputation did not stop him being vilified. After his gaffe, Big Ron came to be regarded as a toxic presence, Ronglish became a tainted tongue and Atkinson never regained his previous prominence. His appearances on television thereafter were restricted to celebrity reality challenges and occasional punditry spots on Manchester United's in-house channel MUTV. Plus an excruciating encounter on a documentary called *What Ron Said* with the Trinidadian-British academic Darcus Howe, who lambasted him with the insistence that the only legitimate penance was to spend the next ten years cleaning

Rio Ferdinand's boots. Ron's response to that was to suggest Howe was 'out of order'. But even as he said it he knew there was only one person in that conversation who had been verbally out of order. And it wasn't Howe.

2004 'Please do not call me arrogant. But I am European champion, I am not one out of the bottle. I think I am a Special One.'

José Mourinho, Stamford Bridge stadium, 2 June 2004.

It was the moment the country fell in thrall to the cult of the coach, the moment we all came to believe that there is only one person who matters at a football club: the manager.

Chelsea had been bought by the Russian billionaire Roman Abramovich the previous June. Perhaps driven by a fear that the booty he had accrued from hoovering up ex-Soviet state assets might not be in his possession for long, Abramovich was a man in a hurry. Nobody could mistake his approach to football-club ownership with the slow, steady build: he wanted to be in charge of the best in Europe and he wanted it yesterday.

His research had informed him that the speediest shortcut to supremacy came in the shape of a young multi-lingual Portuguese who had announced himself to English football followers when his Porto team had won at Old Trafford the previous season. On the way to taking the unfashionable, under-resourced club to ultimate triumph in the Champions League, that night he had cheerfully compromised the integrity of his well-cut suit as he slid along the touchline on his knees in celebration of unlikely victory over

Manchester United. Abramovich wanted a bit of that. To make it happen, he did what a man of his background does: he made the coach concerned an offer he couldn't refuse.*

So it was on a hot summer's day in 2004 that the English press made their first acquaintance with the new Chelsea manager: José Mourinho. It was some impression he made. With film-star looks, a mischievous air and a whip-smart command of the English language, Mourinho was evidently a cut above the growly, jowly managerial norm. And it was clear, whatever facility he might have with English, he had no time for football's default interview setting: false modesty.

'I am a Special One': These words immediately defined him. Well, in fact, not *those* actual words. As he has pointed out many times subsequently, he actually used the indefinite article, claiming himself to be part of a special breed. But by the English press he was gifted the definite: he was unique, and was accordingly dubbed 'The Special One'.

And how quickly Mourinho lived up to his extravagant billing. As a title his was not a hostage to fortune, this was an accurate forecast of what was to come. He took hold of a squad which, under his predecessor Claudio ('the Tinkerman') Ranieri, had been almost but not quite good enough – reaching the semi-final of the Champions League and finishing runners-up in the Premier League – and, with a couple of tweaks and judicious signings (Didier Drogba from Marseille and Michael Essien from Lyon) turned them into serial winners. He scooped the Premier League at the first time of asking in 2004–5, then won it again in 2005–6, undermining the cosy rivalry between Manchester United and Arsenal which had turned the division into a two-horse race.

There have been many volumes written about how Mourinho did it, about his attention to detail, his ability swiftly to affect tactical change, his acute man-management, his shameless application of

---

*Mourinho's salary when he first arrived in West London was £4.2 million, and was raised to £5.2 million in 2005.

mind games. But the short answer is that he did it by elevating the role of the manager to new levels. A man of ferocious intelligence, he had PhD-level understanding of all of the different aspects of his trade, from nutrition and neurology to physiology and psychology. Everything he did, he did a little bit better than it had been done before. And he did an awful lot.

What elite sportsmen thrive on above all is personal improvement. If a coach can demonstrate he can make them better at their chosen calling, then they are forever in his debt. As he made them winners, the Chelsea players loved Mourinho. They loved his training methods (the Icelander Eiður Guðjohnsen spoke gushingly of his to-the-second planning of sessions) they loved his attitude (Joe Cole waxes lyrical on his man-management skills) they loved the man himself (Essien and Drogba both refer to him as a second father). The return for all that love was five trophies in three seasons (two Premier Leagues, one FA Cup and two League Cups).

And the rest of the country loved Mourinho too. His looks, his abilities,

> This intelligent, witty, charismatic and exceptionally good-looking young pipsqueak.

even his coat were the source of drooling admiration well beyond the usual confines of the game. For the first time in football history, he made management sexy. Which really was a special trick. Across the country, he weakened female knees. 'The suit is pure stealth wealth, the shirt is a baby blue and button-down with elegant preppiness, even the socks have a certain minimalist luxe,' panted Polly Vernon in the *Observer Sport Monthly*. While *The Guardian's* Marina Hyde gushed: 'This intelligent, witty, charismatic and exceptionally good-looking young pipsqueak.'

The fact that Mourinho's first spell at Chelsea did not last much more than three seasons remains one of football's great lost opportunities. But Abramovich, never one to keep things the same when they can be changed, tired of him sooner than the rest of us and sent him on his way in the autumn of 2007. After a brief sabbatical, he went to Inter, where he won the treble of Serie A title, Coppa Italia and Champions League. Then he went on to Real Madrid, where, despite Barcelona's pre-eminence, he continued to add silverware to his personal collection, winning La Liga in 2011–12 and the Copa del Rey in 2010–11. Between 2003 and 2012 he did not go a single calendar year without a trophy.

In that time, Chelsea did all right too. Even without the man who kick-started it all, they won the title, the FA Cup, the Europa League and in 2012, to Abramovich's beaming delight, the Champions League itself. In the process, though, the Russian got through eight managers in a failed attempt find an adequate replacement for Mourinho.* But he knew ultimately there was only one way to do that. So in June 2013, after the Portuguese had failed to land the job he always wanted as Sir Alex Ferguson's successor at Old Trafford, the billionaire brought the Portuguese back to Stamford Bridge.

Not everyone thought it a wise move. While the players he leaves behind invariably talk about him in hushed, reverential tones, the same cannot be said of those involved in rival clubs. In his career, Mourinho has picked up as many enemies as he has trophies. And he has collected plenty of trophies. Carles Vilarrubí, the vice-president of Barcelona, for instance, was not voicing an isolated opinion when he greeted the manager's return to Chelsea thus:

> It is not good for English football. If Mourinho behaves like he did in Spain it will only be an unhappy relationship. In his three years in Spain he only created disagreements and arguments. I am happy he is leaving and so is everyone in Spanish football.

---

*Avram Grant, Luiz Felipe Scolari, Ray Wilkins, Guus Hiddink, Carlo Ancelotti, André Villas-Boas, Roberto Di Matteo and Rafael Benítez.

Mourinho, though, preferred to exude contentment as he returned to the very Stamford Bridge suite where he first announced himself to the British public. During his second introductory press conference, he was asked how he would now describe himself as he began his return stint in charge at Chelsea. He thought for a second before smilingly declaring himself to be: 'The Happy One'.

2005 'A message for the best football supporters in the world: we need a twelfth man here. Where are you? Where are you? Let's be 'avin' you!'

Delia Smith addresses the crowd during half-time of a match against Manchester City, Carrow Road, Norwich, 28 February 2005.

As she stepped out onto the Carrow Road greensward, it appeared that Britain's best-selling food writer, the woman who changed a nation's eating habits, had been at the cooking sherry. During the half-time break in a match Norwich City needed to win if they were to remain in the Premier League, a match moreover in which they had squandered a 2–0 lead, Delia – everyone calls her Delia – swayed down onto the pitch clutching a microphone and exhorted the crowd to up their vocal efforts for the second half. Never mind that she was staggering on her feet as if buffeted by a force ten gale, never mind that she was slurring her words, never mind that the words she slurred made little sense, she was determined no one was going to stop her from addressing the crowd. But then why would they? Norwich City was her property, she could do with it as she pleased.

Delia had injected into the club a hefty chunk of the cash she had made from teaching Britain how to boil an egg when she became majority shareholder back in 1996. It was a largely a romantic gesture. Michael Wynn-Jones, her husband and the publisher of her cookery magazines, was a lifelong Canary, and watching the club slide into financial disarray was making him despondent. Between them they decided the best use of her millions was to underpin his favourite football club. They became joint chief shareholders and immediately began the process of revitalising the place. Delia took hold of the catering, Michael sorted the boardroom. Within a few years, they had overseen promotion to the top division. In May 2004, Norwich City became a Premier League club.

The trouble was, barely nine months later the soufflé had sunk. A swift return to the First Division was beckoning. Norwich really had to win all their remaining home matches if they were to have a hope of staying up. And in this one, with the score now 2–2, the chances of victory were rapidly evaporating. As the manager Nigel Worthington worked on the players in the dressing room, Delia decided she would stir up the crowd, season them a little, bring them to the boil. So she issued instructions to the man in charge of the public-address system and, accompanied by her husband, she tripped her way down to the pitch.

For a woman who had made her name and fortune through her ability to communicate, this was not the most coherent of public utterances. Though she later denied it, everyone in the ground assumed she had been enjoying the ample boardroom hospitality. A poll of Norwich fans afterwards revealed that 65 per cent of those questioned found her speech 'excruciating', 27 per cent thought it was 'funny', while just 8 per cent reckoned her attempt at motivation was 'inspiring'. Given what happened in the second half, it is a surprise that as many as that thought her intervention inspirational: Norwich went on to lose the game 3–2.

> Maybe in the heat of the moment I didn't choose the best words.

'My message to the fans was a totally spontaneous appeal from the heart aimed at trying to do everything we could to get behind Nigel Worthington and the team,' she explained in a club statement released a couple of days after footage of her appeal had gone viral. She did, however, concede that 'maybe in the heat of the moment I didn't choose the best words.'

For Norwich, it was not the end of the embarrassment. They were relegated and subsequently sank further, into League One. Delia, however, remained loyal to the operation. Despite an attempted hostile takeover, she stayed on, stirring a further £2 million of her boiled-egg earnings into the business. By 2011 she had her reward. Under the shrewd management of Paul Lambert, the club achieved a double promotion and were back in the Premier League.

And Delia decided to mark that elevation in her by-now trademark manner. At a civic reception at Norwich city hall, as the fans chanted her name on the pavements down below, she grabbed hold of the public address microphone once more and reprised her 2005 effort. 'C'mon, let's be 'avin' you!' she yelled to great applause. Her husband, standing alongside her, was then interviewed live on air by a journalist from the local BBC radio station. 'Anyone would think she'd invented the bloody phrase,' chuckled Mr Wynn-Jones.

Delia wasn't done, though. Grabbing the radio mic from her husband, she went on to call the Norwich manager Paul Langbert, instead of Lambert, and mistakenly encouraged the fans to toast 'staying up' instead of promotion. She then proceeded, cheerily, to turn the Norfolk air blue: 'Just think of this wonderful thing. We haven't gotta go in the frigging play-offs next year.' At which point the radio reporter handed back to the studio with the wise words: 'I think this is as good a place as any to leave it, don't you?'

If only he had been holding the microphone in 2005.

2005 'Rafa, I think you've got twelve out there.'

Liverpool's Jamie Carragher gives his manager Rafael Benítez a maths lesson at half-time during the Champions League final vs AC Milan, Atatürk Stadium, Istanbul, 25 May 2005.

If ever stirring half-time words were required in a football match, it was in the Liverpool dressing room at the mid-point of the Champions League final of 2005. Three-nil down against a Milan team including such gilded talents as Andriy Shevchenko, Kaká and Andrea Pirlo, Liverpool were in danger of humiliation. Here they were in their sixth European Cup final and they were playing like novices. Two goals from Hernán Crespo and one from Paolo Maldini had sent the Italian contingent into a frenzy of celebration. Not just the fans, either. The Liverpool players could hear from down the corridor the sound of their opponents in their dressing room already enjoying what appeared to be certain victory. Even some stalwart Anfield regulars had lost faith: several had already departed from the stadium to make the long journey back to the centre of Istanbul, their heads hanging in embarrassment at what they had just witnessed.

Those who left really ought to have known better. Especially as Liverpool had made a habit of confounding expectations in Europe that season. No one had expected them even to make it to the group stage when they had lost the home leg of their qualifying round to the Austrian minnows Grazer AK. Certainly no one had predicted that they would beat Juventus or indeed Chelsea in the quarter- and semi-finals respectively. But a strike from their Spanish winger Luis García which José Mourinho to this day refers to as a 'ghost goal' had won them the right to play in their first final since the horrors of Heysel (see pages 134–8). And their manager Rafael Benítez was anxious that, having got so far, they did not now depart with a whimper.

And there was further motivation for turning round this disastrous half-time scoreline: if Liverpool were to enjoy Champions League football the following season, their only route to qualification was to win the competition. They had finished sixth in the Premier League and would be otherwise ineligible. Benítez knew something had to change if nights like this were to be enjoyed in the future.

It was not a tub-thumping speech, his. It did not involve recrimination or name-calling. Unlike Brian Clough he did not punch anyone in the stomach, unlike John Sitton he didn't try to start a fight with his centre-back. Instead, he was calm, rational, coherent. Although his English was not perfect, he managed to communicate exactly what was required. He began by suggesting that the scoreline was misleading. Liverpool had had as many chances in the first half as the Italians. The difference was that Milan had taken theirs. There was no reason, he believed, that chances would not be forthcoming in the second. What was required now was their ruthless execution.

In order to do that, Benítez decided to bring the right-back Djimi Traoré off and replace him with an extra forward man. So he told Traoré's fellow Frenchman Djibril Cissé to strip off in preparation. But then he was told by his physio that Steve Finnan, his left-back, had damaged a groin muscle. So Benítez told the reluctant Irishman he was to come off and told Traoré to put his kit back on.

Then he was struck by another idea. 'I'm going to bring Didi [Dietmar Hamann] on,' he announced. That would be the way to close down Andrea Pirlo, who was running the show – bring a German into the reckoning. He instructed Hamann to prepare himself to harry Milan's elegant playmaker at every opportunity. With the changes sorted, he then told his team simply to play with pride. They had done so well to get where they were, they didn't want to spoil it all with a performance that might depress their loyal band of followers.

It seemed like a good plan. There was just one problem. With two substitutes getting ready and only one player removed, Benítez was inadvertently attempting to play with an extra man. Playing twelve against eleven might be one way of getting the better of the Italian champions, but it somewhat went against the traditions of the game. Benítez, though, was clearly blind to his mistake. He was too busy slapping each of his men on the back, encouraging them to further effort.

When Carragher pointed out the arithmetical mix-up, the manager at first could not see it. There followed a brief moment of comedy as the two of them counted the players, before the Spaniard, with a smile, acknowledged he was being a little over-ambitious: he told Cissé he would have to wait to come on.

> Vladimir Šmicer created an unlikely record: the only player to score on successive days in the same match.

Moving to a five-man midfield might have been a spur-of-the-moment tactical switch, but it soon bore fruit. With Steven Gerrard and Hamann nullifying Pirlo, Liverpool found themselves back in the game. In what the Milan manager Carlo Ancelotti would later describe as 'six minutes of madness' Liverpool scored three times in a sudden, unexpected, magnificent flurry. It took a mere 360 seconds to effect the most glorious turnabout in European Cup history. First Gerrard headed in a John Arne Riise cross on 54 minutes, then Šmicer struck just 120 seconds later, before, on 60 minutes, Alonso put home the rebound, having missed a penalty kick awarded for a foul by Gennaro Gattuso on Gerrard. And with the scores now level, there were still thirty minutes remaining of normal time.

Neither side, however, could find the decisive strike. Nor throughout half an hour of extra time could an inch be found between them. The Liverpool 'keeper Jerzy Dudek's double save from Shevchenko right at the death took his side into a penalty shoot-out.

As kick-off had been at 10 p.m. local time in order to fit in with broadcasting schedules in the rest of Europe, by now it was getting very late indeed. While Dudek reprised his predecessor Bruce

Grobbelaar's spaghetti-legs antics from the 1984 European Cup final shoot-out against Roma in the Liverpool goal, Milan's players looked tired. Serginho shot over the crossbar for Milan before Hamann scored for Liverpool. And when Pirlo fluffed his side's second spot kick and Cissé scored, Liverpool were 2–0 in front. Jon Dahl Tomasson reduced the deficit to 2–1 and Riise then failed to convert his kick. When Kaká scored it was 2–2. But after Šmicer scored, Shevchenko needed to convert his kick to keep Milan in the frame. Dudek blocked his straight shot with his left hand despite having gone down to his right. Liverpool, almost unbelievably, were champions of Europe.

When he succeeded with his spot kick, incidentally, Šmicer created an unlikely record: as his penalty was taken long after midnight, he became the first player in the history of the game to score on successive days in the same match. For Benítez, though, there was a far more significant achievement: he had secured the club's fifth European title in his first season in charge at Liverpool. That was some success. And how he managed it with only eleven players on the pitch at any one time only he will ever know.

2006
'He said very tough words about my sister and mother. I tried not to listen, but he kept repeating them. I do not express regret because that would mean he was right to say that. There was a serious provocation. My act is not forgivable, but they must punish the true guilty party, and the guilty party is the one who provokes.'

Zinedine Zidane on his head-butt on Italy's Marco Materazzi, World Cup final, Olympiastadion, Berlin, 8 July 2006.

Zinedine Zidane, the finest player of his generation, had carried France to the 2006 World Cup final. His performance in the victory over the Brazilians in the quarter-final had scaled such heights that it was described as 'monstrous' by Pelé. And he was being complimentary.

The match was to be the great Frenchman's swansong. He had announced beforehand that, whatever the result, he would retire once it was over. And what a way to go, in the World Cup final – the first since 1978 to feature neither Brazil nor Germany – in front of 80,000 fans and an estimated global television audience of some 715 million.

For a figure of his stature, it was entirely appropriate that Zidane should depart with the world watching. This, after all, was the player who had scored the finest goal in the history of Champions League finals, a rip-snorting volley for Real Madrid against Bayer Leverkusen in Glasgow in 2002. This was, too, a man whose elegance and artistry had inspired two film-makers to follow him through a game and use the resulting footage as a eulogising documentary.* This was a player, in short, who deserved the most exalted of send-offs.

He began the final as if keen to engrave his name indelibly on the history of the game. Leading the French side out as captain, within eight minutes, he had scored from the penalty spot. But, after Italy had equalised on nineteen minutes through their centre-back Marco Materazzi, the game had sunk into a scruffy stalemate. Zidane's elegance was an increasing irrelevance as Italy stifled and smothered, playing the Italian way, parking a fleet of buses in front of their goal.

Then, in the eightieth minute, after an incursion into the Italian box had, like so many before, come to nothing, Zidane was trotting slowly back to his own half, with Materazzi at his shoulder, when he suddenly stopped. He turned and, without any warning, pounded his forehead into the giant Italian's chest with a force that sent him toppling like a felled oak.

It took Horacio Elizondo, the Argentine referee, a moment to realise what had happened. Maybe he needed to be alerted to the incident by the fourth official, watching television footage in the stands. But, after consulting with his linesman, he showed Zidane the red card. France's greatest-ever player, three times FIFA's World Player of the Year, recipient of the *Legion d'honneur* from a grateful nation for his World Cup-winning exploits in 1998, made his ignominious way alone back down the tunnel, passing the trophy where it stood on a plinth on the pitchside. As he did so, he was seen on television picture wiping a tear from his eye. He knew his legacy had been horribly compromised.

In the game's immediate aftermath, it was all anyone could talk about. The Italians took home the cup after a penalty shoot-out, but it was Zidane's assault which dominated the conversation, it was Zidane's assault that was immortalised in popular culture, parodied in everything from a chart-topping French pop song to an episode

---

* *Zidane: A 21st-Century Portrait*, by the film-makers Philippe Parreno and Douglas Gordon.

> Something must have
> been said to Zidane. He
> is actually a reserved
> and inoffensive person.

of the American animated sitcom *Family Guy*.

'Something must have been said to Zidane. He is actually a reserved and inoffensive person,' said Franz Beckenbauer, the 1974 World Cup-winning captain and former coach of Germany, who could not resist adding a sly dig at his Gallic rivals. 'He weakened his team. We know how sensitive the French are when they lose their captain.'

The French president Jacques Chirac, meanwhile, who had watched the match at Berlin's Olympiastadion, hoping that he might be able to associate himself with victory as he had done in 1998, was not prepared to criticise:

> I don't know what happened, why Zidane was punished. But I would like to express all the respect that I have for a man who represents at the same time all the most beautiful values of sport, the greatest human qualities one can imagine, and who has honoured French sport and, simply, France.

That was pretty much what everyone thought: if Zidane had been pushed into a reaction as extreme as that, one which spoiled beyond repair his final appearance, then the provocation must have been extreme. A poll published in France's *Le Parisien* newspaper showed that 61 per cent of the 802 people questioned forgave their skipper his indiscretion.

Immediately, media outlets around the world studied footage of the incident to try to establish what it was that was said to provoke him to such extremes. Watching the two of them engage in a clipped exchange on the pitch, some claimed that Materazzi had delivered a racial slur, accusing the Algerian-born Zidane of being a Muslim and a terrorist. Others suggested the Italian had called the Frenchman a rapist, and even, according to one source, a paedophile. Such was the swirl of rumours over the next few days about what exactly was said and to whom, it was even mooted – somewhat outlandishly – that FIFA might strip the Italians of the trophy were it discovered that they had won by using racist language to undermine their opponents' best player.

Zidane himself was initially reluctant to be too specific. In a press conference three days after the event, he preferred to focus on the mouthy Materazzi rather than his own ill-discipline. He thought the Italian deserved at least as great a punishment as he had endured. But eventually the facts began to emerge. They came in part from Materazzi's autobiography, but mainly from a comprehensive study by lip-reading experts of footage taken from every angle by FIFA's own cameras.

And it appears the exchange was along these lines. Zidane, a fluent Italian-speaker after his time playing for Juventus, complained that Materazzi had been all over him at a corner. He told him that if he wanted his shirt that badly, he would give it to him after the final whistle. Materazzi responded by saying that he would prefer to take the shirt off the back of Zidane's whore of a sister. Zidane asked him to repeat himself, which Materazzi did, along with a few choice expletives. Zidane walked away. Then turned and unleashed his headbutt. Materazzi went down as if under sniper fire.

So that was it: the great Frenchman had been provoked ten minutes before the conclusion of his career by the kind of cheap playground insult that he must have heard a thousand times on a football pitch and previously ignored. This time, this last time, however, he snapped.

According to Eric Cantona, a man who had first-hand experience of violent reaction to verbals (see pages 187–90), it is not what is said that makes a player explode, it is the circumstances. 'Provocation we always had,' Cantona once told me. 'Millions of times people say these things, and then one day you don't accept it. Why? It's not about words. It's about how you feel at that moment. One day you react, but the words are exactly the same as those you have heard a million times, so it is impossible to say why you react.'

Maybe for Zidane – who, in truth, was no stranger to the red card in his career – his judgment was clouded by the knowledge that this was the end. Maybe it was the imminent tolling of the bell that would mark the end of his career as a professional footballer that sharpened his sensitivity.

As for a legacy, the one he left was probably not the one he had hoped for. In October 2013 a bronze statue immortalising his assault was unveiled in Qatar as part of an exhibition of art inspired by great moments of World Cup history to mark the country's winning bid to host the competition in 2022. It stayed in place for barely a week before it was removed following a barrage of complaints. You suspect one of them came from Zinedine Zidane, a man who, when it comes to his part in the 2006 World Cup final, would rather forget.

2006 'England did nothing in the World Cup. So why are they bringing books out? 'We got beat in the quarter-finals, I played like shit: here's my book.' Who wants to read that? I don't.'

Joey Barton, interview in *The People*, 9 December 2006.

It was a brilliant bit of repositioning: from violent thug who had done time for common assault to football's leading intellectual, from a man with a propensity for stubbing cigars in other people's faces to someone with a fondness for quoting Nietzsche. Joey Barton's rebranding was a testament to the power of social media. He built up a following of more than two million on Twitter with his musings on everything from David Cameron's political judgment to Dietmar Hamann's alleged refuelling habits. In everything, he said what he thought without the intervention of fear, favour or spell-checker. He quickly established himself as a rare beast in football: a man who ventured beyond the confines of the pitch, albeit without taking the precaution beforehand of checking in what he was about to step.

But back in 2006, his chippy Scouse aggression evident in every tackle, the young Manchester City midfielder was just beginning to make a name for himself. And it wasn't a nice one. Back then, Barton was a dirty word. Yet what was evident in his observation about the England World Cup squad's literary aspirations was that he already had an opinion. Besides, there was no denying Barton was right about the book business. Gambling that England might do well at the 2006 World Cup, a number of members of the squad had put their names to ghost-written tomes to be published in time for the Christmas market. As it happened, England performed to their post-1966 World Cup type, surrendering tamely to Portugal in yet another penalty-shoot-out fiasco after a 0–0 draw in which a less-than-fit Wayne Rooney was sent off for planting his studs in Ricardo Carvalho's groin.

But contracts had been signed and processes invoked, so the books came out even if they had little to celebrate. Volumes attributed to Rooney, David Beckham and Frank Lampard hardly added to the literary canon. Rooney's – ghost-written by an embarrassed Hunter Davies – was spectacular in its lack of insight. Though the money involved – the player received some £5 million for a four-book deal – made such concerns irrelevant.

However, it was Ashley Cole's memoir that was the most risible. Called *My Defence*, it was published in a blush-free flurry just a couple of months after England's damp squib of an exit from the German tournament. Effectively one long whine of self-justification for the player's defection from Arsenal to Chelsea, it was an astonishing own goal. One sentence in particular sealed the player's reputation as football's premier spoiled child. It detailed a phone conversation he had with his agent, Jonathan Barnett, about an offer of a new contract made by Arsenal's managing director, David Dein:

> When I heard Jonathan repeat the figure of £55,000 I nearly swerved off the road. 'He is taking the piss, Jonathan!' I yelled down the phone. I was so incensed. I was trembling with anger. I couldn't believe what I'd heard.

As First World problems go, getting incensed at being offered a wage of £55,000 a week is up there with the calamity of not finding ripe avocados in your local Waitrose. Sympathy was not widely forthcoming; not for nothing was Cole thereafter known as 'Cashley'. Barton was undoubtedly right: it would have been better if Cole and his international team-mates had kept such thoughts to themselves.

At the time he said it, however, Barton's opinion was not widely appreciated. He was, after all, an unreconstructed street yob, the step-brother of a man serving a life sentence for a racist murder, and was thus reckoned to have little to say of value. But after doing time himself for a nasty assault outside a fast-food restaurant in Liverpool in 2007 and being convicted for viciously attacking his team-mate Ousmane Dabo in 2008, Barton underwent extensive therapy. He was admitted to Tony Adams's Sporting Chance clinic, where he impressed with his willingness to embrace behavioural change.

He emerged as a man who valued the idea of communication. An early adopter of Twitter, he used it to reinvent himself, tweeting furiously on a huge range of subjects. Look closely and his quickness of temper was still evident in some of his social-media jousts. Nonetheless, many people saw him in new light. He was invited to discuss politics with Jeremy Paxman on *Newsnight*, he was lauded by *The Guardian* and given a column by *The Big Issue*. He looked like a man who had managed to find accommodation with his demons.

Then he was sent off in the final tumultuous game of the 2012 season after attempting to head-butt half the Manchester City team (though in fairness, he was by now playing for Queens Park Rangers). For many it signalled that Barton's supposed change of demeanour was superficial, manufactured, a piece of theatre; and that he

> Surely it was possible to be simultaneously thoughtful and headless, insightful and stupid.

remained a thug at heart. Others were less dismissive. Surely it was possible to be simultaneously thoughtful and headless, insightful and stupid, brainy and brain dead. Is that not part of the human condition?

Barton will no doubt tell us all about it when his own book comes out. Suggesting that hypocrisy is not a failing restricted to those he condemns on a daily basis on Twitter, Barton has signed a deal on his autobiography. With characteristic self-aggrandisement he chose as his collaborator not some time-serving football hack. Instead he is working with Matthew Syed, the former table tennis international and *Times* columnist, a man who has difficulty finding sufficient room in his skull to accommodate his outsized brain. Still, at least the pair won't be trying to sell it on the back of another English failure in the World Cup: the odds on Barton ever getting an England call-up are about the same as Nigel Farage's chances of acceding to the presidency of the European Union.

2007 'Tim Lovejoy: What would would you have been if you hadn't been a footballer? Peter Crouch: A virgin.'

Exchange on *Soccer AM*, Sky Sports studios, Osterley, 27 January 2007.

It was the remark that secured Crouch the votes in a poll to find the funniest man in football (though given the poll was conducted to promote Sky's *League of Their Own* quiz show, 'funniest' has to be taken as a relative term). It was probably this gag as much as his robot dance in celebration of scoring for England that cast him as Prince William's favourite player.

But what really makes Crouch's remark stand almost as tall as the man himself is how unusual it was in tone. Sportmen don't tend to do self-deprecation. When asked the same question, David Beckham took it rather seriously and reckoned he would have become a painter. The great Wimbledon champion Roger Federer insists that if he had not picked up a tennis racket, he would have become a footballer. Crouch, on the other hand, preferred to send himself up. As he did so, he brilliantly played on the public's misconception of him.

But then, Crouch is not like other footballers. At 6 feet 7 inches in height and about as wide as a tin-tack, he is not built like one for a start. His spindly legs alone are taller than Lionel Messi. When he runs, his shirt seems to billow around a concave chest. Compared to Diego Maradona – all stocky power, vast backside and low centre of gravity – he looks, with his long torso and giraffe-like limbs, to be a member of a different species. A surprisingly skilful player ('a good touch for a big man' is the usual pundit's formulation when referring to his technical ability) he is also capable of getting himself into some odd positions. A photograph of him undertaking a scissor kick at the 2006 World Cup, in which his angular frame arranged itself into something that looked alarmingly like a swastika, went viral.

He also comes from a different world from most players. The son of a successful advertising copywriter, he was brought up in middle-class comfort in Ealing, having spent much of his early life in Singapore, where his first phrases were in Mandarin, taught to him by his nanny. He was raised to understand the power of words. So it was that when Tim Lovejoy asked him the question, he was ready with an answer that neatly played on the notion that he is an outsized freak who would not be remotely attractive to women were it not for his fame and wealth.

In fact, I've always been perfectly comfortable with the way I am.

The reality is that Crouch is a handsome man who never had much of a problem picking up girls even before he became a public face. He may be a beanpole, but he was always perfectly capable of stooping to conquer. 'I think I did all right, yeah,' he told the *Sunday Telegraph*'s John Preston in 2010. 'People tend to assume I was terribly self-conscious about my height. In fact, I've always been perfectly comfortable with the way I am. And if anyone gave me any stick, they soon found I was quite capable of giving it back.'

The truth is, as he became a nationally recognised figure, he had more of a problem keeping away from women than attracting them. The tabloids were frequently filled with rumours of his infidelity to his partner, the model Abbey Clancy; the interview with Preston was conducted two days before a set of allegations – about a holiday fling with a wannabe WAG – were printed. As a man of substance – his agent once loudly boasted that Crouch, earning some £70,000 a week at Liverpool, Portsmouth and Tottenham, employed a personal staff of seven – he was frankly beating them off with a stick. Yet still, the legacy of that one sharp witticism has remained with him. It is the one thing that people endlessly remind him of. 'I only said it as a joke, obviously,' he says. 'But it seems to have, you know... escalated a touch.'

2008 'First I went left, he did too. Then I went right, and he did too. Then I went left again, and he went to buy a hot dog.'

Zlatan Ibrahimović, explaining how he dummied an opponent, January 2008.

As might be suggested by the solipsistic title of his hilariously immodest autobiography – *I Am Zlatan Ibrahimović* – the giant Swedish international is not someone who embraces humility. Take his memory of his ill-starred time at Barcelona between 2009 and 2011: 'I was unhappy,' he explains. 'But I carried on being brilliant.'

Modern professional football provides comfortable sanctuary for the narcissist. This is a pursuit in which self-belief can quickly develop into self-love; every club has a player who, were he made of chocolate, would have long ago licked himself to death. And no one does it quite

I was unhappy... But I carried on being brilliant.

like the sizeable Swedish striker. Apparently channelling the spirit of Derek Zoolander, Ben Stiller's magnificent filmic study of ludicrous self-absorption, Ibra has never feared self-parody. Wealthier than Croesus, paid €15 million a year at Paris St Germain, he has commanded the highest cumulative transfer value in football history. Flitting from Ajax to Juventus, Inter, Barcelona, Milan and latterly PSG, he has made an art of flaunting his riches. This is the man who bought an island off the coast of his homeland, filled it with African wildlife and every summer invites his friends to join him there on hunting expeditions.

It is a far cry from where he came from. Born on the wrong side of the Swedish tracks to refugees escaping from war-ravaged Bosnia, with junkie half-siblings and an alcoholic father, he used his innate skill mixed with a sizeable dose of ghetto cunning to evade poverty. Chippy, angry and under no doubt that the world is out to keep him from achieving his natural place at the very top of things, he raged against authority of every kind, from teachers to football coaches. If there is one thing he has always refused to do, it is conform. Once, when he was playing for Malmö's youth side, the father of a team mate circulated a petition demanding Zlatan be removed from the squad. 'It was mental,' he writes in his autobiography. 'OK, I'd had a fight with the dad's son. I'd head-butted him if I'm honest. But I cycled over to the hospital afterwards and begged for forgiveness. A petition, though? Give me a break.'

That line – 'but I cycled over to the hospital afterwards' – is beautifully reductive. You can imagine the scene: a young footballer hospitalised by a team-mate, lying there in Accident and Emergency with a shattered nose, his distraught family at his bedside beseeching the club to do something to ensure no other player falls victim to this feral child in their midst. Yet in Zlatan-world, of course it is the father who is in the wrong. After all, Zlatan said sorry. And he is Zlatan. You have to accept the rough with the smooth.

Not that, in his dealings with others, the man himself is prepared

The cheek of it! Zlatan? Drive an Audi?

to give and take. Take his relationship with Pep Guardiola, whom the rest of the world regards as being among the best coaches around, but who Zlatan describes as having all the charisma of a pair of curtains. Things did not get off to a good start between them. When Ibrahimović signed for the club, the then newly appointed Barcelona boss took him to one side and quietly informed him that Barça players don't turn up for training in a Porsche or Ferrari and that it would be best if he drove his official Audi on club duty. The cheek of it! Zlatan? Drive an Audi? It was only thanks to his amazing levels of self-control that Ibrahimović didn't refer his new boss to the European Court of Human Rights on the spot.

As José Mourinho pointed out in the spring of 2014, when Chelsea played PSG (whom Zlatan had joined in 2012) in the Champions League quarter-final, the biggest shame of Ibrahimović's career was that he never played in England. What a signing he would have been for any English club. High maintenance, for sure, but his goals, his skills, his sheer presence would have electrified the Premier League. Every newspaper would have been obliged to recruit a Zlatan correspondent just to keep up with him. And what quotes would have ensued. Take the time I encountered him in the mixed zone after a PSG game. A colleague asked him, in English, what he thought of the club's newly adapted 4-3-3 playing system. 'I like,' said Zlatan by way of response. Emboldened, the reporter came back to him to try to ascertain its virtues, perhaps to get some insight into its subtleties, about the way it suited the player's proclivities. So he asked the follow-up question: 'Why is it so good?' To which Zlatan rose to his full 6 feet 5 inches and stared in contempt at his interviewer down the full length of his magnificent nose.

'Because I say so,' he said, before quickly flouncing off, presumably to his Ferrari.

2008 'Owned by Americans, managed by a Spaniard, watched by Norwegians.'

Banner flourished by Everton supporters during the Merseyside derby, Goodison Park, Liverpool, 27 September 2008.

As a measure of where the Premier League stood nearly two decades after its inception, this sarcastic Evertonian banner was bang on the money. For many disillusioned fans, this was what the national game had become: a money-making opportunity for wealthy foreign owners, a trend that was increasingly divorcing football from its grass-roots.

Richard Scudamore, the league's chief executive, however, would have taken the banner as the richest of compliments. He was proud of the manner in which a domestic game once moribund and insular had transformed itself in under twenty years into one whose renown spanned the globe and whose fan base was multinational.

There was no doubt by 2008 that the Premier League was the country's leading cultural export. Once Britain manufactured ships, locomotives and cars and dispatched them around the world. In 2008 it was flogging sporting tribalism packaged for the small screen. The Premier League is the most widely viewed sporting competition in history, with television rights sold to every territory on Earth bar North Korea and Albania (and the Albanian black-out would come to an end in 2014; thereafter the only place where you could escape coverage of the top tier of English football was Pyongyang). Why wait for four years to watch the world's finest footballers gather together to play the beautiful game when you can see it every weekend in the Premier League, the weekly World Cup?

Fans, owners, players, managers: everyone wanted to crash the Premier League party. Not least at Anfield on a match day, where

Liverpool's international standing was evidenced in the Babel of foreign voices chattering around the stadium, mingling with the local Scouse twang. It wasn't just Norwegians who claimed association with Liverpool. The club's lucrative summer tours of the Far East were greeted with an unabashed enthusiasm rarely encountered outside a boy band's fan base; Liverpool FC was reckoned the second biggest sporting brand in India after cricket's Indian Premier League; there is even a branch of the official supporters' club in the Iranian capital Tehran. On match days the Anfield pavements are jammed with visitors from Dublin and Dubai, Singapore and Seoul, all snapping each other by the Shankly gates. The steady flow of foreign fans filling Liverpool's hotels and bars is said to bolster the Merseyside economy by as much as £20 million a season.

But with the global perspective came the global speculators. By the mid-2000s, English football was regarded as the hottest sporting commodity in which to invest, one which promised two things for owners: stonking profits and worldwide exposure. Plus, in the case of the billionaire Russian Roman Abramovich at Chelsea, a highly visible bolt-hole should he need a getaway from his homeland; his enemies, he believed, would think twice about assassinating the owner of a major English sporting institution.

By 2008, more than half of the chairmen in England's top division were foreigners. Among them were a couple of oligarchs, a phoney pharaoh and a corrupt former prime minister of Thailand seeking to evade domestic justice. There were four clubs – including Liverpool – whose largest shareholders were Americans, all of them owners of US sports franchises, drawn here by the appealing lack of restriction in the governance in the English game.

For the sceptic, like the man waving his flag at Goodison, such rapid globalisation was not something to feel happy about. It had loosed the historic moorings of English football. No longer connected to its origins, its purpose dissipated in the search for international markets, the domestic game's authenticity had been diminished.

Digging their heels against the incoming tide, at Everton they liked to think they were still keeping things real. The manager at the time, David Moyes, relished the underdog opportunity that came with the club's comparatively straitened financial circumstances. Chaired by a local fan made good (the theatrical impresario Bill Kenwright) whose wealth would be pushed to cover the annual mooring charges for Abramovich's yacht, playing in a once-grand stadium that showed its age with every passing season, this was a club which set great store by remaining true to its roots. They labelled themselves the People's Club. As opposed to the Speculators' Plaything across Stanley Park.

> Bill Kenwright's wealth would be pushed to cover the annual mooring charges for Roman Abramovich's yacht.

As it turned out, as Liverpool's hardcore support quickly came to realise, whatever your affiliation, the two Americans in charge at Anfield at the time were nothing to celebrate. They were a right pair of chancers, absolutely fulfilling the lowest expectations of those who believed the English game was selling its soul without heed to the nature of the purchaser. From the moment they arrived on Merseyside – joining in the singing of 'You'll Never Walk Alone' with all the conviction and fluency of a seven-year-old sitting A levels – Tom Hicks and George Gillett Jr could not be mistaken for lifelong fans. Hicks evidently had no inkling of the true cultural value of the property he had bought. You could tell that by the way he shamelessly admitted he had been obliged to Google Liverpool's European history ahead of the 2007 Champions League final (in which Milan avenged their catastrophic 2005 defeat – see pages 278–81 – by beating the Reds 2–1).

To buy Liverpool, Hicks and Gillett had used the same leveraged buy-out methodology that had allowed their compatriot Malcolm

Glazer to load the bill for his purchase on the books of the previously debt-free Manchester United. But they were to be overwhelmed by the worldwide crash in the summer of 2008, which dried up their sources of ready credit. In the teeth of the worst recession in a generation, they were soon desperately attempting to sell their Merseyside asset in order to shore up other parts of their tottering empires. The fact that the two loathed each other to the point they could barely conduct a conversation added further grist to the worldview of the Everton banner man: when you sup with the devil, you need the longest of spoons.

So it was, ahead of a local derby which is generally conducted more like a family argument than a civil war, that the Evertonian banner-maker addressed the fissure which at the time went to the heart of football: local against global, social benefit against the profit motive, real as opposed to ersatz. Mind you, being owned by a Scouser, managed by a Glaswegian and watched by Liverpudlians didn't help Everton that sun-drenched early autumn afternoon. They were beaten 2–0, both Liverpool goals scored by the visitors' number nine, Fernando Torres. Who, at the last time of looking, was a Spaniard.

2008 'Which one of you is Simon Bird?'

Joe Kinnear, St James' Park, Newcastle, 1 October 2008.

It opened with that brusque but seemingly straightforward inquiry seeking out the *Daily Mirror's* man in the Northeast. When Bird revealed himself, Joe Kinnear, the freshly appointed manager of Newcastle United, was succinct in his follow-up. 'You're a c***,' he roared.

And so began one of football's most entertaining melt-downs, a rant that was symptomatic of a club which, like an item of sportswear bought from one of the Newcastle chairman Mike Ashley's Sports Direct high-street emporia, was apparently falling apart at the seams. In the circumstances Bird's response to Kinnear was a model of restraint. 'Thank you,' was all he said.

But if anything, his genial reaction seemed merely to provoke the Watford-reared Irishman yet further. In a script apparently penned by Quentin Tarantino, Kinnear went on to deliver a six-minute tirade crammed with fifty-two four-letter words. Which works out at one per 6.9 seconds, the kind of rate of expletive delivery that would impress *The Thick of It*'s Malcolm Tucker or an Australian slip fielder. 'I'll say it to your face, you're absolutely fucking out of order. You ain't got the fucking balls to be a fucking manager,' he yelled at Bird.

Kinnear's stated objection was to a piece the journalist had written in the *Mirror* which revealed that the first thing the temporary Newcastle manager had done on arrival was to give his players three days off. Bird contended that seemed rather odd given that Kinnear had been granted only a six-week-long tenure. Or, as the man himself put it: 'Fuck, you're saying I turned up and they fucked off. Fuck off.'

Looking back on it now, however, Bird believes that Kinnear's unrestrained blast was motivated by something more than just annoyance at his article. The press had latterly given voice to the fans' growing worries about Ashley's stewardship of Newcastle, accusing the owner of traducing the club's heritage in pursuit of a quick buck. Kinnear's appointment was seen as irrational: without a job for the previous four years, he had done little of significance since he left Premier League Wimbledon in 1999, following a heart attack. Ashley, it was claimed, had merely brought in an old mate to act as his yes-man. Bird believes Kinnear arrived in his press conference stoked up by his chairman, sanctioned from above to fire off both barrels at the pesky pressmen on his boss's behalf.

As the manager blundered on, issuing banning orders and insisting he would never again speak to Bird or any of his colleagues, the Newcastle press officer, trying to supervise events, could sense that this was developing into a less than auspicious piece of public relations. 'What is being said here is off the record and doesn't go outside,' he kept repeating. But Kinnear was unconcerned. 'Print what you fucking like,' he seethed.

The pressmen did just that. Digital recording machines had just started to be introduced to football reporting and within moments of Kinnear stomping off to his office, steam escaping from his ears, the press conference was out on the Web in full broadcast quality. And what a sensation it caused. Kinnear's attempt to give Bird the bird got hundreds of thousands of hits from the moment it was uploaded to YouTube. His effing and jeffing provoked mirth everywhere from Land's End to John O'Groats. Though possibly not in Newcastle city centre, where the locals held their heads in their hands in despair.

And no wonder. After Kevin Keegan's recent resignation, United now appeared a club in disarray, owned by the uninterested super-rich, managed by the sweary. It was not an image that was quick to dissipate. But, despite the aggression of that opening salvo, Kinnear's banning orders never materialised. Like a dad failing to discipline his wayward children, the new manager did not follow up any of his wild threats to the media. Indeed, Bird recalls, from that first day, Kinnear continued to address journalists, never ducking any questions. Though sometimes his answers were a little economical with the truth. In one press conference, he talked about his time as manager of Nepal's national team. Reporters were impressed by his story of having quickly to scramble out of the country under cover of darkness after his employers – the Nepalese royal family – were all assassinated. Then someone checked the dates and discovered Kinnear had left his job in the kingdom a good decade before the royal bloodshed. In June 2001, at the time the murders took place, he was, in fact, manager of Luton Town.

> What is being said here is off the record and doesn't go outside.

By February 2009, perhaps even to Bird's disappointment, it was all over. The hapless Kinnear, his blood pressure hardly assisted by his behaviour, suffered another heart attack and stood down (mercifully recovered from his heart problems, he was later to return to Newcastle as Director of Football, a post in which he further demonstrated his cutting-edge knowledge of the club by referring during a radio interview to the star player Yohan Cabaye as Johan Kebab). In his place, on 1 April local hero Alan Shearer was appointed on the fool's errand of trying to keep the club in the Premier League. He failed.

As for Bird, his association with one of football's finest comedy moments has not diminished. Ever since it happened, he says that at least twice a week he is assailed on Twitter by a poster suggesting Kinnear was right. Nor is it just the digital green inkers who allude to the events of 2008. When he recently applied to join a tennis club in Newcastle, the receptionist, taking down his details, heard his name and said: 'Simon Bird? As in you're a c***?'

2008 'If you can't pass the ball properly, a bowl of pasta's not going to make that much difference.'

Harry Redknapp, Tottenham Hotspur training ground, 13 November 2008.

Back in the 1970s, the Scotland goalkeeper Alan Rough kept something special in the sponge bag he put in the back of his net. It wasn't a spare pair of gloves. Or another mouthguard. It was a variety of cakes. These he would remove and eat during games, when the action was up the other end of the park. Athletes, tennis players and swimmers had for years recognised that eating well can produce a difference in performance that makes it an essential part of preparation. But football? No, players were allowed to eat whatever they liked, with management apparently unconcerned about their refuelling habits. As Brian Clough once remarked about his magnificent winger John Robertson: 'He's a fat dumpy lad who lives out of a frying-pan, but give him a ball and some grass and he becomes Picasso.'

It wasn't until Arsène Wenger arrived in England in 1996 (see pages 213–16) that England's national game woke up to what was on their plate. The Frenchman was appalled by the rubbish his players at Arsenal consumed. Not just on their nights out or in front of the telly back home but in the staff canteen too. He quickly sorted that out, ensuring it provided only the kind of food that assisted rather than detracted from performance. He then sought to educate his players about what they should be eating at home. Pasta, fresh vegetables and lean meat were fine. Fish and chips, chocolate pudding and deep-fried pizza with a Mars bar topping weren't.

When it became clear that Wenger's approach was bearing fruit (and veg), other clubs began to ape the Frenchman's ways. Managers, looking for every means, however small, by which advantage might he gained, recognised that food formed part of a wider regime change necessary in the game. As the Premier League got wealthier, with more money available for backroom staff, so dieticians became a part of the portfolio of assistance available to most top division managers. While the fans in the cheap seats were still expected to trough on a meat-and-potato pie at matches, the players were educated into the advantages of eating well. Some instinctively knew what was right. Alan Shearer maintained that it was a strict regime of chicken, rice and peas that propelled him to the position of leading scorer in the 1994–5 Premier League season.

Eventually a good diet came to be recognised as part of the accretion of marginal gains, the fashionable coaching philosophy embraced by rugby union's Clive Woodward and cycling's Dave Brailsford. Some, though, were slower than others to adapt. When he went to Manchester United as a teenager in

> He's a fat dumpy lad who lives out of a frying-pan, but give him a ball and some grass and he becomes Picasso.

2004, the Barcelona-reared Gerard Piqué was appalled at what he saw in the dressing room. Despite MUTV, the club's in-house television station, running a series called *Red Devil's Kitchen* in which Patrice Evra demonstrated how to cook his favourite dish of lobster ravioli served with lobster bisque, wild mushrooms and asparagus, Piqué reckoned most of the players wouldn't know the difference between saturated fat and a goalpost. After moving back to Barcelona in 2008, Piqué recalled:

> It was outrageous. Everyone ate what they wanted and when you take into account the English diet you can imagine what I am talking about. Every fifteen days they would put us on what we called the 'spare-tyre machine' to measure our body fat. You would be amazed at how many top players practically broke the machine because their diet was based on beer and burgers.

Yet some managers took the requirement to eat well to the extreme. When he was in charge of Swindon Town, Paolo Di Canio insisted on flying a chef in from Italy on match days to prepare the players' pasta, at a cost of more than £80,000 in a season. Now everyone knows – Patrice Evra included – that pasta is the most efficient way of fuelling the body ahead of athletic endeavour, but it really didn't require a return ticket from Milan to boil up some penne. Especially at a League Two club long crippled by financial problems. But the mercurial Di Canio prided himself on his refinement and good taste in culinary matters. When he moved to Sunderland for a brief, ill-starred managerial sojourn in 2013 he banned ketchup from the staff canteen. It was a move that was used as evidence by unhappy players of his overbearing control-freakery.

Harry Redknapp's training-ground complaint was rooted in scepticism of such over-zealousness. The then newly appointed Spurs manager had been asked in a press conference to comment on remarks made by Fabio Capello about the task facing him when he took over as England coach that autumn. 'I have, for example, impressed upon [the players] the advantages of a Mediterranean diet over ketchup and chips,' the Italian had said, with the aid of a translator, to FIFA's in-house magazine. In response, Redknapp told of how, a couple of hours before kick-off, George Best used to eat a steak, perhaps the least appropriate pre-match meal possible, sitting as it does undigested in the stomach like a ball of concrete. 'Despite that, Bestie did all right, didn't he?' said Redknapp.

> You would be amazed how many players practically broke the machine because their diet was based on beer and burgers.

Actually, what the old traditionalist was arguing against was not so much the desirability of eating well as the growing assumption within the English game that the foreign manager always knows best. He was anxious to defend native-born bosses from the charge that they were antediluvian in their approach and systems.

As it happens, Redknapp, ensconced since 2012 at Loftus Road, is as wedded as any modern manager to the merits of a sensible diet. Since his QPR press conferences take place next door to the players' canteen, it is clear to anyone who turns up to watch him address the media (not always through the window of his Range Rover) that he does not run a regime in which he encourages his players to eat any old rubbish. The menu there is full of light, fat-free, protein-rich energy food.

Even so, Redknapp's comment was a reasonable one. Diet is something that can only ever make a marginal difference. And while marginal differences are worth pursuing once the basics have been covered, on its own eschewing ketchup and eating pasta for breakfast can't turn a dunderhead into a genius. If it could then it would be an easy thing for us all to turn into Lionel Messi: just tuck in to the tagliatelle.

2008

'The full name of this team is Liga Deportiva Universitaria de Quito – a slap in the face for the man who starts the chant 'give us an L'.'

Dave Woods of Channel 5 during commentary on the Club World Cup final, International Stadium, Yokohama, Japan, 21 December 2008.

Football commentators are more usually remembered for their gaffes than their masterly one-liners. The succession of verbal slip-ups and foot-in-mouth mis-sayings published every fortnight in *Private Eye*'s Colemanballs column (named after the granddaddy of sports broadcast journalism David Coleman), present a picture of a profession almost congenitally tongue-tied and inept.

'Viv Anderson has pissed a fatness test': that was John Helm of ITV in 1991. Or 'colour wise, it's oranges and lemons, with the Dutch all in white,' was his colleague Clive Tyldesley's analysis of a Holland against Sweden clash from 2004. And then there was this cracker from ITV's David Pleat at the World Cup Finals in 2002, after a handball by Germany's Torsten Frings against the USA was missed by the referee: 'Germany benefited there from a last-gasp hand-job on the line.'

But, despite the assumptions of the column, sometimes the commentators get it right. More than right. Sometimes it is best simply to sit back and admire. And Dave Woods's line is less a piece of commentary, more an inspired moment of comedy. Whether it was scripted or not, it did something that broadcast journalism rarely manages to do: it made an entire watching nation giggle. Or at least that vanishingly small part of the nation that tunes in to Channel 5.

It was also the one bright spot in a particularly dull match. Manchester United had discovered that one of the rewards for winning the Champions League in Moscow the previous May was that they qualified to participate in FIFA's ludicrously bombastic cross-continental world championship. Whereas everyone can remember Alex Ferguson's team winning the European title in the all-Premier League clash against Chelsea in the Luzhniki Stadium – Cristiano Ronaldo's goal, Frank Lampard's equaliser, John Terry slipping and scooping the crucial penalty over the bar during the shoot-out that followed extra time – few can recall their elevation to world club champions. Simply because Sepp Blatter's attempt to inveigle his way into the territory of club competition has absolutely no historic resonance. Really, it doesn't matter.

> Germany benefited there from a last-gasp hand-job on the line.

As it happens, United won the game 1–0, with a goal from Wayne Rooney. But it is Woods's beautifully reductive analysis of their Ecuadorian opponents' name that sticks in the memory. What makes it funnier than – for instance – Tyldesley's smart observation during United's Champions League tie against Porto ('It must be the first time Ronaldo has been marked by an anagram,' he said as the United forward was shadowed by Porto's Rolando) was that it chimed in beautifully with the fan experience. Anyone who has heard those old-style attempts to get a crowd chanting would have known precisely what he meant. Maybe Woods follows Oxford United. At every home game a supporter bawls out in Brian Blessed fashion 'give us an O' and then proceeds to spell his way through the club's name until he reaches the conclusion: and what have you got? At which point everyone chants out 'Oxford, Oxford'. Frankly, that is boring enough. And Oxford is only a six-letter word. If only someone had taken up Woods's idea at the Club World Cup final and yelled 'give us an L', the chant could have gone on for days.

2009 'Jermaine is really generous. He bought me some Christian Louboutin shoes for Christmas which I love. But the best present he ever got is priceless: a tattoo of my face on his forearm.'

Ellie Penfold, fiancée of Jermaine Jenas, November 2009.

The thing that most accurately dates a photograph of a footballer is not the cut of his shorts, the length of his hair or the luxuriant nature of his facial tufts. It is the tattoos.

Footballers rarely used to be tattooed. Just as the public at large was largely ink-free, unless they had enjoyed a previous career as a naval rating, a footballer's flesh was unadorned up until the end of the 1990s. By the middle of the next decade, however, as tattoo artists spread along every high street, there was barely an inch of a player's skin that remained unpainted. Footballers had sleeves, they had giant serpents zig-zagging across their backs, they had Sanskrit on their necks. In Sergio Agüero's case they had their name written on their forearm in Elvish.

Jenas, then playing for Tottenham, took romantic inspiration for his permanent markings. Ellie's face was there every time he peered at his arm, to be kissed on the rare – very rare – occasions that he scored a goal. Others – like David Beckham – carried their children's names around with them all the time (plus his wife's name in Hindi, apparently misspelt). Robbie Savage has the word 'Mum' on his arm, as a constant reminder. Sweet.

But some of the indelible adornments worn by the modern player are less starry-eyed in their inspiration. Jay Bothroyd, the former Coventry, Wolves, Cardiff and QPR striker, for instance, has the word

'Love' right across his midriff. Which sounds charmingly romantic, you might think, until you discover that the letters are made up of drawings of weapons. The O of Bothroyd's love is a hand grenade.

Inking is by no means an obsession restricted to British players, either. On his homecoming to Santiago in June 2014, the Chilean footballer Mauricio Pinilla wanted something to remember the Brazil World Cup by. Most of us would have been satisfied with a replica football shirt, a pair of flip-flops and half a kilo of coffee beans, but Pinilla was keen on a more permanent keepsake. So he had a tattoo done. Not just any old design, either, but one which memorialised the moment when he crashed a shot against the bar in the closing seconds of Chile's game against the hosts, a strike which, had it been marginally more accurate, would have won the match for his nation. He now has, permanently applied to his temple, a tattoo which reads (in English) 'One centimetre from glory'.

From a distance, meanwhile, the Portuguese Raul Meireles appears to be covered in the sort of random jottings which look like a troupe of chimpanzees have used his torso for notes as they attempt *The Times* crossword. And Liverpool's Danish defender Daniel Agger, a man whose body is adorned by nearly as many drawings as Florence's Uffizi Gallery, became so in thrall to body art he qualified as a tattooist. His personal portfolio includes a Viking battle scene on his back and the letters 'YNWA' on the fingers of his right hand, an acronym for the Liverpool anthem 'You'll Never Walk Alone'. The Italian Daniele De Rossi has what appears to be a road sign inked into his calf. Closer inspection of the cartoon inside a triangular frame reveals it is a drawing of a stick-man diving into another stick man's shins (if stick-men have shins). Beware sliding tackles: well, it's nice to be warned.

Southampton's Polish goalkeeper Artur Boruc's attempt at humour is even less distinguished. He has around his belly button a drawing of a monkey bending over in such a fashion that – and there's no polite way of putting this – his navel becomes its anus. It looks like the kind of thing that a university student might find scrawled on his stomach the morning after a heavy night in freshers' week. Boruc's, though, is permanent. (But then a man who, in his days as a Celtic player, wore a T-shirt proclaiming 'God Bless the Pope' following an Old Firm game, never was the subtlest of operators.)

The Norwegian John Carew was more serious about his inking. He wanted something which reflected his character, his refusal to compromise. So, when he was playing for Aston Villa, he asked a Birmingham tattooist to inscribe round the bottom of his neck the words: 'My Life, My Rules'. And, to demonstrate his class, he wanted them in French. The needle wielder duly consulted an internet translation service and carefully wrote the words *Ma Vie, Mes Règles* across Carew's neck. Nuance, it seems, does not translate on the Web. Unfortunately for Carew, in the plural 'règles' takes on a somewhat different meaning from plain 'rules'. The hapless Scandinavian had managed to tattoo himself with words that translate into English as 'My Life, My Menstrual Cycle'.

Perhaps fearful of such public display, Nile Ranger had his tattoo done in a place normally invisible to the public eye. For reasons best known to the former Newcastle United forward himself, he has a smiley face drawn on the inside of his lower lip. Smart.

Still, neither Carew nor Ranger can compare with some of football's most unhappy inkists: the fans. In 1995, a Newcastle supporter called Robert Nesbitt wanted to demonstrate his affection for the club's striker Andy Cole. So he had an image of the player in action in Newcastle strip applied to his thigh. After enduring a five-hour exercise in pain at the tattoo parlour, however, he walked out to discover that while he was otherwise engaged with the needle, Cole had been transferred to Manchester United. Still, at least he had once played for Newcastle. In 2009, Chris Atkinson, a follower of Manchester City, responded to rumours that Kaká was about to join the club from Real Madrid by having his name indelibly applied to his chest. Kaká signed for Milan twenty-four hours later.

But even that pair are fortunate compared to the young Boca Juniors fan who went into a Buenos Aires tattoo parlour in 2011 and asked to have the logo of his beloved club permanently inscribed across his back. Unbeknownst to him, the tattoo artist was a supporter of fierce rivals River Plate and decided to have a bit of fun at his client's expense. When he had completed his work, the artist told the young man that unfortunately he didn't have a mirror to hand, but the lad ought to show the work to everyone he knew as it perfectly captured what it meant to support Boca. The young chap went home, stripped off his shirt and proudly displayed his new tattoo to his parents. Who wondered, quite understandably, why their son had just paid to have a giant penis tattooed across his back.

2010 'Nobody serious about political change can shirk the fact that the game has to be abolished.'

Terry Eagleton, Professor of English Literature at Lancaster University, writing about football in *The Guardian*, 15 June 2010.

Terry Eagleton, a Marxist academic noted more for his *Literary Theory: An Introduction* than for his enthusiasm for sporting activity, was writing as the World Cup circus set up its tent in South Africa. FIFA had promised that staging the competition would transform the country, give it an unrivalled developmental uplift. By the time the prof's piece was published, however, the only visible evidence of change wrought in the country was in the giant advertising posters featuring various players which greeted arrivals at O.R. Tambo International Airport in Johannesburg.

But it was not so much the peripherals, the relentless commercial paraphernalia that attached itself to football, that Eagleton objected to. The game itself, he insisted, was a paradigm of capitalism, a promoter of all that is wrong with the world, a force less progressive even than the winners of the recent British general election.

> If the Cameron government is bad news for those seeking radical change, the World Cup is even worse. It reminds us of what is still likely to hold back such change long after the coalition is dead. If every right-wing think-tank came up with a scheme to distract the populace from political injustice and compensate them for lives of hard labour, the solution in each case would be the same: football... For the most part football these days is the opium of the people, not to speak of their crack cocaine. Its icon is the impeccably Tory, slavishly conformist Beckham. The Reds are no longer the Bolsheviks.

Mind you, any right-wing think tank would have its work cut out to invent anything to match football's intoxicating charms. The game, Eagleton admitted, offered much that radical politicians do not: an experience of solidarity for fans, a mix of 'glamour with ordinariness', hero worship of stars 'who could easily be you', something 'that enriches the aesthetic lives of people', a game that 'turns ordinary people into experts'.

And that is its problem: football is just too damned intoxicating. How easily the populace is seduced into following a pursuit whose very purpose is unapologetically elitist, its structures Darwinian, its fundamental aim to divide between winners and losers. The collective good plays no part in its rhythm, its goal is entirely solipsistic. It represents the capitalist urge at its most distilled. And so the only sensible course for anyone seeking proper change, proper egalitarianism, proper liberation is to ban it. Though as Eagleton admitted, any political outfit which attempted to do so 'would have about as much chance of power as the chief executive of BP has of taking over from Oprah Winfrey'.

Ever since it was first codified, football has lent itself to political interpretation and exploitation by the ruling classes. In 1938, so keen was Benito Mussolini on the idea that the triumph of the Italian team in that year's World Cup would stand as testimony to the powers of fascism, he told the players before the competition that they would not be welcome home if they lost (they didn't). Seventy-four years on, Eagleton's least favourite politician, David Cameron, ensured that his spin doctors circulated a picture of him, taken in a break during a G7 summit in Washington, raising his arms in triumph as Chelsea beat Bayern Munich in the Champions League final. That he was standing alongside a crestfallen Angela Merkel, chancellor of Germany and long-established fan of the game, only gave impetus to his triumphalism.

> If every right-wing think-tank came up with a scheme to distract the populace from political injustice... the solution in each case would be the same: football.

Eagleton's was a fascinating thesis. And rather demonstrating his argument that football *is* a politically fluid thing, the reaction to his uncompromising polemic found dozens of respondents seeking to use the game as evidence of the superiority of their worldview. Disagreeing fundamentally with the author, Steve Rotheram, the Labour MP for Liverpool Walton, preferred to see football as: 'A mechanism that can be used to tackle one of the single biggest issues in our constituencies: a poverty of aspiration. Its influence on ordinary working-class families is profound. Without football, Wayne Rooney and Steven Gerrard would still be working in Liverpool, struggling to make ends meet, just like every other would-be footballer.'

Dave Zirin, meanwhile, American author of the book *A People's History of Sports*, offered the following analysis:

> Football is, at the end of the day, like a hammer. And you can use a hammer to bash someone over the head or you could use it to construct something beautiful. It's in the way that you use it. It can be brutal. It can be ugly. But it also has an unbelievable potential to bring us together, to provide health, fun, enjoyment, and of course pulse-racing excitement.

Brilliantly, a post on *The Guardian* website suggested that, rather than being an endorsement of the monetarist system, England's abject failure to beat their impoverished rivals Algeria in the World Cup game in Cape Town the very day after Eagleton's piece was published utterly undermined the cornerstone of capitalism: the insistence that financial reward is the only way to encourage performance. 'England today destroyed right-wing meme that more incentives means people work harder. Cut footballers' & boardroom pay!'

It was an interesting theory. After all, participants in the Ryder Cup, golf's bi-annual team competition that pits Europe against the USA receive no monetary return for their efforts, yet seem to try as hard as if there were millions on offer. Maybe that is the way ahead for any future manager of the England team: tell his players they will get nothing for their labours, watch them win the World Cup and then justify it as an act of socialist revolution. It is about as likely to work as anything else.

2011 'Somebody better get down there and explain offside to her.'

Sky TV's Richard Keys discusses the referee's assistant Sian Massey with his colleague Andy Gray, ahead of a live broadcast, Molineux stadium, Wolverhampton, 22 January 2011.

As with many a twenty-first century media scandal, 'linogate' was conducted at breakneck speed. It began with the leaking of a recording featuring the two men who had been at the forefront of Sky's football broadcasting for nearly two decades. They were heard off-air discussing the appointment of the first female referee's assistant to officiate at a Premier League game. Keys sounded affronted by the very fact that a woman was to run the line. Former Aston Villa and Wolves striker Gray harrumphed that women are genetically incapable of understanding the offside law. Keys suggested Massey's appointment was evidence of 'a game gone mad'.

They were not alone in expressing such antediluvian attitudes. In 2003, after Morag Pirie had officiated in a game against Montrose, the Albion Rovers manager Peter Hetherston, redefined the term unreconstructed.

I knew it wasn't going to be our day when I arrived at Links Park and found that we had a woman running the line. She should be at home making the tea or the dinner for her man who comes in after he has been to the football.

Three years later, in 2006, the Luton Town manager Mike Newell was loftily dismissive of female officials. He was furious when assistant referee Amy Rayner failed to award his side a penalty in a defeat by QPR. 'She shouldn't be here. I know that sounds sexist but I am sexist. This is not park football, so what are women doing here?'

As it transpired, Keys and Gray's disparagement was misplaced. Massey, by the very excellence of her decision-making, provided public refutation of their denigration of women's abilities. She has gone on from that debut to establish a reputation as one of the game's most consistent flag wavers, rarely wrong in her judgment. As for Keys's notion that football has 'gone mad', some would suggest that the meritocratic promotion of a young official who performed conspicuously well was one of the few areas in which it retained a modicum of sanity.

Yet to be fairer to the pair than they were to the object of their disdain, Keys and Gray never intended the audience to hear their prejudice. Both may have been paid to give their opinions, but over eighteen years at the helm of Britain's most watched live football broadcast, they had restricted their public statements of opinion to technical observations on the games they were watching. Though the viewing public knew all about their attitude to diving wingers, parking the bus and the two-footed tackle, they had no idea what they thought about women. This was an off-air comment. All too aware of what had happened to Ron Atkinson (see pages 267–71), Keys and Gray were too professional to be caught out by a live microphone. However, someone at Sky was pretty keen the public should find out what they were really like. Whoever it was not only recorded the private exchange, they handed it to *The Mail on Sunday*, thus plunging their colleagues into a national brouhaha.

Looking back, in itself the recording is still not that shocking. Narrow-minded, clearly, but no worse than you might hear down the golf club lounge. The pair's superiors at Sky, however, moved swiftly – some might say precipitately – to quell the ensuing firestorm that accompanied the leak. Keys and Gray were initially suspended from duty for one week. And it might have gone no further than that, had either man been in possession of an ally. But after nearly two decades of work with the satellite broadcaster it appeared that they had made few friends at Sky. So it was that a number of incriminatory private recordings, apparently stockpiled by disaffected staff in order one day to wreak revenge, immediately seeped out into the public domain. There was one of Gray disparaging the lineswoman again, another in which he attempted a feeble chat-up line with a young female colleague and a third in which Keys tried to embroil the pundit Jamie Redknapp in his dirty-old-man talk.

To add to the duo's travails, colleagues were briefing everywhere to the press. The picture painted was of a pair floating on a bubble of inflated self-regard, forever keen to inform staff that they were the ones who counted in this operation. We learned that Keys's favourite put-down of co-workers was that they were lucky to be drinking at the well of success that he and Gray had dug.

> This is not park football. So what are women doing here?

The truth is that Gray and Keys are superb broadcasters – unflustered, unflappable, never stuck for an apposite phrase. But they failed to apply the oldest adage in showbiz: be nice to others on your way up, because you'll need them on the way down. The Sky sexists were renowned for treating colleagues with a contempt evident in their language. Any man who, like Keys was heard to do, refers to a young woman as 'it' is not someone who maintains a deep reservoir of respect.

But still, the history of broadcasting is littered with household favourites who turned out to hold loathsome views in private. If Keys and Gray had not infuriated so many in the workplace, we would have been none the wiser about the reality behind their image of smooth clubbability. As it was, they were very publicly jettisoned by their employers, dispatched from the building with unseemly haste, sacked less than a week after the recording became public, without recourse to appeal.

The relief at no longer being daily confronted by their sense of superiority apparently generated a party atmosphere at the company's Isleworth studios. But surely the pair can't have been removed simply to cheer up the workers. So why were they defenestrated? Keys still speaks of 'dark forces at work' behind his demise. There are those who suggest that Gray paid the ultimate price for suing the *News of the World*, Sky's NewsCorp stablemate, over the alleged hacking of his mobile, an explanation buttressed by reports of Rupert Murdoch dropping hints of 'other reasons' for the P45s during a visit to *The Times* newsroom. Others believe, though there is no clear evidence to suggest it happened, that the Sky hierarchy, anxious to refresh their presentational line-up, but fearful of the scale of any required pay-offs, engineered the leaks to facilitate easier dismissal.

Whatever the reason, Sky immediately went to work to modernise its output, bringing in to replace the pair the brilliant Gary Neville and Ed Chamberlin, a presenter known for his off-screen charm. It worked: their coverage became increasingly regarded as being at the forefront of innovation and insight. Keys and Gray, meanwhile, went off to work for Al Jazeera in Qatar, a society less than renowned for the rigour with which it observes women's rights.

One final thing about the affair: brilliant as Sian Massey has been at her profession, she remains the only female to officiate at a Premier League game. And there are plenty within the sport who would regard that as about as far as things should go (the Russian footballer Andrey Arshavin, for instance, believes that women should be banned from driving a car, never mind allowing them to wield a flag and a whistle). The sad truth is, the departure of Keys and Gray should in no way be regarded – as some within football tried to claim at the time – as the removal of the last vestige of sexism from the game.

2012 'Oooohohohnnnggggoooo!'

Gary Neville appears to be in the midst of an orgasm as Fernando Torres scores the goal that takes Chelsea to the Champions League final, Camp Nou stadium, Barcelona, 24 April 2012.

It is not often that Gary Neville is lost for words. When he retired, the former Manchester United full-back made the transition to television punditry with an ease which suggested he was born to the role. Coupling a sharp mind to a Stakhanovite work ethic, from the first moment he put lips to microphone he proved himself a brilliant analyst on Sky TV, able quickly and succinctly to sum up what was going on, adding to the pictures rather than simply describing them. In the spring of 2014, he spotted why Manchester United were losing to Liverpool within about five minutes of the game beginning, for instance. Which was roughly an hour and a half before the United manager David Moyes worked it out.

But even Neville was reduced to gibbering incoherence by what unfolded in the last minute of the 2012 Champions League semi-final. As Chelsea's Torres galloped from the centre circle and skipped around the Barcelona goalkeeper Víctor Valdés to slip the ball into an unguarded net and send his club to the final in Munich, Neville could only moan as if in the throes of ecstasy. And in doing so, he articulated all that could be said about the most improbable of turnarounds. 'Unbelievable, unbelievable,' Neville yelled when he had finally recovered the power of speech. 'The last eighteen months have been forgotten in two seconds.'

Given what had happened, given the way a fractious and fractured squad of players had combined to outwit the finest club side assembled in the twenty-first century, given how nobody had offered so much as a prayer for Chelsea's chances, he was right: it really was unbelievable.

Eleven months earlier, in his restless five-year-long search for an adequate replacement for José Mourinho, the manager he had so recklessly fired in 2007, Roman Abramovich had hired André Villas-Boas to be Chelsea head coach. A former protégé of Mourinho, Villas-Boas was supposed to be the Special One Mark Two. Abramovich tasked him with the job of refreshing the team that Mourinho had built, of easing the big egos out the door. AVB, as he liked to be called, approached the job with the subtlety of a bull elephant attempting needlecraft: within six months he had so alienated the old guard his position in the dressing room was untenable.

> They weren't about to be inconvenienced by a team featuring John Obi Mikel. Were they?

As is the Abramovich way, no time was given to him to prove he could get it right; he was fired. His assistant, the former Chelsea player Roberto Di Matteo, took over with Chelsea already out of domestic contention, but still, somehow, alive in the European Cup. By dint of simply returning responsibility to the players AVB had ostracised – gnarled old-timers John Terry, Frank Lampard and Didier Drogba – Di Matteo advanced the team through the latter stages of the competition. They needed extra time to bypass Napoli in the last sixteen and then used all their grizzled experience to ease past Benfica in the quarter-final.

But when they were paired with Barcelona in the semis, it was almost universally predicted that they had reached the end of the road. This was Pep Guardiola's Barça at their peak, the tiki-taka* maestros who passed opponents to death. A team boasting the skills of Lionel Messi, 'Xavi' Hernández, and Andrés Iniesta, they had annihilated Manchester United in the final of the competition twice in

---

* The coining and popularising of the onomatopoeic *tiki-taka* to describe Spain's quick and precise passing style is generally credited to Andrés Montes. The late Spanish broadcaster used the phrase during his TV commentaries on the 2006 World Cup.

the previous three seasons. They weren't about to be inconvenienced by a team featuring John Obi Mikel. Were they?

Even when Chelsea won the home leg, with a poacher's snipe from Drogba, still the script was assumed to be written in Barça's favour. Especially when the home side quickly took a two-goal advantage. Especially when Terry got himself sent off for a pathetically ill-conceived assault on Alexis Sánchez. Especially when Drogba clumsily upended Messi and the Argentine got up to take the spot kick.

But Messi's penalty crashed off the bar. Gradually the idea began to form that Ramires's goal at the end of the first half might be enough, after all, to confound probability. With Chelsea playing so deep their defence required the services of an aqualung, Barça kept up a relentless death-by-passing assault. But they couldn't break through; the score remained 2–1 with Chelsea's away goal enough to see them through.

And then, in the very last minute, with every Chelsea player bar one lined up across the edge of their own area, a huge hit-and-hope clearance found the one man not parking the bus. As Torres charged forward with the ball, every assumption, every prediction, every expectation was confounded. And Neville lost the power of speech.

Now all that was left for Chelsea was to head to Munich and take on Bayern who, by a quirk of fate, were hosting the final in their own backyard. Which, surely, would be a step too far even for this astonishing run by Roberto Di Matteo's side. Wouldn't it?

2012 'Agüeroooooooo!'

Martin Tyler of Sky TV reacts to Sergio Agüero's Premier League-winning strike for Manchester City, Etihad Stadium, Manchester, 13 May 2012.

Ever since they paid a sheikh's ransom for the rights to show Premier League matches, Sky had been waiting for a day like this, waiting for an occasion when all the tension, drama and excitement of a nine-month long competition was distilled into one afternoon, waiting for a day when the league behaved like a knock-out competition. Twenty years it took before it arrived, twenty years of victories sealed long before the final day, of triumphs confirmed by others' defeats, twenty years of petering out.

When the Premier League was first mooted, the broadcaster had wanted a critical dénouement every season, so had lobbied for a play-off to decide the title winner. They wanted a footballing Super Bowl to attract subscribers. Those in charge of the competition, however, preferred to maintain the integrity of a league system. It was not until the league entered its twenty-first year that the moneymen were presented with the last-day drama they had always craved. And when it came, the action Sky had to report on a May afternoon in 2012 was simply astonishing.

Throughout the 2011–12 Premier League season the action had fizzed and bubbled, the lead switching between the two Manchester clubs with a frequency that was at times dizzying. The final day arrived, though, with the mathematics extremely simple. City and United were neck-and-neck on the same points. City's goal difference, however, was markedly superior, largely thanks to the 6–1 derby defeat they had inflicted on their crosstown rivals the previous autumn. Any sort of victory for City at home to Queens Park Rangers and the trophy would be bedecked in blue ribbons. United had to win at Sunderland and hope that their oldest rivals somehow blew it.

City, though, were surely not going to blow it, playing at home against a QPR side threatened with relegation, a side that had not won an away match all season, albeit one managed by the former City boss Mark Hughes and containing within their number the erstwhile City hero Joey Barton. Certainly Sky thought that, and had dispatched their senior reporting team to the Etihad. Manchester United, kicking off at the same time on Wearside, were just an afterthought.

'Take it out of context and it looked like a case of dotting the i's and crossing the t's,' Tyler recalls. 'But it was never a formality. In my preparations for the game, I'd taken account of City's history, of their ability always to snatch defeat from the jaws of triumph. It had crossed my mind that I might have to say something if they messed it up.' Even when United scored first it didn't look as though the script was going to deviate from a pre-ordained City triumph, especially when Pablo Zabaleta put the Sky Blues ahead at half-time.

> I'd taken account of City's history, of their ability always to snatch defeat from the jaws of triumph.

It was in the second half that a nightmare possibility began to form in the minds of the more pessimistic City followers. First QPR equalised, then took the lead. Up in the Sky commentary box, Tyler was gripped by a sudden fear he was in the wrong place, reporting on the wrong story. Even when the Nietzsche-quoting Barton turned recidivist and got himself sent off, claiming retrospectively that he 'was doing the professional thing' by trying to provoke a couple of opponents into getting themselves sent off for retaliation, City were labouring, apparently rigid with tension, their volatile manager Roberto Mancini going purple with fury on the touchline at their inability to break down a stubborn QPR backline. Ridiculous as it seemed, City looked as though they were were going to throw away the chance of a lifetime, afflicted by an ill-timed recurrence of that most persistent of East Manchester afflictions – the dreaded 'City-itis'.

As ninety minutes arrived at both stadiums, many of the Sky Blue supporters did not see the board go up to signal that four minutes of time was to be added, mainly accrued by Barton's brainless sending-off. The exodus that had begun with a trickle about ten minutes from full-time was by then in full spate. This was not the usual dash for the car parks to beat the traffic. This was a flight from reality.

The game in Sunderland had already finished, and United were mathematically champions even when Edin Džeko scored an equaliser in the ninety-second minute. But that in itself was not enough: City still needed another goal to clinch the title. At the Stadium of Light, the United team remained on the playing surface, scouring the crowd for news of how their rivals were faring.

'We went to a split screen to show the United players waiting on the pitch,' says Tyler of the Sky coverage that was beamed around the globe. 'Then the director switched to single screen back at the Etihad at the exact moment [Mario] Balotelli received the ball on the edge of the area. You couldn't have post-produced it better.'

As the focus of the television pictures returned to the Etihad, a hopeful punt forward by the substitute Nigel de Jong had landed at Balotelli's feet. Attempting to turn, the Italian slipped and appeared to have lost it. But he stuck out a leg and thrust the ball forward to Sergio Agüero. The Argentine had cost City £35 million the previous summer, and now Diego Maradona's son-in-law had the chance to repay that massive investment in one last-gasp moment of athletic brilliance. He pushed the ball on towards goal, trying to evade a lunging foul from QPR's Taye Taïwo. It caught him on the knee. But he wobbled on. For a split second the stadium held its breath. And up in the television gantry, Tyler gathered his.

'That moment he took a touch gave me the time to get air into my lungs. I knew he wasn't going to go down. I knew he'd want this. What followed wasn't planned. It was a gut reaction.' And what followed was this: as the City man blasted the ball past the QPR 'keeper and ran, delirious, across the pitch, whipping his shirt above his head, the crowd behind him doing as close an impression of collective apoplexy as you could ever hope to see, Tyler opened his throat and roared out his name. 'Agüerooooooo!' he yelled, an ecstatic war-cry that was to become the ring tone on thousands of City fans' smartphones. There was nothing else that would have been appropriate. Nothing else that could have summed up the adrenaline rush of the moment. In the days and weeks to come, the City megastore was to run out of O's as fans bought shirts specially printed with all those extra vowels in the Argentinian's name.

Tyler describes the aftermath of Agüero's Premier League-winning strike:

> Then when I'd said it I let the pictures take over. They spoke far more powerfully than I ever could. The shot of Joe Hart running with his arms spread and having to look over his shoulder to check whether what had happened really had happened: you couldn't better that. Then I said something like: 'Drink this in, you will never see anything like it again.' And I stand by those words. It felt epochal. I don't mind admitting, when we finished, there were tears in my eyes. Not because I'm a City fan, I'm not. But because it was an epic moment and I had something to do with it. It moved me to the core.

For commentator and broadcaster alike it was indeed an epochal moment. Sky's comprehensive coverage of the league had achieved the ultimate reward when nine months of competition was not decided until the very last second of the very last game. Talk about competitive uncertainty. This was drama, this was tension, this was television.

PART VI

EXTRA TIME AND PENALTIES

2013–14

2013 'THE CHOSEN ONE'

Banner unveiled in the Stretford End to mark the appointment of David Moyes as Manchester United's new manager, Old Trafford, Manchester, 26 August 2013.

It is rare enough that a football manager chooses the time of his departure from a club. But to be able then to appoint his successor was a unique privilege for Sir Alex Ferguson.

When he announced in May 2013 that he was to leave his position as Manchester United manager after twenty-seven trophy-bedecked seasons, Ferguson already knew who was going to take over. He had enjoyed a lunch with Pep Guardiola, his relationship with José Mourinho was cordial, and he was known to be an admirer of Carlo Ancelotti. But his mind was made up about who should step into his place. David Moyes, who had steered Everton carefully and productively for the past eleven years was the man he thought best equipped to take on the institution he had built. While it was true that, unlike Guardiola, Mourinho and Ancelotti, Moyes had never won a thing in his career, Ferguson believed the flinty-eyed Scot was more likely to honour his legacy, maintain the traditions of the club, keep things as red. They shared a similar background, they had been members of the same Glasgow youth football club, where they were coached by the same man, their values were identikit. 'He reminds me of me,' the grand old man said of his successor.

> Your job is to stand by the new manager, he said.

At his final, emotional send-off from Old Trafford in May 2013, Ferguson instructed the fans what their future role should be. 'Your job is to stand by the new manager,' he said.

Given what he had delivered, given the glory he had engineered, given the esteem in which he was held, it seemed the least they could do. And while some wondered why a business of United's scale had allowed its most significant piece of executive recruitment in more than a quarter of a century to be conducted on a personal whim, even the sceptics had to admit that Ferguson had fluffed precious few lines in a quarter-century plus of performing at the 'theatre of dreams' (a term coined for Old Trafford in 1978 by Sir Bobby Charlton). Sure, Moyes had been notorious for his caution and conservatism at Goodison Park, where he had acquired the less-than-wholly-flattering nickname Dithering Dave. But Ferguson was convinced he was the right man for the job, that he would grow into United, that his pragmatism was simply a result of the financially reduced circumstances under which he had worked on Merseyside. Ferguson persuaded the board to back his judgment by giving Moyes a six-year contract. This was an appointment for the long haul. And, believing the great manager had got his final decision right, a group of 400 supporters who sit in the Stretford End showed their support by paying for a flag in the new man's honour.

Stretford End Flags, as the group styled themselves, revealed their work ahead of the game against Chelsea. A neat riposte to the nickname of the recently returning Chelsea manager (José Mourinho, aka The Special One; see pages 271–5) it carried a profile picture of Moyes looking stern and determined, alongside the legend 'The Chosen One'. The inference was clear: Moyes had been appointed from on high, Fergie's anointed dynastic successor.

Well-meaning, well-intentioned and supportive the banner may have been. But it also turned out to be less a statement of intent than a hopeless hostage to fortune. Because once up, there was no way it could be taken down. Even when it turned out that, as he urgently semaphored instruction to his players on the touchline down below, the Chosen One was not waving. He was drowning.

From the moment he arrived in Manchester, Moyes gave every indication that he was going to reinforce the old adage about leadership succession, which suggests that the wise man is not the one who immediately follows a triumphant boss, it is the one who comes next. From the very first time he stepped into the Old Trafford technical area, the name of his predecessor there in ten-foot high letters across the roof of the stand in front of him, the scale of the task seemed to overwhelm him.

No one could deny there were weaknesses within the squad he inherited from Ferguson, the back four was ageing, there was a huge gap where a central midfield should be, there was a surfeit of the mediocre and a deficit of the world class. But this was a bunch of players who, having won the title the season before, now suddenly found themselves faltering under the leadership of the new man. From being top of the Premier League pile, they slipped with alarming dispatch.

Everything Moyes did suggested the job was simply too big for him. He foolishly cleared out Ferguson's backroom staff – men of huge collective winning experience – and brought with him his own team of coaches, none of whom had won anything before, a group who failed to inspire players used to serial success. His press statements were underwhelming, his tactics nervy and cautious, his team selections entirely lacking in consistency (in fifty-one games in charge, he chose fifty-one different line-ups). Worse, his training was reckoned by the players to be unimaginative and unsophisticated.

> For the first time in a generation, United were not contenders.

The result was, for the first time in a generation, United were not contenders. They were out of the title race by Christmas, knocked out of all the cups and, by finishing seventh in the final table, not even close to qualifying for the Champions League. Moyes's record was not one he might have been expecting when he took over the job: under his stewardship, 2013–14 was the first season in their history in which United lost home and away to Liverpool, Everton and Manchester City.

A technocrat rather than a gambler, a manager who preferred not to lose rather than to risk everything in the pursuit of victory, Moyes simply did not fit the Old Trafford brief. He was not a manager equipped with the necessary devilment to make United successful. The players quickly lost confidence that he was a man with a plan – and that lack of confidence was evident in every stumble and stutter.

Yet, despite the growing embarrassment of his insipid leadership, the home crowd remained exemplary in its support. 'Every single one of us stands by David Moyes,' was the chant as defeat followed humiliation. It was not the United way to change managers promiscuously. As Ferguson insisted, it was the crowd's job to support the new man, to see him through what would surely turn out to be temporary difficulty. It will come right, Fergie kept reiterating. Just give him time.

But as it became clear there was nothing temporary about this floundering, as Moyes's imprint on United seemed to be one of utter emasculation, as his language of 'do our best', 'try and win' and 'hope we can do something' jarred with United's traditional sense of panache, the discontent began to coalesce around the banner. After a spineless home defeat in the Manchester derby in March 2014, a group of spectators attempted to tear it down. They were stopped by stewards, who were positioned at matches thereafter to guard it. During a game against Aston Villa later that same month, a bunch of fans hired a light aircraft to fly over the stadium trailing a banner which read 'Moyes Out: The Wrong One'. As Liverpool surged ahead in the race for the league title, a sign was held up at Anfield during a game against Spurs by Merseyside fans both praising the qualities of their boss Brendan Rodgers and ridiculing United's selection policy. It read simply: 'Brendan, the carefully chosen one'.

And, since the supporters had no access to the stadium to have it removed from its position on the middle tier of the Stretford End, it turned out the banner was still in place when Moyes was relieved of his duties on Easter Monday 2014, the day after a dire capitulation at his old club Everton. It took three days after the *Manchester Evening News* announced his departure under the headline 'The Badly Chosen One' for it to be quietly taken down, a Stalinistic erasure of the unfortunate Moyes from United history.

One thing the episode might have taught the United hierarchy: when a placard lasts longer than your manager, it might be wise for an organisation to re-assess its recruitment policy.

2013 'I know all sorts. I know that the origin of the phrase 'Bob's Your Uncle' dates back to 1887, when the British prime minister Robert Gascoyne-Cecil (Lord Salisbury) was accused of nepotism for appointing his nephew to the position of Irish Chief Secretary. But I don't know how a Premier League footballer, who considers himself to be a smart guy, managed to turn £8 million into nothing.'

Keith Gillespie in the introduction to his memoir *How Not To Be A Football Millionaire*, published 3 October 2013.

Keith Gillespie – the former Manchester United, Newcastle and Sheffield United winger – reckons, during his fifteen-year football career, that he squandered no less than £7,215,875 on gambling. If you wonder how that can be possible, he admits that at one point his eye-watering losses were running at £100,000 a day as his habit careered out of control.

'That's the thing,' he told me. 'You're always chasing the next winner. I would have a bet on every race going, in the bookies I'd have had slips for two horse races and a dog race all going off at once, I couldn't follow what was happening. It didn't matter, the stake, it was the buzz of winning.'

Despite what his bank statements might suggest, Gillespie is no fool. At grammar school in Northern Ireland he notched up good academic grades; he shares with Frank Lampard that rare distinction for a Premier League footballer of having a GCSE in Latin. These days he is a devoted pub quiz enthusiast, someone whose conversation is peppered with gobbets of oddball information, like that about Lord Salisbury's keep-it-in-the-family employment practices. For a bright man, though, he was an absolute mug when it came to placing a bet. 'Without a doubt I was a stupid gambler,' he admits. 'But then, when you look around, there's not too many clever gamblers. What there is are a lot of rich bookies.'

> When you look around, there's not too many clever gamblers.

Gillespie's addiction to a flutter began when he was part of the great Manchester United FA Youth Cup-winning side of 1992. After he was introduced to betting by a team-mate, he spent most of his extensive spare time following the horses, heading down to the bookies the moment training finished and staying there until closing time: 'Everyone knew where I was. Alex Ferguson had spies everywhere in Manchester, he knew I was there. He probably thought it meant I wasn't getting into mischief.'

And once Ferguson knew what he was up to, he did little to discourage the young player. Indeed, he did the opposite, sending Gillespie, then just eighteen years old, down to the bookies on his behalf. 'I'd have been the runner for the manager, putting his bets on for him,' he recalls. 'I was the runner for the first team's syndicate. It wasn't a big issue.' This was the thing Gillespie discovered: no one thought his incessant gambling was a problem. Ferguson reckoned it far less damaging to Gillespie's playing abilities than other diversions to which young players are prone. And the then United manager was by no means alone in doing that. Across the game, managers have been allowing extraordinary levels of gambling within their dressing rooms, apparently oblivious to its addictive nature. When Gillespie moved to Newcastle – as the financial make-weight in the deal that brought Andy Cole to Old Trafford – he found his new boss, Kevin Keegan, was as tolerant of his failing as the old boss had been.

'It is football's last taboo,' he says of gambling. 'There's that many things players can get involved in, but gambling's probably not taken as seriously as alcohol or drugs. Yet there's heavy gamblers in every dressing room. What I mean by heavy is basically addicted. Loads of players really come unstuck: Michael Chopra, Matthew Etherington, John Terry, me.'

Footballers have gambled since the year dot. Men with an advanced, aggressive, competitive instinct, they have relished the thrill of challenging their team-mates at anything: cards on the team bus, the likely winner of the 2.30 at Fakenham, which of two raindrops will run quicker down a window. It has been ever thus: it was once said of the former England forward Stan Bowles that if he could pass a bookies like he could pass a football he would have been a wealthy man.

But what has changed has been the levels of gambling. As money arrived in the pocket of the modern player, so the amounts being wagered rose exponentially. The old adage about a bet not being worth making unless the loss hurts meant some footballers began to spend huge amounts. Gillespie was not unusual in being overtaken by the scale of his habit. The game is replete with stories of former England captains losing tens of thousands of pounds in card schools, of household names obliged to re-mortgage their home to pay off their debts to the bookie, of men who should be expecting a comfortable retirement facing bankruptcy. Which is what happened eventually to Gillespie. In 2010, he was declared bankrupt despite having earned a seven-figure salary for more than a decade.

And what has upped the scale of losses has been the increasingly ready availability of gambling. Players no longer need to visit the bookie – or even to send a junior along to place the bet for them. Not when they have a smartphone and an appropriate app to hand. Now they can bet whenever they choose without ever being obliged to show their face in public, and lose a shedload of money at the tap of a screen. Gillespie takes up the story again:

> Online betting was an absolute nightmare for me. It made it so easy. I was staking money on anything. Golf, horses, dogs, the darts. Didn't matter to me as long as I stood a chance of winning. And all of it on account with the bookies, who were more than happy to keep extending me credit.

Football is doing very little to protect its employees from the seductive appeal of smartphone betting. In fact it is doing the opposite. The game has become increasingly in hock to betting companies. In 2013–14 four Premier League clubs had a bookie's firm as their shirt sponsor. Most clubs have gambling enterprises as commercial partners. Every ad break during televised matches has Ray Winstone growling at you, urging you to bet in-play ('You will LAHV it!'). At every turn, far from challenging the seductive lure of the bet, the game is encouraging its followers to gamble.

Indeed, in 2014 we were treated to Peter Coates, Stoke City's chairman, talking about how his club would stand by their winger Matthew Etherington after he revealed that he had posted gambling losses totalling the national debt of a small South American country. Not only would they stand by him, Coates insisted, they would encourage him to seek professional help for his addiction. What he didn't do was confront the bookies who had entrapped his player. But then why would he, given that Coates is also the chairman of Bet365, the very same company that has hired Winstone to do his Cockney-geezer *schtick*.

Gillespie, meanwhile, believes there is only one way to stop other players following him into financial ruin:

> You can't ban gambling in dressing rooms, everyone's got a mobile phone. At the end of the day, you can't tell adults how to spend their money. What I'd say to young kids starting out is this: get a hobby. It was the boredom that got me. I bet for something to do. I should have taken up golf to kill the time. If only I'd learned how to putt.

That said, he admits that if he had taken up the game, he would have probably only ended up having a bet with his golf coach about how many shots it would take him to complete a round.

2013 'The hardest part of Roy's body is his tongue.'

Sir Alex Ferguson on his long-term right-hand man, Roy Keane, in *Alex Ferguson: My Autobiography*, published 25 October 2013.

The former Manchester United manager always chose his words carefully. Whether he was indulging in mind games, dropping a few verbal grenades to undermine an opponent, or seeking ways to encourage his players, nothing was left to chance. So when he used his autobiography, published shortly after his retirement, to savage his former great lieutenant spontaneity was not involved. This was pre-planned. This was revenge served up in the most chilled of dishes.

And the choice of phrase – according to Paul Hayward, his ghostwriter, the words were entirely Ferguson's own – was brutal.

Keane, a player who, in his effort in the 1999 Champions League semi-final against Juventus, Ferguson himself once said had given the most magnificent individual performance he had ever encountered, was dismissed as nothing more than a verbal bully. These were words calculated to hurt. 'He can debilitate the most confident person in the world in seconds with that tongue,' Ferguson went on. 'What I noticed about him that day as I was arguing with him was that his eyes started to narrow, almost to wee black beads. It was frightening to watch. And I'm from Glasgow.'

His eyes started to narrow, almost to wee black beads. It was frightening to watch.

Keane would probably smile at that observation. The argument to which Ferguson refers signalled the end of one of football's most successful double acts. Keane was Ferguson's conscience on the pitch, his eyes and ears. For ten years they plotted and planned together, both utterly committed to the same cause. But by the autumn of 2005, Ferguson saw Keane's powers were waning. Age was visibly withering him. He was convinced, too, that the player's increasing petulance in the dressing room was a result of that decline. As had happened with Mick McCarthy in Saipan in 2002 (see pages 255–9), Keane was raging against the dying of the light. No longer able to function on the field of play as he once had, he was becoming increasingly testy, aggressive, verbally nasty.

The end of their relationship came in December 2005 when Keane – at the time absent injured – was recorded by United's in-house television station rubbishing the performance of some of those who were playing in his stead. His analysis was so ferocious the piece was never broadcast. But, when challenged by Ferguson about what he was playing at, Keane stood by what he had said, claiming he was happy for it to be shown in the dressing room. When the tape was played to his colleagues, understandably it caused some disquiet. Ferguson insisted

Keane apologise and his captain refused. Two stubborn men rejected any possibility of compromise and the player left the club immediately.

But if Ferguson thought Keane's powers were in decline, his player thought much the same of his manager. At the time, United had slipped behind Arsenal and Chelsea. Keane saw in José Mourinho and Arsène Wenger more progressive, more engaged, more motivated leadership figures. Ferguson, he believed, was too distracted by outside interests, his dispute with the Irish racing fraternity over ownership of the horse Rock of Gibraltar a symptom of his diminishing focus. A man always restless in his quest for fulfilment, the Irishman saw in Ferguson a manager who had grown sleek with complacency.

As divorces went, this was not amicable. The animosity between the two erstwhile comrades rumbled and grumbled for the next eight years, as Keane first went into management, then into the ITV studios as the broadcaster's principal pundit. Keane did not change his opinion about his old boss, even though Ferguson brilliantly revived his fortunes by creating his last great United side and winning the Champions League in 2008.

The spat was never made public until Ferguson's book erupted like a particularly virulent boil. Though Keane announced he had no intention of reading the tome, when he heard what had been said about him, he predictably retaliated. His eyes narrowing to Fergie's 'wee black beads', he told the ITV cameras that Ferguson was a man who preached loyalty but didn't understand the meaning of the word. Later, in a documentary with his old adversary Patrick Vieira, he insisted that the best manager he had ever worked with was Brian Clough, a man under whom he won precisely nothing. And when picking his best-ever United side, he pointedly left out Ferguson favourites like Ryan Giggs and Paul Scholes.

That was the final indication of how far the two had parted company. Because it must take some bitter disillusion for anyone seriously to select a greatest-ever United line-up and not pick Scholes.

2013 'I think the only people who should play for England is English people. If you've lived in England for five years it doesn't make you English.'

Jack Wilshere at a press conference ahead of England's World Cup qualifier against Ukraine, 9 October 2013.

Wilshere was responding to a question about Adnan Januzaj, who had just made an impressive debut for Manchester United. Despite sparkling in the Premier League, the young midfielder had not yet committed himself to any international cause; he had never played a minute's representative football in any age group. And it seemed half of world football was anxiously trying to sign him up. Born in Brussels to Kosovar/Albanian parents, his complicated heritage meant he was immediately eligible to turn out for no fewer than four national sides: Belgium, Serbia, Albania and Turkey. But the FA had worked out that, since he had not committed himself to anyone else, he might still be theirs. So they were fluttering their eyelashes in his direction, suggesting that he might wait out the required five-year residential qualification period and then play for England.

As one of the country's leading young performers, Wilshere was asked if he thought that the national squad would benefit from Januzaj's recruitment. The Arsenal man was not impressed with the idea. For him, the England team should be just that: a selection of the best Englishmen available. Not an amalgam of whoever happened to being passing through Heathrow. Surely there was enough native football talent around without going down the route of the England cricket and rugby sides, eager as they are to select anyone the moment they step off the plane from Johannesburg.

Somewhat unfairly, his vision of how a national side should be chosen was immediately ridiculed as being apparently scripted by the English Defence League. The South African-born-and-bred – though genetically half-English – Kevin Pietersen queried his conclusions on Twitter: surely, half of the sporting heroes competing under the Union Flag would be excluded if Wilshere had his way?

The fact is, Wilshere's was a view that failed to take into account the changing circumstances in which the modern game is played. Across world football, old-style demarcation lines have been blurred by immigration. Displaced from their homeland by war or economic necessity, players have long been turning out for countries far from where they were born. In any international competition these days you will find Ghanaian Italians, Bosnian Germans and Brazilian Croats.

> Across world football, old-style demarcation lines have been blurred by immigration.

Indeed, it was happening all around Wilshere in England too. He himself had been selected for the under-21s at the same time as Wilfried Zaha, who came to London from the Ivory Coast – formerly a French colony – as an eight-year-old and a decade later had committed himself to play for his new country rather than for his country of birth. The Kingston-born, London-bred Raheem Sterling was vigorously pursued by Jamaica before opting for England. And let's not forget Owen Hargreaves, born in Canada to Welsh parents, who learned his football in Germany before becoming England's stand-out player in the 2006 World Cup.

In a way it was ever thus; the game's international selection has long been flexible. On 5 January 2014 football lost the great Eusébio. He was born and raised in Mozambique, a country for which he had boyhood dreams of playing. But his homeland was then a Portuguese colony. When it turned out he was a more than useful footballer, the colonial masters insisted he apply his ability to the cause of Portugal. Which he did with effortless distinction, winning the *Ballon d'Or* in

1965, leading the scoring in the 1966 World Cup and twice picking up the European Cup with Benfica (in 1960 and 1961). With no apparent self-awareness, during his peak the Portuguese authorities had him designated a national asset so that he could not be transferred to play for a club outside its borders. Never mind that he was snaffled from elsewhere, the Portuguese public adored their 'Black Pearl'. Just as you suspect the English would have loved to see Adnan Januzaj in a white shirt. Or at least they would if he had not, a couple of months after Wilshere spoke, selfishly decided to commit himself to Belgium.

2013 'Arsenal is like an orchestra, but it's a silent song, yeah? And I like heavy metal more. I always want it loud! I want to have this: BOOM!'

Jürgen Klopp, the Borussia Dortmund coach, in an interview published in *The Guardian* ahead of a Champions League tie with Arsenal, 3 November 2013.

If there were ever a floodlight failure at the Westfalenstadion in Dortmund, there would be no problem carrying on with the game. Just stand Borussia's manager on the touchline and get him to smile: that full-beam grin from the most substantial set of gnashers in world football would ensure everyone could see what they were doing until the power was restored.

Klopp's grin cheered up football throughout the second decade of the twenty-first century. A footballing cavalier in an era of roundheads, he is a manager who believes in the game's romantic core, in building things rather than buying things, in keeping a connection between those in the stand and those on the pitch. After a stint working for television as Germany's Gary Neville (before Gary Neville became Britain's Gary Neville) Klopp took on the Dortmund job at the end of the 2007–8 season, when the club had finished thirteenth in the Bundesliga. At a place where fan input is enshrined in the club's constitution, he created a powerhouse of a team that for a time surpassed the commercial juggernaut of Bayern Munich. He won the German Cup in his first season and added the Bundesliga title in 2011 and 2012. He then guided his club – an operation whose standing, scale and revenue is several divisions below the superpowers of the European game – to the Champions League final in 2013.

And along the way, he made everyone with whom he came into contact smile. A man of vibrant emotion, he behaves like a fan on the touchline, feeling every second of every game, occasionally erupting in volcanic spasms. He is the same off the pitch, a vibrant, passionate, funny presence. A living, breathing, chuckling inversion of the traditional stereotype of the dour, humour-bypass German, his press conferences are soundtracked by laughter, while his post-match interviews (in particular the one after his team beat Málaga in the last seconds of a Champions League quarter-final in April 2013) have become instant YouTube hits. Klopp has become a cult figure in Germany, now largely known by his middle name Norbert. In 2013 a pop song by Matze Knop entitled 'I Wanna Be Like Jürgen Klopp' was a big hit in Germany. The man himself was seen cheerfully dancing to it at a club function.

> A man of vibrant emotion, he behaves like a fan on the touchline.

After meeting him, *The Guardian's* David Hytner wrote that any interview should come with stage directions because in conversation Klopp constantly flings himself around the room to make emphasis: 'For me, he is *Sir* Arsène Wenger, he is really something, I love him,' Klopp adds, before miming a polite handshake. 'But I'm this guy, with high fives. I always want it loud. I want to have this...' Klopp makes the sound of an exploding bomb.

But gesticulation is only part of the Klopp way. As he has gone about his business of winning trophies, he has added hugely to the canon of great footballing quotes. Here are half a dozen of his best:

- *When BVB last won here most of my players were still being breastfed.*
  Relishing an unlikely victory by his young Borussia team at Bayern Munich, 2011.

- *Yes, it's true I underwent a hair transplant. I think the results are really cool, don't you?*
  Frankly confronting rumours in the media about his barnet enjoying some surgical assistance, 2012.

- *I'm a bit proud of my first red card as a coach. I approached the fourth official and said: 'How many mistakes are allowed here? If it's fifteen you have one more.'*
  Even his transgressions are framed as a joke, 2012.

- *We will wait for him like a good wife waiting for her husband who is in jail.*
  Explaining his approach to the German international Mats Hummels' extended injury problems, 2013.

- *Mkhitaryan fits us like an arse in a bucket.*
  Speaking of his new signing, the Armenian Henrikh Mkhitaryan, in 2013.

- *Mourinho says I speak too much? That's what one of my teachers used to tell me. I don't care, I don't think about this. I'm not intelligent enough to understand what it should be... but it's no problem, now I'll shut up, and everything is OK.*
  Responding to taunts from the mind games master ahead of

Dortmund's Champions League semi-final with Real Madrid in April 2013.

And everything *was* OK, Dortmund won the tie 4–3 to progress to the final against Bayern, an affair which turned Wembley Germanic. And though Klopp's team lost 2–1 at Wembley, that didn't stop him grinning. 'The only thing I can say is it was great... the whole atmosphere in the stadium was brilliant... Only the result was so shit.' This is, without doubt, a fan at heart.

2013 'My *quenelle* was very misunderstood.'

Nicolas Anelka talking about the gesture he made after scoring a goal for West Bromwich Albion against West Ham United, Upton Park, London, 28 December 2013.

Nicolas Anelka marked his strike in a 3–3 draw with West Ham like this: he sought out the touchline television camera and very deliberately, while maintaining full eye contact with the lens, placed his gloved left hand on his extended right arm just above the elbow, as if in a chopping gesture. For everyone watching the game in England his gesture had absolutely no significance. It just looked like the sort of semaphore managers use to instruct their players to switch position. It went so far over the collective British head, nobody even noticed what he had done. After all, Anelka hadn't scored a goal in the Premier League for over two seasons: maybe that was what he always did.

The French journalist Philippe Auclair, the London-based Premier League correspondent for several Parisian news outlets, however, was rather more alarmed. He was watching the game live and knew exactly what Anelka was doing. He also insisted, when it was more widely reported what the gesture signified, that the reaction would be significant. 'This will cause a real stink,' Auclair tweeted moments after Anelka had trotted back to the centre circle, wearing the smirk of a naughty schoolboy.

Auclair was right. When he did his salute, Anelka was fully aware that the Premier League was now an international property. His gesture was not aimed at the English audience, it was directed at those watching back home in France. The next morning, his apparently innocent celebration was the lead item on every news channel in his homeland. Because whatever it might have looked like to English observers, Anelka wasn't making random movements with his hands. These were absolutely deliberate. What he had done was to *glisser une quenelle*. And in France that has a very specific meaning.

> This will cause a real stink.

A *quenelle* is a small, seasoned ball of fish or meat bound with fat and eggs. But Anelka wasn't turning all Michel Roux on the Upton Park crowd. The *quenelle* is also the name of a salute invented by the French comedian Dieudonné M'bala M'bala. So proud is Dieudonné of his handiwork he has copyrighted it, ensuring everyone knows who came up with it and why. The culinary *quenelle* is thought to look like a suppository, so the comedian regarded it as a 'kind of *up yours* gesture to the establishment'.

Comedy is a very specific taste and it might be that Dieudonné's jokes don't travel well. But from a distance it looked as though there is little that is funny about him or his salute. The man is an avowed anti-semite. In fact in 2012 he starred in a film called *L'Antisémite*, which was financed by the former Iranian president Mahmoud Ahmadinejad, a man who wants to see the state of Israel wiped off the map. In his stage act, Dieudonné has long claimed that capitalism is a worldwide conspiracy driven by Jewish interests (which sounds uncomfortably close to a theory once promulgated by certain German politicians of the 1930s).

'All of them [Jewish people] are slave-traders who've moved into banking, show-business and, today, terrorist action,' is one of the lines in his act. He concludes his stage show with a song poking fun at the Holocaust and has a particular beef with the popular Parisian radio reporter Patrick Cohen, who just happens to be Jewish. He once said of Cohen: 'When I hear him, I tell myself, you know, gas chambers... too bad.'

Maybe we're missing something in the translation. But while it might not be what we would consider remotely funny, Dieudonné's brand of polemical anti-semitism has found considerable traction among French youths of North African descent living in the *banlieues* of Paris and Marseille. Mostly Muslim, they have a distaste for Israeli actions in the Occupied Territories and are easy targets for those seeking to stir up wider anti-Jewish sentiment.

Even as the authorities moved against him, banning him from live shows and twice charging him with inciting racial hatred, so Dieudonné became a symbol of anti-establishment rebellion among the young. Pictures of lads doing the *quenelle* at Auschwitz, outside the Holocaust Museum in Berlin, or in front of Parisian synagogues became commonplace on social media.

And then Anelka gave the gesture its biggest publicity boost: he took it on to an international stage. Yes, other players like Manchester City's Samir Nasri and Liverpool's Mamadou Sakho had been photographed back home with fans doing the salute, but Anelka's televised action was of a different order. What he did at West Ham, deliberately exploiting the global reach of the Premier League, took the *quenelle* to a much wider audience.

As the media storm swirled around him, Anelka claimed he had no idea the salute meant anything pejorative, he was just doing it as an 'act of solidarity' with his old mate Dieudonné who was having a hard time back home in France. All wide-eyed and innocent, he told a French newspaper:

My *quenelle* was very misunderstood. I have no record of racism or anti-semitism, there is no evidence to support it. I have never had a problem with the Jewish community, and besides why would I have? There are so many questions and no answers. Because some people have performed [the *quenelle*] in front of a synagogue, then the gesture is suddenly meant to be racist and anti-semitic in any place and in any situation? Sorry, I'm not swallowing that. I've tried to swallow it but it won't go down.

While the FA promised an investigation, West Brom stood by him, even when their shirt sponsor, the property search engine Zoopla, withdrew financial support from the club. The company is owned by Alex Chamberlain, a businessman of Jewish descent who was not keen to see his logo in such close proximity to a symbol of rampant anti-semitism on international television.

Eventually, the FA – following a careful and well-researched inquiry – found Anelka guilty of making inappropriate political gestures and banned him for five matches, accompanied by a fine of £80,000. After their initial inertia, West Bromwich Albion moved against him when he didn't turn up for training during his ban and sacked him for breaking the terms of his contract. As for the gesturing Anelka, he returned to France and was pictured with Dieudonné, whom he described as 'closer than a brother'.

> I have no record of racism or anti-semitism. I have never had a problem with the Jewish community.

2014 'He is a specialist in failure.'

José Mourinho on Arsène Wenger, Chelsea training ground, Cobham, 14 February 2014.

José Mourinho took a while to warm up on his return to English football. For a few months he was a picture of diplomacy, tact, niceness. But eventually he couldn't help himself. The bile was rising, there was no holding back. So when, at a routine press conference ahead of an FA Cup tie, the Chelsea manager was asked for his response to Arsène Wenger's suggestion that his (i.e. Mourinho's) endless public insistence that his side were not title favourites was born out of a 'fear to fail', the Portuguese unleashed both verbal barrels in the direction of North London.

'He is a specialist in failure. I'm not,' Mourinho said. 'So if supposing he's right and I'm afraid of failure, it's because I don't fail many times. So maybe he's right. I'm not used to failing. But the reality is he's a specialist because, eight years without a piece of silverware, that's failure. If I did that in Chelsea I'd leave and not come back.'

> Eight years without a piece of silverware, that's failure.

He could not have been more damning in his analysis of the Arsenal boss's career, trophy-free since he won the FA Cup in 2005. There was not even a respectful nod to the Alsatian's not inconsiderable pre-2005 achievements; the Chelsea boss was ruthless in his dismissal.

That has long been the Mourinho way: he does not engage in the clubbable assumptions of professional solidarity. He targets opposition managers in the gimlet-eyed search for a weak spot. The exploitation of vulnerability is his method of choice. He has made a habit of disparaging the managers he has succeeded at clubs. He routinely ridiculed Claudio Ranieri, his predecessor when he first joined Chelsea. Roberto Mancini, who preceded him at Inter, he accused of bequeathing a squad thin on talent, bereft of a winning mentality. Manuel Pellegrini at Real Madrid he claimed was small-time, a nearly man destined to come second. And Rafa Benítez, his long-time antagonist, was wincingly dismissed for his efforts at Chelsea in the season before Mourinho's second coming. Winning the Europa League, Mourinho said, was something the Spaniard should be embarrassed about doing at a club of Chelsea's stature.

As tactics go, it is one of Mourinho's most transparent. Slag off the man who came before you and then you can blame him if things go wrong; and if things go right it only enhances your legend: given how the previous guy messed up, what you did in such unpromising circumstances is little short of miraculous. It's a ploy politicians have been using since time immemorial.

But despite his antagonism towards all those who came before him, his biggest ire has long been directed at Wenger. When he first arrived in England, Mourinho quickly worked out that the Frenchman was not the most popular member of the elite coaching corps. Not a part of the establishment corralled by Alex Ferguson, he was seen as aloof, distant, not One of Us by many of those in the Premier League. He didn't share a glass of wine after a match, for a start. The man simply didn't have many allies.

Mourinho was consequently as sharp about Wenger as he was deferential to Ferguson. And when Wenger issued one of his paranoid complaints about Chelsea receiving favouritism from authority in 2005, the whiff of cordite was evident in Mourinho's response. 'I think he is one of these people who is a voyeur,' he said. 'He likes to watch other people. There are some guys who, when they are at home, have a big telescope to see what happens in other families. He speaks, speaks, speaks about Chelsea.' Eight years on, Mourinho resumed his attack on Wenger:

He loves to look at this football club. I thought between 2007 and 2013 was enough time for him to forget this. But it looks like he always likes to look at this. Am I afraid of failure? What is that? I believe at the end of the day I'll be [represented as] the unpolite guy, the one who's aggressive in his words. But of course not: he is saying we're not candidates because we're afraid of failure. Failure of what? Not winning a title this year? Or in two years? I have a lot of respect for him. But failure is not winning a title in seven or eight years. That's failure. Am I aggressive in my words? I don't know.

He added that he would not hang around at a club if he was not accumulating silverware. 'If I don't win a trophy in four years, I don't want a new contract. It's as simple as that,' he said. 'I don't think a manager should be embarrassed when he gives everything, tries everything, dedicates himself to the club, the project and the collective dream. If you don't get results, that's football. But for my mentality, there is a limit. There is a limit. And you have to be strong enough and proud enough to admit when it's enough.'

Pre-prepared and scorchingly delivered, his demolition of Wenger was immediately spun round the world. Even as he said it, the press room at Chelsea's luxurious training complex was filled with the sound of keyboards clattering as the words were tweeted and filed. It was the harshest of dismissals, but the words stuck.

And by an unhappy coincidence, Wenger notched up a remarkable landmark when he took his side to Stamford Bridge on 22 March, just a few weeks after Mourinho's put-down. It was his thousandth game in charge of Arsenal, an achievement lauded in glowing tributes from the press and from his peers (though not from Mourinho; he was lukewarm and sarcastic). It was a fixture which at the time was regarded as if not a title showdown, then at least one which gave indication of the two sides' relative credentials for lifting the Premier

League trophy. And for Wenger it was a brutally chastening experience. When Chelsea won 6–0, the home crowd were not remotely shy about crowing in victory, joyously repeating Mourinho's disparagement.

For Wenger, though, there was a reprieve. On 17 May 2014 his Arsenal side won the FA Cup, beating Hull City 3–2. Which meant that in the 2013–14 season he had won one trophy, while Mourinho had won precisely none. Not a bad result for a specialist in failure.

2014 'It is a surprise to be relegated after asking him to be moved?'

Former Fulham owner Mohamed Al-Fayed claims that the removal of his Michael Jackson statue by Shahid Khan, the new chairman, led to the club being demoted from the Premier League, National Football Museum, Manchester, 6 May 2014.

Mohamed Al-Fayed was speaking at the unveiling of his Michael Jackson statue at the National Football Museum, where it took its place among a welter of such fascinating football exhibits as the ball from the 1966 World Cup final and George Best's sideways-laced boots. Quite why a sculpture of a pop singer was deemed appropriate for the country's biggest collection of footballing memorabilia is a question that will doubtless occur to anyone who sees it there. But not to Al-Fayed. After all, the former Harrods boss felt it the most natural thing in the world to erect the statue outside Fulham's Craven Cottage stadium. And much to Al-Fayed's chagrin, Shahid Khan, the man who paid £150 million to buy the club in August 2013, insisted, the moment he took over, that the piece be removed from its position outside the Riverside stand. An incandescent Al-Fayed claimed the action had had immediate and fateful consequences. After thirteen years in the Premier League under the Egyptian's stewardship, the club was relegated to the Championship at the end of the 2013–14 season.

'I have put a lot of time and money to create an image of such a great character, a great entertainer, a great gifted guy,' ranted Al-Fayed. 'And he was a Fulham fan. Don't forget that.'

Al-Fayed commissioned the work in 2011, two years after the entertainer's untimely death. When it was first unveiled it caused consternation among Fulham supporters. Many of the Craven Cottage fans considered it an off-the-wall decision to place a statue of the troubled singer-songwriter in their ground. However much Al-Fayed's long-term PR man, the former BBC journalist Michael Cole, insisted there was nothing cheap about its construction ('I'm not going to tell you how much it cost, but I can assure you it was a lot of money') it was immediately dismissed by many as an embarrassment, a poorly executed shop-window mannequin. Brashly coloured and oddly proportioned, it looked like something that might be encountered at a crumbling end-of-the-pier waxworks exhibition. Besides, many Fulham supporters wondered what Jacko had done for the club to be so honoured. Putting his likeness outside the stadium seemed about as appropriate as having a statue of Scott Parker at Neverland. Al-Fayed, though, insisted that the work was hugely popular:

> To have him and put him on the Riverside and people enjoy him there was great thing. I had floodlights on him, non-stop; people pass on riverboats specially to have a look and take pictures. He was a great entertainer, a great singer and at the same time he was a Fulham fan. He attended several important matches, sitting next to me, walking around, saluting the fans. Great character. For him not to be there now, I feel sorry for the fans.

Indeed, while the removal of the statue may have undoubtedly improved the Thames-side view, its departure was a visual reminder of the change of ownership at the club. For sixteen years Al-Fayed's slightly potty regime held sway, its benevolent eccentricity a clear mark of Fulham being somehow different. On match days the chairman was a notable presence, marching around the pitch ahead of kick-off, waving

> I'm not going to tell you how much it cost, but I can assure you it was a lot of money.

his black-and-white scarf above his head, serenaded by fans delighted by his stewardship, which had guided the club from the fourth tier when he took over to more than a decade as a fixture in the Premier League. As he made his way, with due pomp and circumstance, to his seat in the directors' box, the supporters chanted 'give him a passport' in support of his campaign to secure British citizenship. How he beamed back at them. Behind the scenes, he was equally visible, forever offering the players blue mints from his pocket (which he insisted were Viagra), and bringing a succession of oddball celebrity contacts into the Craven Cottage dressing room: if it wasn't Michael Jackson it was Tony Curtis.

And with every such batty action, Al-Fayed confounded expectations. Nobody thought he would be like that when he first acquired the freehold in Fulham FC in 1997, just a few months before his son Dodi was killed in the same car accident in Paris as Princess Diana. He was greeted with widespread suspicion by the Fulham faithful. In truth, there was a lot to be suspicious about.

When he took over, the club had been going nowhere and there seemed nothing in its footballing potential that might attract such a ruthless businessman, someone who had outflanked 'Tiny' Rowland to engineer a takeover of Harrods, an arriviste and social climber with no history of football support. Mocked by *Private Eye* magazine as the 'Phoney Pharaoh', Al-Fayed was once described during a High Court hearing as 'deeply dishonest and with an evil habit of vindictively pursuing those who he regarded as his antagonists'. His purchase of Fulham was widely depicted as a real-estate deal, that his eyes were solely fixed on Craven Cottage's superb Thames-side location, reckoned at the time to be worth something north of £100 million. Not a bad return, it was thought, for an initial £6.25 million investment.

And yet, almost immediately, he began to undermine such preconceptions. He not only delivered on a promise to project the club into the Premier League within five seasons, he did so a year early. He invested in players. He didn't interfere in dressing-room decisions, giving a succession of progressive managers – Jean Tigana, Chris Coleman, Roy Hodgson – the room to develop.

But what really changed minds was when, after moving to a ground-share with QPR at Loftus Road, he returned the team to a refurbished Cottage in 2004. Now that really did come as a surprise. The assumption was that, the moment the club moved out, Fulham's historic home would be redeveloped into housing, netting Al-Fayed a major fortune. Instead he revamped it into an all-seater stadium, which he incrementally improved over the next decade.

By now he was fully acknowledged as one of football's leading eccentrics. His oddness permeated everything around the club. I once arranged to interview him for a magazine profile. But instead of him appearing at the appointed time, his PR adviser – the latterly notorious Max Clifford – showed up. Clifford said I could ask him anything I wanted and he had been given the owner's blessing to answer on his behalf. There followed the most surreal half-hour, in which Clifford not only used the first person in his answers ('I want Fulham to be the best club in the country') as if he was playing the role of Al-Fayed, but also began to affect the Egyptian's Middle Eastern accent. By the end of the interview, Clifford was enjoying himself so much that not even Rory Bremner could have carried off a better impression of the Harrods boss. It was the kind of behaviour unlikely to be encountered at Arsenal.

There was one thing the PR-man-turned-impressionist said that could not be denied. When asked why Al-Fayed had bought the club, Clifford ended a bravura performance with the words: 'because I love Ful'am from de bottom of my 'art and I love de fans even more dan zey love me'.

This was what seemed to have happened to Al-Fayed at Fulham: if he did indeed initially buy it for its development potential, he was quickly seduced by the place's old-school values, with its half-timbered stands, its peerless views across the Thames and 'Diddy' David Hamilton as the matchday compère. He seemed genuinely fond of the club. And, in return, there was a lot for the fans to be fond of in his ownership: the Premier League consolidation, the Europa League final in 2010 (which Fulham lost to Atlético Madrid), the succession of gifted international players, from Steed Malbranque and Louis Saha to Dimitar Berbatov, all largely secured on the back of the £187 million in interest-free loans made available by the owner.

'When I took over Fulham, everyone in the world told me I was mad, that I would spend money and the club would go nowhere,' Al-Fayed said when, by now aged eighty-four, he finally relinquished responsibility for the place, selling it to Shahid Khan, the American owner of the Jacksonville Jaguars. 'It breaks my 'art to sell, but sometimes you have to listen to the clock.' And when he went, the Fulham fans immediately realised what it was they had lost. He may have been certifiable, he may have installed quite possibly the worst piece of public art at any football ground in the country, but they loved him. The fact is, what Al-Fayed proved at Fulham over the years was that the Beatles were wrong: in football you really can buy love.

> When I took over Fulham, everyone in the world told me I was mad.

2014 'JAWS III'

Headline in *The Daily Mail* the day after Luis Suárez had bitten an opponent in the Brazil World Cup, Arena das Dunas, Natal, 24 June 2014.

In a World Cup distinguished by magnificent attacking flair, by hatfuls of goals and comebacks and last-minute winners, by drama and glory, by stadia alive with colour and bouncing with noise, the defining image was not one created by shimmy, or dribble or piledriver free kick. It was one shaped by molar. The stand-out memory of the tournament was Luis Suárez's toothy assault on Giorgio Chiellini. It was the moment the Uruguayan attempted to dine on shoulder of Italian.

The facts are incontrovertible: while playing for his national side at the World Cup in Brazil, the sublimely talented striker bit an opponent. Watching his dental mugging again (and it is hard to avoid; footage of the incident has played on an almost continuous loop on televisions across the world), what is immediately striking is how utterly weird it is. As a sense of moral perspective seems to be the prevailing requirement when dealing with this particular player's misdemeanours, it has to be said that he isn't actually endangering the Italian's life. His toothy intervention is not remotely threatening to the Italian's future career. He is not attempting to break Chiellini's leg or tear the ligaments on his knee. He is just biting him. Yes, what the world was treated to on that steaming June night in Brazil's equatorial Northeast was the sight of a twenty-seven-year-old adult biting a fellow professional. How bizarre is that? He is not a toddler. He is a grown man. He has children of his own, to whom he is apparently devoted. If they went around biting people, like the good father he no doubt is, he would tell them to desist. Yet here he was doing it himself.

Imagine if that had happened in your office. Jeremy from Accounts gets into a dispute with Geoff from HR about hand towels in the gents and bites him. Immediately some of his colleagues step in and say: yes, he may have bitten Geoff, but you have to remember, Jeremy is a brilliant accountant. And he comes from Bromley, so he doesn't quite understand the nuances of the local culture. Actually, that wouldn't happen. Jeremy would be fired and everyone in the office would scratch their heads. A grown man had just bitten another grown man: work that out.

What was oddest of all about Suárez's attack was that this was not a one-off. This was the third time the forward had used his capybara-sized incisors on a fellow professional. In November 2010, while playing for Ajax, he had snacked on Otman Bakkal of PSV Eindhoven. He was consequently banned for seven games. In April 2013 he tried to take a chunk out of Branislav Ivanović of Chelsea while playing in Liverpool's colours. This time he was banned for ten matches. Just over a year after his nibble at Ivanović, something he had admitted at the time was 'inexcusable', he was at it again, this time on the biggest stage of all.

> This was the third time the forward had used his capybara-sized incisors on a fellow professional.

The sadness was, he had arrived in Brazil after enjoying the best season of his career; his thirty-one goals in 2013–14 had taken Liverpool to the brink of the Premier League title. His disciplinary record during that time had been exemplary: no biting, no fouling, no snarling. Just scoring.

Until that season he had divided opinion in England. Roughly the split went like this. To Liverpool supporters he was a demi-god; his spirit, determination and refusal to be beaten a modern embodiment of the characteristics they believe central to their club. His every transgression was forgiven because of his rare ability to win games. To everyone else he was a whining, moaning, diving, psychotic biter, a man whose inability to control his gnashers was matched only by his inability to prevent racist bile from spewing out of his mouth. It was some reputational chasm.

But that season he seemed to bridge the gap. As coruscating display followed coruscating display, as goals poured forth, opinion softened. It was – perhaps grudgingly – recognised that here was a special talent. Besides, he appeared to have learned from his attack on Ivanović. He looked like a reformed character. A man who had grown up before our eyes. He was voted double footballer of the year, by his peers and England's football writers.

Ahead of the World Cup he had this to say about his previous transgressions: 'When you have children and family, you want to change for them because maybe in a few years' time, your children can see on the internet what their dad was doing. I am an easy guy off the pitch and on the pitch I knew I had to change because I love football.'

The man had apparently changed. And he began the competition reprising the form he had displayed in the Premier League. Initially injured and missing from Uruguay's limp opening defeat against Costa Rica, he had come back to eviscerate England with two astonishing goals. Single-handedly he had revived his nation's fortunes. He was potentially the star of an utterly compelling competition, a figure as potent as Neymar, Arjen Robben and the magnificent Lionel Messi.

But then, towards the end of Uruguay's final group game with Italy, the suggestion of change appeared to be a chimera. The red mist descended once more. Once more he behaved like a petulant toddler denied a favourite toy. To widespread astonishment, once more he bit out. Such was the swiftness of his attack, the referee missed it. Despite Chiellini's protestations, the player remained on the field to participate in his side's victory celebrations, as they danced in joy with their supporters at progressing to the next round.

And when the subject of his biting was raised after the game, his Uruguayan colleagues immediately pretended nothing untoward had happened. Fully appreciating his value to their team, the last thing they needed was to have him suspended from action. So they reckoned it all someone else's fault. The manager Óscar Tabárez accused a BBC man who asked him a question about it of having an agenda. He was English, after all. Suárez's team-mate Diego Lugano, meanwhile, blamed Chiellini. The Italian was a crybaby, he said, a cheat, a disgrace to the game. Apparently for pointing out that he had been bitten by an opponent, Chiellini was undermining the moral values of sport.

This was a reprise of what happened when Suárez racially abused Patrice Evra of Manchester United in 2011, calling the Frenchman 'negrito' seven times and pinching his skin to emphasise the point. The then Liverpool manager Kenny Dalglish rallied round him, making his colleagues warm up before a match in Team 'Luis T-shirts' to show solidarity. The suggestion by some Suárez defenders was that there had been no abuse, and that in any case if Suárez had said something, it was only because he was operating within different cultural parameters, which needed to be respected. Never mind the fact that in England racially abusing a fellow professional – racially abusing anyone, for that matter – is regarded as a disgusting thing to do, instead of accepting this and dealing with it appropriately, with Suárez the excuse-mill went into overdrive. It always does.

Perhaps the most telling reaction to his World Cup snacking came from the player himself. He brushed off the incident as if it were perfectly unremarkable, claiming: 'These things happen all the time on the pitch.' Well, not all the time, actually, Luis. Only when *you* are on the field. Not that he was on the field much longer at the World Cup. Acting retrospectively on the damning evidence of the television footage, FIFA's disciplinary committee banned him from all football for four months. He was thus given plenty of time to ponder the consequences of his stupidity, watching from the comfort of his home in Montevideo the 2014 World Cup he should have been gracing with his skill.

What causes Suárez to behave like that may be a failure of anger control, or it may be something more substantial. But the truth is, until he is prepared to accept it, confront it and not simply issue lame apologies scripted by his agent in the attempt to maintain him as a marketable asset,

> These things happen all the time on the pitch.

he is not going to overcome it. If those close to him, those he trusts, keep telling him what he is doing is fine and it's only the English media with their agenda and whiney Italians that are complaining about it, then he is hardly likely to change.

Nor is there any urgency if he is snapped up by Barcelona on a huge transfer free. He has made it to the top behaving like he has: it does not suggest he needs to change. Yet one thing was abundantly clear about what happened in Natal: brilliant as he may be, Luis Suárez needed immediate help if he were not to tarnish beyond repair his standing in the game. Though some might say, the fang of God had this time gone too far ever to be happily redeemed.

2014 'BRACE YOURSELF – THE SIXTH IS COMING'

Slogan seen painted on the side of the Brazilian team bus as it arrived in the Estadio Mineirão, Belo Horizonte, ahead of the World Cup semi-final against Germany, 8 July 2014.

Never mind how much they were instructed to assume the brace position, no one in Brazil saw this coming. And when the sixth duly did arrive, courtesy of German substitute André Schürrle and bulging the back of Júlio César's net, it sent shock waves through the country. Soon followed by a seventh German goal, scored by the same player, it marked a rout that was as humiliating as it was unexpected. Brazil beaten 7–1 in their own backyard, in their own World Cup tournament, at their own game? No defeat in football history can have hurt like this one. Not even the Maracanã disaster of 1950 – the previous occasion in which Brazil had failed to win a home World Cup (see pages 43–5) – came close to matching this for trauma.

Of course, 'the sixth' the slogan on the bus claimed was on its way was not an uncanny prediction of this devastating scoreline. It referred to World Cup wins. Brazil had won the championship five times – in 1958, 1962, 1970, 1994 and 2002 – and the 2014 competition was billed as the one which would elevate the nation to a point way above the Italians with their four, or the Germans with their three, never mind the Argentinians and Uruguayans with their paltry brace apiece. From the moment the crest on the captain Thiago Silva's shirt – decorated as it was with five stars – was beamed up onto the big screen ahead of the opening game of the tournament, adding the sixth became the national obsession.

It was, incidentally, an obsession which the politicians responsible for bringing the World Cup to Brazil were more than happy to encourage. For President Dilma Rousseff, who had gambled her political future on the success of the tournament, winning the trophy, embroidering that sixth star on every team shirt, became essential. For her and her colleagues, victory was the only thing that they could use to gainsay the demonstrators who had spent the year leading up to the competition filling the streets with protest at the unsustainable cost of it all, the only thing that might ease re-election.

When it was first mooted, this was meant to be a tournament that would showcase Brazil as a modern, thrusting, ready-to-do-business economy. After all, Brazil was the 'B' in the group of so-called BRIC* countries, the up-and-coming new kids on the global economic block. In an interesting twist of logic, hosting the world's premier football competition would, it was argued, provide a golden

---

* The acronym stands for Brazil, Russia, India and China.

opportunity to prove that this was a country that no longer defined itself solely through football. But as the tournament began, it became obvious that the £8 billion outlay had produced precious little in the way of tangible economic benefit. The infrastructure projects it was supposed to generate never materialised. In the northeastern city of Fortaleza, for instance, of a city-wide metro system that was meant to be completed in time for the competition, barely half a mile was laid down, now abandoned and left rotting in the tropical sun. So behind schedule was it, it made Edinburgh's infamous new tram line look like a model of delivery. But then it was not alone. Not a single piece of wider infrastructure development that was promised was completed.

When it became clear all that £8 billion would deliver was a bunch of hugely expensive white elephant stadia (the one in Brasília alone cost £600 million and as yet there are no plans in place for its future use), the World Cup focus changed. Now it was sold as the chance to prove that Brazil was the best in the world at something. Winning the trophy, adding that sixth star to the crest on the national jersey became the sole imperative. Sure, it may have cost a bit, was the insistence from those in charge, but – hey! – it will be worth it when we're all dancing round Rio with the cup. Winning would set in motion the biggest party on Earth.

And so winning became all that mattered. After attempting to reposition itself, this was a nation more dependent on the prestige of footballing excellence than ever. For the politicians who had staked so much on the project, victory was essential. If they couldn't provide the bread, they at least had to ensure they supplied the circus.

And for a month, how the locals partied in expectation. Never has a nation embraced a sporting event as patriotically as the Brazilians did their World Cup. The entire country was smothered in green and yellow. The explosion that was waiting to greet ultimate victory would have been heard in Buenos Aires. But it never came. Instead of fireworks, after the semi-final there was the smoky odour of a damp squib. And how it hurt. No one thought a joyous month-long carnival of colour and noise would end in such humiliation, such embarrassment, such disgrace as happened in Belo Horizonte.

True, most Brazilians were aware that their 2014 line-up was not a vintage one, the squad available nothing to compare with the glorious tradition of the past. This was not 1970 redux. Any team that relied on the hapless Fred as its principal source of goals could hardly be expected to set the world alight. Fred? Frankly, as Neil Custis put it so succinctly in *The Sun*, if they were going to hire a Flintstone, Barney would have been a better bet.

> No one thought a joyous month-long carnival of colour and noise would end in such humiliation.

But as the competition reached its climax, the locals had convinced themselves that a mixture of passion, desire, and collective hope would drive this less-than-stellar team of theirs to success. How woefully, painfully short it fell of that elevated goal. From the very moment when David Luiz, the stand-in captain, bellowed out the national anthem holding aloft the shirt of his colleague Neymar (who was absent after fracturing his spine in the quarter-final), everything that could go wrong in that semi-final did go wrong. Hoping to unleash a rip tide of emotion that would wash the Germans aside, all that collective singing did was fog the focus. Luiz in particular looked to be a man who had completely misplaced his tactical nous. Overwhelmed by the occasion, he provided all the resistance of a damp paper bag to the free-flowing Europeans. And his lead was picked up across a team poorly selected and poorly managed by Luiz Felipe Scolari. Every player in yellow appeared hamstrung by emotion. Manchester City's Fernandinho, whose snappy interventions had bruised Chile and Colombia in previous rounds, seemed incapable of making a tackle. Luiz Gustavo was equally absent, Dante about as much use as a papier-mâché crash helmet, Oscar and Hulk simply abject. If it were possible, the wretched Fred, the falsest of number nines, looked even worse than we imagined him to be.

And this against a German side of fluency, pace and tactical flexibility, the very epitome of the modern game. Suddenly all the frailties of the Brazilian team, which had been papered over in the unconvincing stagger to the semi-final, emerged at once. In the absence of their creative inspiration Neymar and tactical anchor Thiago Silva (suspended after receiving two yellow cards in previous rounds) they were horribly exposed. After just ten minutes Thomas Müller was the first to breach the Brazilian back line, from a poorly defended corner. There then followed a devastating seven-minute spell, during which Germany scored four times. FOUR. The stats make barely credible reading:

22 min. 08 sec. Miroslav Klose: Germany 2 Brazil 0
23 min. 58 sec. Toni Kroos: Germany 3 Brazil 0
25 min. 07 sec. Toni Kroos: Germany 4 Brazil 0
28 min. 49 sec. Sami Khedira: Germany 5 Brazil 0

Brazil's defence appeared to be made up of a bunch of clowns from the nearby circus who had somehow inveigled their way onto the pitch, dressed in yellow shirts. It was that embarrassing. The old footballing hands in the BBC World Cup studio were flabbergasted at what they were witnessing (see page x). Alan Hansen didn't mince his words: 'In twenty-two years as a pundit, and forty years in the game, I have never seen anything like it.' Gary Lineker encapsulated the momentous nature of this drubbing:

This was not just one of the game's super-powers beating a smaller nation, this was Brazil for crying out loud, a Brazil side hosting the World Cup for the first time in sixty-four years.

Germany's elation is matched by Brazil's desolation. We have seen something truly astonishing.

'RABBITS 1 HERRS 7' was the headline in *The Sun* the next morning, capturing in a single phrase the yawning chasm between the two sides. A chasm which Scolari had had neither the personnel nor the tactics to bridge. *Guardian* correspondent Barney Ronay summed it up neatly as Brazil's 'jogo collapso'.

The Brazilian crowd, initially so pumped up with patriotic fervour, now turned on their former heroes. These players had not only let them down, they had shamed the tradition on which the nation had been reared. They booed their team off the pitch at half-time. Then in the second half, as the sixth did indeed arrive (closely followed by the seventh) they became more specific in their targets. 'Fuck you Fred,' they chanted as the team in yellow so conspicuously betrayed them. And 'fuck you Oscar'. Not to forget, adding a political dimension, a somewhat direct message to the country's president: 'fuck you Dilma'. She was not to be forgiven for this humiliation.

They then switched their attention to the one team out on the Belo Horizonte pitch that was playing the game as they wished to see it played, as they played it themselves on the beach and in the *favelas*. How they cheered Bastian Schweinsteiger, Sami Khedira, Toni Kroos and Mesut Özil, serenading them like champion bullfighters. Though in every '*olé*' that greeted every German pass, you could hear the anguish. The end came not in glory but in humiliation. Poor Brazil: the carnival really was over. Now all they had to look forward to was the Olympics.

INDEX

PICTURE CREDITS

The majority of the images in this book are used with the kind permission of GETTY IMAGES.

The publishers are also grateful to the following for permission to reproduce images:

CORBIS: 1st plate section, page 8, bottom.

MIRRORPIX: 1st plate section, page 7, bottom right; and 2nd plate section, page 3, top.

NEWS INTERNATIONAL: 2nd plate section, page 4.

PRESS ASSOCIATION: 1st plate section, page 4, bottom.

WIKIMEDIA COMMONS: 1st plate section, page 3, bottom right.

Details of the images that appear at the start of each of the book's six parts are as follows:

PART I (page 1): An illustration by S. T. Dadd of a match between Oxford and Cambridge, 1889.

PART II (pages 22–3): Players jump for the ball in a match between Arsenal and Preston North End at Highbury, London, 1 March 1922.

PART III (pages 66–7): Gordon Banks punches the ball away during an Argentine attack in the England v. Argentina World Cup quarter-final, Wembley, 23 July 1966.

PART IV (pages 160–61): Steve McManaman, Alan Shearer and Jamie Redknapp celebrate Paul Gascoigne's goal during the Group A match between Scotland and England at Wembley, 15 June 1996, during the 1996 European Championships.

PART V (pages 230–31): Sergio Agüero scores in extra time v. QPR to win the Premier League for Manchester City, Etihad Stadium, Manchester, 13 May 2012.

PART VI (pages 326–7): Uruguay's Luis Suárez celebrates his second goal during the Group D match between Uruguay and England at the Corinthians Arena, São Paulo, 19 June 2014, during the FIFA World Cup.

The vignettes dotted through the text are taken from:

A vintage illustration from *The Illustrated Sporting and Dramatic News*, featuring scenes of international football at Glasgow, *c*. March 1884, including various players, action scenes and spectators.